Early Praise for *Zero Chance of Passage*

President Bill Clinton, Founder of the William J. Clinton Foundation and 42nd President of the United States:

In *Zero Chance of Passage,* Ember Reichgott Junge delivers a fascinating and detailed account of the bipartisan movement to revive the American education system. As she breaks down the misconceptions surrounding charter schools and sets the historical record straight, readers will learn what too few have known: charters simply wouldn't exist without Ember Reichgott Junge.

Former US Senator David Durenberger (R-Minnesota):

Every education policy leader in America simply must read this eyewitness account of the birth of a great Minnesota idea. Supported by a degree of bipartisanship too seldom seen today, charter schools have changed the way the country defines and delivers public education.

Nina S. Rees, former Assistant Deputy Secretary at US Department of Education and adviser to Vice President Dick Cheney:

This book is required reading not just for those interested in learning more about the history of charter schools but for learning how a dedicated legislator can bring an unorthodox idea to life with the support and dedication of a grassroots-driven advocacy community.

Caprice Young, former CEO, California Charter Schools Association:

Any understanding of the charter school movement begins with this story. It's a fiery political tale, full of the characters and the intrigue accompanying any serious effort to make the world better. My graduate students loved this book as it drove real dialogue around what is required to define real public education.

Lori Sturdevant, Editorial Writer and Columnist, *Star Tribune*:

With *Zero Chance of Passage,* Ember Reichgott Junge demonstrates that she is a talented storyteller as well as a skillful legislator. She brings personalities and ideas to life as she describes the power of special interests, the maneuvers of conference committees, and the value of bipartisanship in making Minnesota the first state in the nation to authorize chartered schools. *Zero Chance* offers an object lesson to any would-be engineer of systemic change. It's a reminder that persistence, patience, and compromise are essential ingredients of reform.

John Merrow, Education Correspondent, PBS NewsHour, and President, Learning Matters, Inc.:

Zero Chance of Passage—written by one of the founders of chartered schools— grows more fascinating with every page. Anyone interested in chartered schools ought to read this book. And those who imagine they already know all there is to know about them must read it. Even though I participated in the seminal meeting in 1988 and have been reporting on these schools ever since, I found myself saying "I didn't know that!" dozens of times while reading Ember Reichgott Junge's compelling history.

Andrew J. Rotherham, Co-Founder and Partner, Bellwether Education Partners and Education Columnist for *TIME* Magazine:

Ember Reichgott Junge offers a history of the nation's first public charter school law that will engage policy wonks, political enthusiasts, and all who care about improving public education. She couples research and history with her own personal experience as a major player in that effort to produce an important contribution to the literature about expansion of school choice in America.

Richard D. Kahlenberg, author of *Tough Liberal: Albert Shanker and the Battles Over Schools, Unions, Race, and Democracy*:

Ember Reichgott Junge provides an enthralling behind-the-scenes depiction of the birth of charter schools two decades ago. She reminds us that the original vision centered around empowering teachers to try new things to help students—a goal, one hopes, that will re-emerge as a driving force in the charter movement's next twenty years.

David Osborne, author of *Reinventing Government:*

People are often confused about charter schools: Are they private schools or public schools? Were they a Republican idea or a Democratic idea? Ember Reichgott Junge's superb book answers those questions, describing just how the idea became a reality. Charter schools are a classic "third-way" strategy: they embrace innovation and market forces while preserving equal opportunity, regardless of income.

Dr. James N. Goenner, CEO, National Charter Schools Institute:

Ember's story reminds us that the original idea behind chartering was about much more than schools. What Minnesota did was pioneer a bold strategy other states could use to redesign their educational systems and defy the "givens" of the status quo.

Sandra F. Cimmerer, eighth-grade teacher, Shakopee, Minnesota public schools:

As a veteran public school educator, it was intriguing to learn of the charter school journey. Having an additional option within the public school arena that facilitates experimentation with methods to teach our students can only strengthen public education overall, and help bring about expanded solutions to the challenges of increasing achievement, learning, and understanding for all our public school students.

Tom Gonzalez, 1995 graduate of City Academy High School, the first chartered school in the nation:

Reading the history of how we became a school gave me a real sense of pride. I was especially proud after learning that most of the traditional educational institutions expected us to crash and burn. We did the exact opposite: we created a movement.

Josephine C. Baker, former Executive Director and Chair of the DC Public Charter School Board:

Zero Chance of Passage is a book that needed to be written. It offers a serious look back at the essential elements of chartered schools and enhances the future of chartered schools moving forward.

10-22-13

To Linda & Ron MacDonald —

    With great appreciation
for your leadership in public
education in bringing innovation
to the sector and your support
in bringing new charters to
Washington — you are today's
pioneers!   Warmly,
                    Emlee Reichgott
                    Junge

ZERO CHANCE OF PASSAGE

The Pioneering
CHARTER SCHOOL STORY

EMBER REICHGOTT JUNGE

BEAVER'S
POND
PRESS

Charter Schools
Development Corporation

Photo of President Bill Clinton meeting with a student at City Academy charter school in St. Paul on May 4, 2000 by Joe Rossi, *St. Paul Pioneer Press.*

Cover photo by Tom Olmscheid. Black and white capitol photos in photo inserts by Tom Olmscheid and David J. Oakes.

ISBN 13: 978-1-59298-476-3

Library of Congress Catalog Number: 2012905645

Printed in the United States of America

First Printing: 2012

16 15 14 13 12   5 4 3 2 1

Cover and interior design by James Monroe Design, LLC.

**Charter Schools
Development Corporation**

Beaver's Pond Press, Inc.
7108 Ohms Lane
Edina, MN 55439–2129
(952) 829-8818
www.BeaversPondPress.com

BEAVER'S
POND
PRESS

To order, visit www.BeaversPondBooks.com
or call (800) 901-3480. Reseller discounts available.

For standing firm in his vision to improve public education
for more than five decades and for giving new meaning
to the power of a "policy entrepreneur,"
I dedicate this book to Ted Kolderie, the godfather of chartered schools.

Contents

Introduction 1

Part I: The Decision

    1. Has It All Come Down to This?. 13

Part II: The Origins of Chartering

    2. Governor Rudy Perpich and the Brainpower State. 21

    3. The Origins: Chartered *What*?. 33

    4. The Dinner Napkin 47

    5. The Template: The Citizens League 53

    6. Ted Kolderie: Withdrawing the Exclusive Franchise 59

    7. Creative Writing: The First Chartering Legislation 67

    8. Focus on "Change" Becomes Central
       to Public Conversation. 71

Part III: The Minnesota Story—Blueprint to Legislative Passage, *Not* Civics 101

    9. Transforming Ideas into Legislation:
       A Painstaking Process 83

    10. The Hearings Begin: The Players Line Up 89

    11. Chartering and the House:
        Below the Radar. 101

12. The Unions Rise Up. 109

13. The Unions: Breaking Up Is Hard to Do. 121

14. The Conference Committee: Ground Zero 129

15. The Decision Revisited: "Pigs Get Fed, and Hogs
Get Slaughtered" 139

16. Passed by "An Absolute Hair" 153

17. The Morning After. 165

Part IV: From Idea to National Movement

18. Charters Explode onto the National Scene. 175

19. The Rise of the "New Democrat"
—Governor Bill Clinton 181

20. The Republican Pragmatist—US Senator
David Durenberger 189

21. Chartering: Not "Voucher Lite". 199

22. Starting Chartered Schools: "Electric Expectations" . . . 205

23. The Unexpected Ally—US Senator Ted Kennedy 213

24. Chartered Schools: The Bleeding Edge of Change. 219

25. Shaping the Chartering Message:
Setting the Tone for the Future 229

26. The First New Chartered Schools:
Outside the Mainstream 233

27. Chartering Evolves in California:
"A Policy Redwood". 239

28. States Lead, Congress Lags. 249

29. 1992 Election: Politics at Home
and in Washington, DC. 255

30. *Mandate for Change* 261

Epilogue: A Personal Journey through Chartering—
Twenty Years of Highs and Lows 267

Acknowledgments. 277

Appendix I: Commentaries 281

A Serious Risk of Missing Its Potential: Ted Kolderie . . . 281

Coming Full Circle: Louise Sundin 288

Appendix II: Viewpoints 304

Public Viewpoint: Facts and Findings 312

*The Freedom to Be Better: Speech to
Democratic Leadership Conference.* 316

*Speech at City Academy Chartered School
by President Bill Clinton May 4, 2000* 321

Why MEA Opposes Chartered Schools 324

Appendix III: Biographies and Chronologies 328

Biographies. 328

Chronology. 334

States with Chartering Laws by Years Passed 338

Appendix IV: Legislation 339

*1991 Minnesota Law Creating Chartered
(Outcome-Based) Schools* 339

The innovation of chartering is just beginning.

Introduction

I woke up one morning in December 2010, and it hit me like a bolt of lightning. Next year was the twentieth anniversary of the passage of the first chartered school law in Minnesota. If I were ever to write the story of chartered schools, the time was now.

Love 'em or hate 'em, chartered schools have endured for twenty years. Today 70 percent of the American public supports chartering. In the 2011–2012 school year, the number of students attending public chartered schools across the nation surpassed two million, with another 400,000 students on waiting lists. Approximately 5,600 public chartered schools are open in forty-one states and the District of Columbia. To a surprising extent, chartering has taken hold in some large urban districts. According to 2010 data from the National Alliance for Public Charter Schools, chartered schools serve at least one of every five public school students in twenty different school districts, including those in New Orleans, Louisiana; the District of Columbia; Detroit, Michigan; Kansas City, Missouri; Dayton, Ohio; and Flint, Michigan. These students' progress has been documented in multiple ways.

How did this happen? What has sustained this redesign in public education through years of controversy? What lessons about chartering must we learn if it is to be sustained and grown over the next twenty years? What contributions has the chartering sector made to public education in general? What insights can be applied to redesigning other public services?

This book will not focus on whether "chartered schools" have been successful. The literature is filled with studies that support every point of view on that question. No. This book will tell the pioneering story of chartering from its early origins, the turmoil of its legislative passage in Minnesota, and its explosion onto the national stage within weeks thereafter. There are many lessons to be learned from this story. Chartering is here to stay. It is a fundamental reform of our public education system. We must understand its past if we are to inform the future of chartering around the nation and world.

In writing this book, I hoped to achieve three things that will shape the future of chartering:

1. Set the historical record straight.

2. Reclaim the urgency of why chartering came to be.

3. Reshape the conversation around chartering for the next decade.

Frankly, this is a better story than I initially expected to write.

After working from 1989 to 1991 as the senate author of the chartering legislation in Minnesota, I was devastated when the bill finally passed into law in 1991—I thought it was too compromised to allow a chartered school to open. I thought I'd failed all who'd traveled the road with me and that I'd forced a continuing battle over multiple years to improve the legislation.

Twenty years later, I now recognize that without this compromise in 1991, chartering might never have happened at all. And the success of the first chartering legislation was a result, in part, of the political winds of the times. Frankly, chartering might not have happened in another political era—certainly not in the political times of today.

I expected this story to be an account of "Us against Them"—education reformers versus the teacher unions. I was a union-endorsed DFLer. (In Minnesota, the Democratic Party is known as the Democratic-Farmer-Labor, or DFL, Party.) At the time, I saw the unions as overly aggressive opponents of new legislation that would provide new opportunities for kids. To me, the contrast in our positions was black and white. Not so.

Twenty years later, I found many shades of gray in this story. And I learned that the story of chartering and unions continues to evolve today in new and innovative ways. That, above all, gives me hope that this book can help allay the ongoing battles and controversy around chartering that continue in many areas of our nation today.

Setting the Historical Record Straight

Over the years, I've been heartened by increasing bipartisan acceptance of chartering in Minnesota and around the nation. At the same time, I've been disheartened by widespread lack of understanding of chartering and why this change in our public education system came to be. I've heard policymakers from other states proclaim that chartered schools are nonpublic schools developed by supporters of private school vouchers. Democratic lawmakers have asked why I support this "President Bush initiative." Others believe chartering arose from urban "ultra-left liberals" to address specific challenges of urban schools with student populations of color. Myths about chartering abound. This lack of understanding has fed into the confusion and controversy that still exist today around chartering. For example, in national polling as late as 2006, only 34 percent of the American public identified chartered schools as public schools. Thirty-seven percent defined them as private or religious schools, and the rest didn't know.

I wrote this book to record the pioneering story of chartering as it happened in the words of the people who were there. I am grateful that fifteen people involved in the creation and passage of chartering legislation added their historical perspective in interviews for this book in 2011. I am grateful to Ted Kolderie, a policy entrepreneur who has never held elected office but whose persistent vision guided us on the long trek of chartering. In the least of his contributions, Kolderie recorded much of the history of chartering in memoranda. When I retired from the Minnesota Senate in late 2000, I brought home a large file drawer full of papers and documents filled with Kolderie's memos, printed articles he provided from around the country, and his records of (endless!) meetings during that time period.

If there are three key historical points I hope people take away from this story, they are these:

1. Chartering is a *bipartisan* policy initiative.

2. Chartering came from the *middle* of the political spectrum.

3. Chartering came from *outside* the traditional political system.

As a legislative author of chartering who lived through this daily history, I thought I had a good idea of what went on twenty years ago. Not true. I realized in writing this book that I knew just a fraction of this history. For instance, I was always astonished that the chartering idea spread to the national scene so quickly after passage in Minnesota. Years later, no one was more surprised than I—or Kolderie!—to learn that Arkansas governor Bill Clinton had been traveling the country with Kolderie's "exclusive franchise" paper in hand, talking about chartered schools, even as I and others struggled to pass the bill back in Minnesota. That's why it's important that this history be recorded now. None of us involved in the birth of chartering knew the whole story. We each contributed parts of it. This book brings the whole story together for the first time.

There is another reason to preserve the historical legislative record: it doesn't currently exist in a public forum! A law student recently asked me about the legislative history of chartered schools in Minnesota. She said she couldn't find anything on the legislative audiotapes at the Minnesota Historical Society. She was right. Very little is there. "Outcome-based schools," the original term in the legislation for chartered schools, was mentioned only a handful of times in debate in the house and the senate, often in the context of a much larger debate on a much larger education funding bill. That's it. Passage of chartering legislation was anything *but* Civics 101. If anyone is to believe the chartering story, we need to write it down. Now.

Reclaiming and Restoring the Urgency

Over the last twenty years, I've watched the growth of the chartering sector with great pride. I've also watched the growth of chartered schools with increasing concern as to their future.

For me, the breakthrough innovation in chartering was always about the law itself—the restructuring of the dynamics of the public education system. It was less about the schools themselves. I expected some chartered schools would do very well while others would not succeed. The purpose of the chartering legislation was to give freedom to parents and teachers to create new schools outside the existing system. These schools would offer new opportunities for students. Chartering would become the "research and development" sector of public education. These schools would be held accountable through performance-based outcomes in a contract overseen by an authorizer, such as a state board of education. The authorizer would require chartering leaders to deliver quality education results. If they did not do so—or their innovation did not work—they would be closed. (How many district public schools close for accountability reasons? They don't.)

Chartered schools allow the "freedom to be better." To me, that means two things: the freedom to excel and to innovate. Both are fundamental to the origins of the chartering movement. Quality and innovation work hand in hand. There are many examples of this integration in chartering. Longer school days, year-round schooling, customized learning strategies, technology options, and subject-focused schools (such as environmental or arts schools) have seen great success in urban, suburban, and rural chartered schools around the country.

That being said, I have two concerns about how chartering has evolved. First, there are too many poorly performing chartered schools not living up to high standards of quality. If chartering is to succeed into the future, charter authorizers *must* close poorly performing schools. Period.

As Newark mayor Corey Booker said at the 2011 National Charter Schools Conference, "If we begin to protect charters just because they are charters, we have failed as a movement. We cannot condone mediocrity. . . . Those charter schools need to improve or move aside and let someone else do the job." At the same national conference, Doctor Howard Fuller, director of the Institute for the Transformation of Learning at Marquette University and board chair of the Black Alliance for Educational Options, did not mince words: "Bureaucratic creep has come into the [chartering] movement. We need to push people to be honest and innovative. . . . As a movement we must shut down every school that is ill-serving our kids. . . ."

That brings me to my second concern. In our quest to close poorly performing schools, I worry that some may ignore the other fundamental issue that brought chartering to where it is today—the opportunity for innovation. Certainly, schools that profess to offer innovative learning must also be schools of quality. But is there a risk that innovation may be squelched by divergent definitions of quality or start-up timelines that don't allow innovations to take hold? Many people today, even *within* chartered schools, have no idea why charters came to be. Chartering advocates cannot forget why we are here: to improve delivery of public education by allowing "the freedom to be better." We can't become new protectors of the status quo or of the mediocre. What system could ever make progress if it were limited to doing only what has worked well in the past?

We can't be afraid to close down a school that is not worthy of being open. We cannot be afraid to push educators in chartered schools to create high-performing, high-quality schools. We cannot be afraid to push them to innovate and try new ways of learning, new ways of organizing, new ways of managing, and new ways of motivating. We mustn't be afraid to push them to meet the needs of students, especially those students whose needs are not being met in district public schools.

We must understand our history to reclaim it. For chartering to thrive into the future, we must restore the urgency that brought it about twenty years ago.

Reshaping the Chartering Conversation of the Future

As we move into the third decade of chartering, the concept appears to be stalled in delayed adolescence. If we are to reclaim the urgency of chartering, we must also redirect the conversation for the next decade. We need to create a different conversation.

Chartering is not about a particular kind of school. It is not about the success or failure of any one learning strategy. It is a process, not an end in itself. It is about creating new opportunities for children and stimulating the larger public education system to do the same. Here are some questions to ask if we want to further public education in this country for all public education students—including students at chartered schools:

1. What changes have taken place because of chartering? What new strategies, discussions, and learning technologies has chartering stimulated? Can research help here, perhaps more than it has?

2. How have chartered and district schools shared strategies and innovations and learned from one another?

3. What innovations and positive results can chartering bring about in the next twenty years for the entire educational system?

4. What are we doing in the chartering sector that we can and must stop doing?

5. What outcomes have we not been able to achieve, even with the freedoms of chartering? How can we achieve those outcomes?

6. How can we find and build on common ground with those who have opposed—or still oppose—chartering?

7. How can rapidly developing digital technologies be accommodated and encouraged in all public schools?

8. How can the principles of chartering apply to other governmental services?

In successful redesign of government services, asking the right questions is more important than coming up with the perfect solutions. That is what brings stakeholders to "the next right answer." Think of the creativity we could generate across the public school sector with robust discussions around these questions.

Some of this, of course, is already happening. New learning technologies are flourishing, such as setting and enforcing high expectations (e.g., KIPP schools). Some district schools work in partnership with charters, even colocating in the same building. Teacher cooperatives have formed with professionals who seek ownership and freedom in helping students learn in new and creative ways. Examples abound. We just don't hear much about them.

Today the conversation is often one of controversy, because we are focused on the wrong questions. It's not about which school or system is better or which learning method is better. We are expending enormous energy and resources on these debates, and little comes from it in the way of improving public education. It takes boldness to rise above and redirect this conversation. But with skilled, courageous, and committed leaders, we can do so. Educators in our district schools and chartered schools all want the same thing: to deliver quality public education to our children. Our nation depends on it. Let's stop the battles about which is the better way. Let's change the conversation to how we can invest that energy into creative ideas and teaching opportunities that benefit all children in public education.

In a commentary following this story, former Minneapolis Federation of Teachers president Louise Sundin provides an insightful, fresh start to that conversation, and it's an example of how this union continues to lead. Recently the state of Minnesota approved the Minnesota Guild of Public Charter Schools, a single-purpose chartered school authorizer, which was proposed by the leadership of the Minneapolis Federation of Teachers. This is the first such union-initiated authorizer in the country.

What can chartering cause in the next twenty years? Start with a new conversation. The innovation of chartering is just beginning.

Part I
The Decision

Nelson offered his compromise amendment.
The committee adopted it. The gavel came down.
The bill was closed.
Tears welled in my eyes.
I was bitterly disappointed.

*Don't worry—we have the votes to kill it
on the house floor.*

TEACHER UNION LOBBYIST

1

Has It All Come Down to This?

MAY 17, 1991

I was numb. I stared straight ahead at the ten members of the Education Funding Conference Committee seated at a large table in front of me. I didn't see them. I was lost in thought and on the verge of tears. I knew what was coming. Had we made the right decision? Would we ever know?

We'd come to the last week of a five-month legislative session. Everyone was sleep deprived. Legislators, lobbyists, and staff were all in "survival" mode. The Education Funding Conference Committee members had already spent days—and very late nights—hammering out hundreds of other budget issues affecting Minnesota learners. Some members were testy; others, downright cranky. For me, the entire legislative session had been an emotional roller coaster. I, too, was in survival mode.

The room was packed. It looked like a cargo of hollow-eyed passengers at the end of a long, overseas flight. Papers were strewn everywhere. Candy wrappers, remnants of sandwiches, and loose shoes lay scattered about the room. People had stretched themselves out over several chairs, trying to catch a quick nap. They never knew when the conferees might make their decisions, so they held twenty-four-hour vigil.

People who cared deeply about the future of this chartering legislation filled the room. The supporters were education visionaries who had worked on the legislation since at least 1988. The main opponents were the two powerful teacher unions in the state, which had played a key role in removing the chartering legislation from the two previous years' omnibus education funding bills.

The only major decisions left now in the 1991 omnibus education funding bill were in Article 9, which included the chartering provisions. The question wasn't so much whether chartering legislation would pass, but what it would look like. Would it resemble the senate bill that allowed parents and teachers to form autonomous public schools and create new opportunities for kids? Or would it be much less than I and the others had hoped for? Feeling more than anxious, I feared house resistance would water down the language so much that chartered schools would exist in name only, with no real distinction between them and traditional district schools, and with no possibility for success.

Had it all come down to this?

I thought about the twists and turns the chartering legislation had taken to reach this decisive moment. Three long years had elapsed since I first introduced legislation in the Minnesota Senate to create public chartered schools. In 1989 and 1990, the senate had passed chartering legislation as part of its omnibus education funding bill; the house had not. And in those years, the house had then rejected the chartering provisions in conference committee. But now in 1991, for the first time, it appeared there were the necessary votes from both the house and senate for chartering to pass the conference committee.

Once the two omnibus education funding bills got to conference committee, all of us who supported the chartering bill thought we were, at last, close to passing it into law. But the reality is that in lawmaking and politics, things can turn on a dime. And that's exactly what happened.

We supporters had expected pushback from the teacher unions. But none of us anticipated such aggressive resistance. The unions focused their pressure where we were most vulnerable—on DFL members of the Minnesota House. The two unions unleashed their lobbying force in phone calls, letters, and visits. Their members armed themselves with blatant untruths about the bill and my supportive colleagues. I became firefighter-in-chief, working day and night to put out the fires that seemed to blaze everywhere. Opponents were now labeling us as "anti–public education." These same opponents claimed chartered schools would destroy public education as we knew it by draining scarce dollars from the already struggling system. Forgotten in all this were the new opportunities we could create for students, their families, and, yes, teachers.

DFL representative Ken Nelson of south Minneapolis became the target. He was chair of the house Education Finance Division, and he had worked closely with DFL representative Becky Kelso, the house author of the chartering bill. Nelson had also authored the chartering legislation with me the first two years. Everyone knew he was the deciding vote. Nelson appeared to me to wither under the storm, and for good reason. The unions were powerful, especially in urban areas like south Minneapolis, which he represented.

He absolutely wanted to change the educational system in Minnesota and make it work better for kids. To his credit, he wasn't going to let the chartering legislation go down for a third year. So, he searched energetically during this volatile time for a compromise he could offer the unions to modify the bill and temper their opposition. But many supporters of chartered schools, I among them, felt Nelson's compromise gutted the bill. It meant starting a chartered school would be nearly impossible for anyone. Chartering supporters felt it would leave us with the status quo. Children would have no new choices to access.

And now the ten conferees sitting in front of me would decide its final fate. After three years of intense and painful advocacy from supporters of the legislation, it all came down to this: *Do we pass severely compromised legislation into law, or do we withdraw the bill, work another year to build support, and pass stronger legislation next year?* We had no time to think. I was in denial. How could our work have come to this? I couldn't blame Ken; the legislation would never have gotten this far without his leadership, but there had to be a way around this.

As reality set in, I became angry. Actually livid. I had personally worked with union leaders and made significant changes to the legislation within the last month to accommodate some of their concerns. Now it was clear that this battle wasn't about compromise; it was about blocking the legislation completely. How ironic that it was Albert Shanker, the president of a national teacher union, who had first introduced me to the idea of chartered schools as a way to empower teachers. I couldn't help but feel that no matter what path we chose, the unions had won and the children had lost. It was gut-wrenching. I felt as if I were personally failing those who had traveled this long journey with me. I had to make a decision.

Should we go forward? Many, many colleagues had put their votes on the line for this. The last thing I wanted was to ask colleagues to take a controversial vote and end up having nothing to show for it. On one hand, the proposed amended legislation was so gutted, it would likely have no problem passing the house floor. And maybe, just maybe, after chartering became law, we could improve that law in the future. But on the other hand, could there ever be a true chartered school, given the constraints of the compromise? Were we setting up this new system for failure? That could harm our chances to improve it in the future. Would it be better to withdraw the legislation? Could we really come back next year with a stronger case and more public support?

The conference committee chair gaveled the meeting back to order. The room silenced. The outcome took only a few minutes. Nelson offered his compromise amendment. The committee adopted it. The gavel came down. The bill was closed.

Tears welled in my eyes. I was bitterly disappointed. I rushed to the door to find safe haven.

"Don't worry—we have the votes to kill it on the house floor."

I could hardly believe my ears. It wasn't an idle threat that I overheard in the hallway. The two teacher union lobbyists were deep in conversation, and they knew how to count their votes.

PART II
The Origins of Chartering

I took out a pen,
reached for a clean napkin,
and jotted down the elements we would need to include in
such a bill:
Who goes to the chartered school?
Who decides if a school gets a charter?
Who holds those new chartered schools accountable?
How do we ensure they are nonsectarian?
How are they funded?
What if they fail?
What if they succeed?

A true visionary, Governor Perpich acted on his beliefs.

2

Governor Rudy Perpich and the Brainpower State

1985–1988

According to the history books, Minnesota DFL governor Rudy Perpich had nothing to do with passage of chartering legislation in Minnesota. In reality, he had *everything* to do with it. Perpich's vision allowed more public school choice. Without the mandate for more choice, chartered schools would likely never have been created.

I admired Perpich. A true visionary, he acted on his beliefs. He saw Minnesota as the "Brainpower State" and was committed to making it so. Minnesota voters elected Perpich to his second nonconsecutive term as governor in 1982, the same year I was first elected to the Minnesota Senate. As an Iron Ranger from northern Minnesota, Perpich enjoyed strong labor support. Between his two terms as governor, he worked in the global business community for four years for Control Data Corporation in Vienna. This work greatly influenced him.

Besides admiring Perpich, I also enjoyed a satisfying personal relationship with him, as I was one of few Croatians in the legislature, a heritage we shared. He was always respectful and kind to me, even though I was only twenty-nine when I started my senate service. I'm not sure if Perpich was a direct influence, but in 1984 I left my law firm and began a stint as in-house corporate counsel at Control Data Corporation. I really liked Perpich's ability to partner with business, and this became even more important when the Minnesota House of Representatives switched from DFL to Republican control in the 1984 election.

After President Ronald Reagan's National Commission on Excellence in Education published *A Nation at Risk* in 1983, policymakers were put on notice that the nation's educational system was failing to meet the national need for a competitive workforce. Examples of academic underachievement noted in the now-landmark report were sobering:

- Average Scholastic Aptitude Test (SAT) scores fell over fifty points in the verbal section and over forty points in the mathematics section during 1963–1980.

- Studies of student achievement in the 1970s revealed that in comparison with other industrialized nations, American students never ranked first or second on nineteen academic tests, but ranked last seven times.

- About 13 percent of all seventeen-year-olds in the US were considered functionally illiterate, with that percentage running as high as 40 percent for minority youth.

- Nearly 40 percent of seventeen-year-olds tested could not "draw inferences from written material"; only one-fifth could write a persuasive essay, and only one-third could solve a math problem requiring several steps.

These statistics greatly troubled Perpich. While many governors looked to the commission's recommendations regarding increased course and graduation requirements, he didn't.

"He wasn't so big on standards," recalled Dan Loritz, then assistant commissioner and director of governmental relations for the Minnesota Department of Education. "Rudy [said] that he'd seen too many people who failed tests and passed life—and too many people who passed tests and failed life." The governor was interested in creating more competition in education, which would be the access to excellence.

His own personal experiences and those of his family moved the governor to action. When he was chair of the National Governors Association in 1989, he wrote the following in the foreword of the book *Public Schools by Choice,* edited by Joe Nathan:

> Education was my passport out of poverty. I am a first generation American. On entering the Hibbing, Minnesota, Public Schools, I did not speak English. My teachers taught me English and many other things. They helped me develop the confidence which led to my running for local school board, the State Legislature, and finally, Governor. Education reform has been a special passion for me. . . .
>
> It was an experience with my son and daughter many years ago that sparked my interest in choice. In the 1960s our children attended the excellent public schools in Hibbing. After my election to the State Legislature, we moved to the Minneapolis-St. Paul metropolitan area. During that first

legislative session, we rented a house without considering the schools our children would attend. Our children found that their classes were mostly a review of what they already had learned in Hibbing. But, when my wife and I talked with teachers and school administrators, we learned that we had *no* options for more challenging assignments or moving our children to another classroom or school.

During the next legislative session, our family looked *first* at schools before deciding where to rent a house. Unfortunately, few families can move from district to district until they are satisfied with the school.

That is why I recommended in 1985 that we allow Minnesota families to select among various public schools, as long as their movement did not harm desegregation efforts and the receiving district had room. The plan was not warmly received at first. In fact, one legislator who sponsored the bill said it was a little like trying to rearrange a cemetery.

In 1985, with the Minnesota House of Representatives in Republican control, Perpich launched "Access to Excellence," a comprehensive education reform agenda that seemed downright radical at the time. One initiative was postsecondary enrollment options (PSEO), legislation that would allow eleventh- and twelfth-grade public school students to enroll part-time or full-time in nonsectarian courses at Minnesota public and private colleges and universities and at public vocational-technical schools, at no cost to the student. Public funds would follow the students, who would earn both high school and college credits. The purpose of the program was to promote rigorous educational pursuits and provide a wider range of choices for students.

Another initiative within "Access to Excellence" was open enrollment, legislation that would allow public school students (ages five to eighteen) to attend any public school of their choice in the state of Minnesota, as long as their movement did not harm desegregation efforts and the receiving district had room. Again, the purpose was to provide greater access to choices for public school students. It was important that neither initiative required new spending during tight budget times.

Both proposals were based, in part, on recommendations from a study commissioned by the Minnesota Business Partnership. They were also based, in part, on recommendations made by a small group of reformers who engaged in discussions with the governor before the new year—and beyond. This group consisted of Ted Kolderie, Joe Nathan, Curt Johnson, and Verne Johnson, among others. Former governor Al Quie was also involved as a longtime proponent of school choice. In 1983, as a member of Reagan's National Commission on Excellence in Education, Quie had tried unsuccessfully to get choice recommendations into the *A Nation at Risk* report.

Both of Perpich's proposals—postsecondary enrollment options and open enrollment—created an immediate firestorm of protest from nearly all education groups. Most of the firestorm focused on open enrollment. A *St. Paul Pioneer Press* newspaper poll in 1985 indicated that opposition wasn't limited to educators; Minnesotans opposed the governor's open enrollment plan by nearly two to one.

Why? Senator Tom Nelson, then chair of the senate Education Aids Subcommittee, addressed the issue more than twenty-five years later in an August 21, 2011, *Pioneer Press* article by Megan Boldt: "It was a new paradigm. . . . People didn't like it for two reasons. One was because funding was based on enrollment. You'd lose money. But two, if you lost too many students, you'd lose face."

I did not become part of this story until 1988. In 1985, still a first-term member of the Minnesota Senate Education Committee, I watched from afar with curious interest. My admiration for the governor grew as I better understood his vision for education. My admiration for my bipartisan legislative colleagues also grew as I watched them perform legislative cartwheels to get the governor's controversial initiatives passed.

Take PSEO. Republican house majority leader Connie Levi—with support from Quie—sponsored the new postsecondary initiative and made it her top priority from Perpich's package of reforms. She got the initiative into the house omnibus education funding bill. In the DFL senate, however, the bill never moved. But the senate omnibus education funding bill included another Perpich initiative—a statewide arts school, which never moved in the house. Nelson authored the senate bill. Perpich was now in the catbird seat—that is, the enviable position where the legislature was trading for two things he wanted. Levi and Nelson got together, made the deal, and both PSEO and the arts school became law in 1985.

As I reflect on those years, I realize I hadn't even heard of the term *chartered schools* at that time. But in reality, chartering was already happening. In a May 2011 interview, Loritz said, "The truth of the matter is that postsecondary enrollment options was essentially the first charter: Colleges were granted a charter to operate eleventh and twelfth grades. And the arts school was another charter. The state had created a school by granting it a charter."

The educational establishment, solidly focused on open enrollment, responded angrily, alleging that PSEO had been "slipped through" the process. Loritz remembers well the fallout. "Everybody was mad in the education community. So the governor sent me to meet with the unions, School Boards Association, and everyone else, which I did. They were *so* mad. I'd never seen them so mad."

"Our first reaction to PSEO was, 'Well, here's another challenge to our jobs,'" recalled Louise Sundin in an August 2011 interview. Sundin, who became president of the Minneapolis Federation of Teachers union in 1984, recalled that declining enrollment was a huge issue at the time. She explained what was happening:

I think 1979–1984 was the big drop in students in Minneapolis. [Superintendent] Richard Green closed eighteen schools, and we all got reassigned, and we lost a lot of teachers. That was, of course, pretty traumatic for teachers. We weren't the only place where this was happening, so teachers were concerned for their jobs. So the first reaction to PSEO [and later to charters] was they'll take more kids out of public schools, and we'll lose more jobs yet. That was a pretty big deal.

The Minnesota Federation of Teachers also challenged PSEO (unsuccessfully) in court. "It was the fact that kids could go to religious [postsecondary] institutions," Sundin explained. "It was based on the philosophy that there shouldn't be public funding going to religious institutions for any reason. That's why we challenged it in court."

With emotions running high, Loritz told the education groups he would recommend creation of a governor's discussion group on education. Moreover, the discussion group would have approval power for anything the governor proposed in the future. Loritz recalled,

What happened was, the governor called the groups together. But he also invited Ted Kolderie, Joe Nathan, Verne Johnson, Al Quie, and a whole bunch of folks who were on the reform side of the agenda. When Rudy called them together in the summer of '85, [the groups] got up and threatened to walk out. Rudy just looked at them and said, "If you walk out, no deal. I will bring whatever you agree to, but you have to agree to it with these people."

For the balance of 1985 and for the 1986 legislative session, the governor didn't bring anything new to the legislature because the group didn't want anything. Instead, the governor focused on protecting PSEO from repeal. PSEO passed in May 1985. The governor knew he had to get PSEO into operation by fall of 1985 or risk its repeal in the 1986 legislative session. With the bill signed on June 27, 1985, the start of the school year was only a month and a half away. Perpich insisted that his staff move quickly.

At the governor's direction, Loritz dispatched Bob Wedl and Jesse Montano of the Minnesota Department of Education to launch a rigorous effort to implement the program, including the development and implementation of comprehensive guidelines to assist secondary and postsecondary institutions, a telephone information hotline, and regional meetings around the state. The two were to make sure that students enrolled in the program by September. They did. When the 1986 session rolled around, plenty of students and parents could testify in support of PSEO. The vote to repeal wasn't even close.

A constituency for PSEO was building, and support for it was heard during the 1986 elections. That was likely a factor when the 1987 governor's discussion group recommended support for the postsecondary program, as well as support of a voluntary version of open enrollment. Resistance to mandatory open enrollment still existed. Voluntary open enrollment, however, was less threatening to opponents. Districts would volunteer to open their doors to allow students to enroll or take leave of their schools. No district would be required to participate.

In 1987, voluntary open enrollment passed into law, even with the House of Representatives now back in DFL control. Once again, Perpich moved quickly to build a constituency. According to Loritz, the governor sent letters to 160 school superintendents identified as entrepreneurial or innovative leaders and encouraged them to sign on. Ninety-five districts agreed.

In my years in the senate, I learned never to underestimate the power of choice. When citizens can make their own decisions about what is best for them and their children, they do. A number of students took immediate advantage of open enrollment opportunities offered in those ninety-five districts. By the school year 1987–1988, more than five thousand students had enrolled in PSEO. Stories of "reenergized" students emerged and were shared with legislators. Other existing choice options—such as alternative schools, where students ages twelve to twenty-one who did not succeed in one public school could attend another—were already thriving in some parts of the state. As always happens with customer satisfaction, a constituency of support for these public school choices emerged.

This is where I enter the story. I still smile when I think about how mandatory open enrollment finally passed in 1988. The Minnesota Business Partnership had approached me to sponsor a bill they had developed. Among its proposals was mandatory statewide testing. Near the end of the comprehensive bill was legislation implementing mandatory open enrollment. As a second-term senator and first-term member of the influential senate Education Funding Division (now chaired by Senator Randy Peterson, upon Nelson's retirement), I was blissfully unaware of the past history behind passage of open enrollment. I had no qualms about sponsoring the bill.

No one expected the bill to pass during the short, nonbudget 1988 legislative session, but we hoped to reshape the debate around Perpich's vision for what constituted "mandatory" open enrollment. We would make clear that under his vision, a student would always have the right to leave a school, and school districts would always have the right to close their doors to accepting new students—for example, if there wasn't room.

I did not expect what happened next when I introduced the Minnesota Business Partnership's bill. A firestorm of opposition erupted—not about open enrollment, but about the mandatory statewide testing in my bill. Clearly, testing legislation wasn't going anywhere . . . fast.

Far more interesting to me, however, was that in all the firestorm about testing, virtually no one came to talk with me about the mandatory open enrollment portion of the bill. *Not even the governor's staff.* It was as if we had fought that battle and it was over. Done. I talked with Peterson. Could we possibly add mandatory open enrollment as an amendment to the 1988 omnibus education funding bill? Was the timing right?

We agreed to try. As chair, Peterson was fully supportive; he had to be for this to work. Our senate Education Funding colleagues—of both parties—were quite strong on public school choice, so they were willing to help. I presented the amendment to the senate committee. Unlike the previous year, in which legislators debated the issue ad nauseam, little discussion ensued in 1988. The senate adopted the provision and mandatory open enrollment became part of the omnibus education funding bill headed for the senate floor.

The media took four days to figure out what had happened. By that time, the senate had passed the omnibus education funding bill by a wide margin and had sent it to the conference committee. The senate had done its job. Peterson would take the lead in conference committee. As the debate about open enrollment belatedly raged on in the media, I looked to Perpich and Loritz to help "enroll" the house. Frankly, I couldn't contact either of them. I knew the house had taken no action on open enrollment, and the house had the most vigorous opponents to open enrollment during past years. I thought it would take a "Hail Mary pass" to get something like this adopted in conference committee without the governor's active support.

Then, out of the blue, the deal was done. Open enrollment would be phased in for all school districts throughout the state over two years. The larger school districts would go first, and the smaller ones would follow. Only years later would I learn that the deal had already been secretly cut between Loritz and Representative Ken Nelson, chair of the house Education Finance Division, who was waiting for statewide open enrollment to show up in the conference committee. Loritz and the governor had intentionally stayed clear of the issue, for fear that the governor's other initiatives would be held "hostage."

At session end, to the surprise of many—including me—open enrollment for all public school districts was the law of the state of Minnesota, the first such law in the country. And Representative Nelson would soon become a key legislator in passage of chartered schools.

The best answer so far is charter schools.

ALBERT SHANKER

3

The Origins: Chartered *What?*

OCTOBER 1988

It was October 2, 1988. I sat on a rock, enjoying the fall sunshine at beautiful Madden's Resort near Brainerd, Minnesota. I was pleased to be one of a handful of legislators the Minneapolis Foundation had invited to their fourteenth-annual Itasca Seminar. This year the theme was public education. I looked forward to a stimulating discussion and some fruitful networking with a distinguished group of business, education, and civic leaders from around the Twin Cities.

The roster of speakers was also impressive. It included Albert Shanker, president of the American Federation of Teachers (AFT), and Sy Fliegel, a well-known educator who had helped turn around a large group of failing schools in Harlem, New York. John Merrow II—education correspondent for *The MacNeil/Lehrer NewsHour* and columnist for *Children,* a magazine for parents—served as facilitator as well as presenter. Merrow was not only a communicator in the world of education, but was experienced as a teacher in a high school, a college, and even a prison. Minnesota had become a national leader in education reform. That may have been why so many national leaders joined us for the seminar. Governor Rudy Perpich's vision for making Minnesota the "Brainpower State" was paying off.

I was then vice chair of the senate Education Committee. I suspected the Minneapolis Foundation had invited me to the Itasca Seminar because I had sponsored the 1988 legislation creating mandatory open enrollment. Senator Randy Peterson and Representative Ken Nelson, both instrumental in passage of the public school choice legislation, were also attending the seminar. Business leaders from the Minnesota Business Partnership—which had developed my open enrollment bill—were in attendance. Ted Kolderie was there. So were key union leaders. One was Sandra Peterson, president of the Minnesota Federation of Teachers, who also happened to be both my constituent and my friend. Another was Louise Sundin, vice president of the American Federation of Teachers, in addition to serving as president of the Minneapolis Federation of Teachers.

I wasn't sure what we would hear from AFT president Shanker. I wondered if he would have concerns about open enrollment. But the next morning I found Shanker engaging. He offered his audience visionary ideas for improving public education and the teaching profession. "Eighty percent of students do not learn in traditional settings," he said. "They just don't fit." He also talked passionately and enthusiastically about empowering teachers.

At their recent national convention, Shanker said, AFT delegates had been inspired by the prospect of having hundreds, even thousands, of school teams actively looking for better ways to produce more learning for more students by using different methods, technologies, organizations of time, and human resources. He asked two questions: How could teachers be part of a consistent way to make innovation an ongoing and valued part of the school community? And how could the system partner with teachers to encourage risk taking and change?

"The best answer so far," Shanker concluded, "is charter schools."

Charter schools? I'd never heard the term before. Shanker had introduced the idea in a speech to the National Press Club in Washington, DC, on March 31, 1988, and also in his July 10, 1988, *New York Times* column entitled "A Charter for Change." He said that over time, he expected charter schools to "stimulate a different and more effective school structure."

Key elements from that column included:

- "Some official body," like a school board, grants the charter.

- Charter grantees are teams of teachers with visions to construct more relevant educational programs or revitalize programs.

- The charter usually calls for "exploration into unknown territory and involves a degree of risk to persons undertaking the exploration. . . . There's no guarantee that a charter school will find better ways of educating students."

- "A charter implies both the idea of a franchise and competition."

- The charter school has its own budget on the same per-pupil or per-staff cost basis as the rest of the schools, but it can use the budget to have staff explore new roles.

- A charter contains "specific directions for the grantee and a definite length of time to complete the activity."

This new information fascinated me. In all our legislative work to expand public school open enrollment, legislators focused on expanding choices for kids. Shanker was introducing a new concept: Why not expand choices for teachers?

It is important to note here that Shanker's proposal was for "charter schools." He was focused on the schools themselves. The concept he introduced later evolved into legislation that focused on the *process* of chartering, not on the schools themselves. Schools that receive a charter in that process are called "chartered schools." The distinction is subtle but important, and "chartered schools" will be the frame of reference for this book.

Years later, I learned that Shanker developed his proposal for charter schools in the context of a much larger shift—some would say "momentous"—toward defining teaching as a profession. According to Sundin in her interview,

> In 1983, when *A Nation at Risk* was published, that was a big turning point in the AFT, and it was a big turning point in the path that Shanker took us down. In 1985, as a result of *A Nation at Risk,* instead of reacting negatively or reacting defensively, Shanker [delivered a National] Press Club speech, in which he outlined all the parts of a true professional model for teaching.

Shanker delivered that now-famous National Press Club speech on January 29, 1985, three years prior to his National Press Club speech about charter schools. Shanker proposed the concept of a voluntary national certification system that could certify teachers as outstanding veteran practitioners in specialty areas, much as the medical profession does, and he said that these board-certified professionals should be entitled to more pay. Included in this was the proposal of an "internship" program for teachers.

Greg Humphrey, who worked with Shanker as AFT legislative director, called the decision to endorse the basic thrust of *A Nation at Risk* "absolutely momentous, a watershed moment" for the AFT. As quoted on the website of the Albert Shanker Institute, Humphrey continued,

> Context is essential to understanding what a risk Shanker was running by publicly backing the "Nation at Risk" message. [President] Ronald Reagan had come into office three years earlier and put unions squarely in the crosshairs when he destroyed the air traffic controllers union in 1981. It was "The Empire Strikes Back," and the conventional wisdom in the labor movement was to circle the wagons and never give an inch.

Sundin described it this way in her interview:

> In the 1960s until the '80s—till Reagan took over—we were into blue-collar unionism power. And we needed that power to undo the inequities that were built into the expectations of our work. Married women weren't hired or they were fired because they might get pregnant. If they got pregnant, they got fired. High school teachers were paid more than elementary teachers, and male heads of households were paid more than single females. All those inequities we didn't have any power to change, until we actually used the tactics and strategies of blue-collar unionism—think United Auto Workers.

A Nation at Risk is when we made this gigantic U-turn to start patterning ourselves after the professions. That was a pretty screeching U-turn. And it still is [today] a difficult one for a lot of our members and a lot of our leaders.

Sundin points to this context to explain why teachers and unions reacted as they did during the time and why there were tensions.

[The professional model] was a totally new concept. It was not placed on a foundation of really anything yet that had been developed in the educational model. The only thing in Minneapolis Public Schools, for instance—and we were ahead of everybody else—[was that] in 1985 [Superintendent] Richard Green and I started the Task Force on Professionalizing Teaching. Our first act was to invent the mentor program. From the mentor program we continued to develop all the pieces of the professional model, up to professional pay, which was in maybe 2000. So for fifteen years, following the [1985] Press Club speech, we were systematically putting [it] together. In 1988 we had very little talking about professionalizing teaching, little talking about all these ideas of Shanker's.

This historic shift in the teaching profession was an important lesson for me in writing this book. It helped me put our education policy work in perspective and better understand the union point of view. I thought back to a dinner I'd had around 1987 with a classmate from St. Olaf College. She'd received a degree in education and spent over a decade teaching science in an urban district. Now she was working in the corporate office of a local health-care entity.

"Was it the money?" I asked.

"No," she said. "It was the freedom."

My classmate had grown more and more frustrated with the administration of her school district as she sought to implement her creative ideas in curriculum and teaching methods. "My ideas were not valued. I was not respected as an educator. My hands were tied. I lost my passion. I had to leave, for fear my frustration would affect the experience for my kids."

What I was hearing was that my friend wasn't being treated as the professional that she was. Her story made this notion of "more choices for teachers" resonate with me. It seemed a natural extension of our legislative work with open enrollment, even though at the time of our conference, I didn't have a clue as to what more choice for teachers would look like. I did consider that opening up those choices would provide me with a great opportunity to work with teachers and better understand their ideas about improving public education.

The whole idea attracted me. I'd grown up in the suburban legislative district I represented as a senator. That meant that in 1988, I was representing the very teachers who'd taught me. In fact, the executive secretary of the local union—the Robbinsdale Federation of Teachers (RFT)—was Barry Noack, my former ninth-grade social studies teacher. To make things cozier, the current president of the Minnesota Federation of Teachers, Sandra Peterson, was also a Robbinsdale teacher, having served as president of the RFT herself.

Peterson, Sundin, and I all heard Shanker's charter schools speech at the 1988 Itasca Seminar. In her 2011 interview, Sundin described how she received the speech:

> In Al's usual fashion, he was throwing these ideas out. [Charter schools] happened to be one of them. It wasn't anything that anyone was prepared for. It was, in some ways, premature. If it had happened later, after we had started articulating the professional model, and we had started

putting the pieces together, and teachers had started accepting the change or the enhancement or the power of professionalism—instead of just the power of power—then I think it would have fit.

In his Itasca Seminar speech, Shanker acknowledged he didn't create the idea of chartering. He credited Ray Budde, a little-known educator, with the original chartering concept. Budde was a teacher, then a junior high principal in Michigan. In the late 1960s, he was teaching educational administration at the University of Massachusetts when the dean reorganized its school of education. Budde wrote later that he always had a strong interest in "the way things are organized" and in "how things work or don't work in organizations." At the annual meeting of the Society for General Systems Research in 1974, he presented some ideas for the reorganization of school districts. He titled his paper "Education by Charter: Restructuring School Districts."

Think about that: Budde introduced the notion of chartering as early as 1974. But nobody took the notion seriously. At that time, no one recognized a problem significant enough in our system of public education to require such restructuring. So those who knew about Budde's idea simply shelved it.

Then came *A Nation at Risk* in 1983. Now, everyone was talking about restructuring. As Budde reflected years later in "The Evolution of the Charter Concept" in the September 1996 issue of *Kappan*, he dusted off his 1974 report, and the Regional Laboratory for Educational Improvement of the Northeast published it as a book. He proposed that teams of teachers be "chartered" directly by a school board for a period of three to five years. "No one—not the superintendent or the principal or any central office supervisors—would stand between the school board and the teachers when it came to matters of instruction," he wrote. Budde sent the book to people he thought might find it interesting—among them, President George H. W. Bush. Then he waited. And waited.

One Sunday in July that year, Budde's wife put down the newspaper and said, "Hey, Ray, you've made the *New York Times!*" She showed him Shanker's July 10, 1988, column reporting the support of the American Federation of Teachers for the idea of teachers setting up autonomous schools. The best name for these schools, he said, came from Ray Budde—*charter schools.*

It is only fair to point out that the original concept of chartering Budde offered was actually for chartering departments or programs—where groups of teachers would receive educational charters directly from the school board and would carry responsibility for instruction, such as creating a new kind of math or English program. No mention was made of the idea of chartering whole schools. His concept dealt only with *existing* schools, not *new* schools. It was not about less regulation.

Later, as chartering new schools became a reality, Budde wrote Ted Kolderie in 1992 that he had come to believe that "there has to be a formal, legal change that would . . . remove power from most central office positions and flow funds directly to schools" and that these changes would have to be "grounded in state law." Budde acknowledged a gradual change in his thinking in his 1996 *Kappan* article. Said Budde, "'This is not what I originally had in mind' has changed to 'There are more powerful dynamics at work in creating a whole new school than there are in simply restructuring a department or starting a new program.'"

Shanker built upon Budde's concept and introduced the idea of teachers starting new schools—though within existing school buildings. In fairness to Shanker, his concept of chartering meant that some official body, like a school board, would grant a charter in accordance with a procedure agreed upon with the teachers' bargaining agent. According to Sundin,

Shanker's view was that charters would be created by groups of teachers and parents who had an idea for a better mousetrap—an idea for a way to better educate kids. Shanker created the concept where teachers are leading the effort and remain within the union. In that model, parents and teachers would lead that effort, not boards or some of the people who [today] created charter schools for political or [other reasons].

These distinctions—that teachers would be the sole decision makers for the chartered school while remaining within the district union bargaining agreement—would emerge as key differences between Shanker's vision of chartering and what later would become the first chartering legislation in the country.

Joe Nathan, a longtime proponent of chartering and public school choice and founder of the Center for School Change at the University of Minnesota in 1988, points to other important contributions to early chartering origins. He notes that as early as 1968, an African American psychologist named Kenneth B. Clark became fed up with school districts, saying that African Americans could not depend on the traditional power structure—traditional school districts—to get them the kind of education they needed. So in an article entitled "Alternative Public School Systems" in the *Harvard Educational Review*, Clark called for new kinds of public schools operating outside school districts. He wrote,

Alternatives—realistic, aggressive, and viable competitors—to the present school system must be found. The development of such competitive public schools will be attacked by the defenders of the present system as attempts to weaken the present system and thereby weaken, if not destroy, public education. This type of expected self-serving argument can be briefly and accurately disposed of by asserting and demonstrating that truly effective competition strengthens rather than weakens that which deserves to survive.

Nathan explained in an April 2011 interview that

> Clark was calling for regional state schools, federal regional schools, college-and-university-related open schools . . . for schools set up by companies, for schools set up by unions, [and] for schools set up by the army. In other words, he . . . [was calling] for public schools outside the district structure.

Nathan became interested in education reform issues when he was an aide in the Minneapolis school district and a public school teacher and administrator in the St. Paul school district, where he helped start the St. Paul Open School. He became frustrated about public education "from the inside," and in 1983 wrote a book entitled *Free to Teach*. In this book, he suggested the public education system provide broader opportunities for teachers and parents to create new kinds of public schools. Note the word *new*.

The book came to the attention of Tennessee governor Lamar Alexander, who hired Nathan to coordinate an education project for the National Governors Association for the next two years. In 1986, in his chairman's summary of the governors' conclusions, Alexander stated, "To sum up, the governors are ready for some old-fashioned horse trading. We'll regulate less if schools and school districts will produce better results." At that 1988 Itasca Seminar, Nathan shared that governors' report. "This set the policy environment in the states," said Nathan. "This set the idea of 'less regulation in exchange for better results.'" This differed, said Nathan, from Budde's concept, which was focused on district activity and did not include the idea of less regulation at the state policy level.

In 1987, when Nathan returned to Minnesota from his work with the National Governors Association, he observed an ongoing public relations campaign in Minnesota called "Ah, Those Marvelous Minnesota Public Schools." "This was a huge PR campaign to try to convince people that [the warnings of a failing public education system in] *A Nation at Risk* didn't apply to Minnesota," he recalled. Nathan talked with the Minneapolis Foundation, among others, about what they might do. "The Minneapolis Foundation decided it was time to introduce into Minnesota some pretty radical ideas," said Nathan. So plans got underway for the Itasca Seminar, with a focus on public education.

Around this same time, from February through December 1988, the Citizens League, an organization of civic-minded people committed to improving public policy, had established a study committee that was fleshing out the chartering concept. This was done under the leadership of volunteer committee chair John Roll-wagen, CEO of Cray Research, and executive director Curt Johnson. Kolderie was a member of the committee. After Shanker spoke at the Itasca Seminar, Kolderie had the opportunity to bring the work of the Citizens League committee to his attention. Kolderie drove Shanker back to the Twin Cities airport. During the afternoon drive of over three hours, Kolderie explained how the Citizens League committee was shaping the chartering idea. He solicited Shanker's comments and said he'd keep Shanker in the loop thereafter as the idea evolved.

This may be one of the most significant "takeaways" from this story of chartered schools: Contrary to myths currently promoted across the country, politicians from neither the right nor left created the concept of chartering. In fact, policymakers did not generate the idea at all. No. It arose from visionary and insightful educators, civic leaders, and "policy wonks." All of who were focused—for all the right reasons—on finding ways to improve public education. They did not have partisan political agendas. What they did share was a strong commitment to improving public education so learners could learn better and teachers could teach better.

All these ideas were in the mix at the engaging three-day Itasca Seminar in October 1988. But one speaker stood out. Sy Fliegel had already put these ideas into action.

The legislation creating chartered schools was born on a dinner napkin.

4

The Dinner Napkin

OCTOBER 3, 1988

As I mulled over this new chartering idea proposed by Albert Shanker, a subsequent presentation at the Itasca Seminar captivated me. Sy Fliegel, deputy superintendent of District 4 of New York City, was the person behind many of the exciting and dramatic changes in the East Harlem schools since 1974. In 1973, these schools were the "worst" in the city. By 1988, students were transferring from prominent west Manhattan schools to attend the twenty East Harlem alternative and traditional high schools.

District 4 grew out of the opportunity created when the New

York School District went through a terrible battle in the 1970s. This battle resulted in the New York School District's decision to create community districts. The new community board could hire its own community superintendent, and the new superintendent could remake the elementary and junior high schools in that area. The board in District 4 hired district superintendent Anthony Alvarado. He brought in Fliegel, Deborah W. Meier, and others.

Alvarado and his team created a network of small schools of choice in the community. In a March 4, 1991, issue of *The Nation,* Meier described what happened in District 4. Starting in 1974, within ten years the new structure "totally changed the way 15,000 mostly poor Latino and African-American youngsters got educated, without pulling the rug out from either parents or professionals." The results were drawing visitors from around the country. According to Meier,

> Alvarado and his Alternate Schools Director Sy Fliegel gave such schools extraordinary support in the form of greater flexibility with regard to staffing, use of resources, organization of times, forms of assessment and onsite advice and counseling. When people in the "regular" schools complained of favoritism, Alvarado and Fliegel assured them that they'd be favorites too if they had some new ideas they wanted to try. Some even accepted the challenge.

In his 1988 Itasca presentation, Fliegel explained things a little differently from Meier's description in *The Nation.* He said, "Don't ask too much permission. That makes others take responsibility. If you want to do something different, they will be reluctant to take that risk. So they are likely to say no. Just do it. If it works, you can give them the credit."

As described by Fliegel, the people in District 4—principals, teachers, parents, students—no longer equated schools with real estate. For them, schools were about relationships. Small groups of teachers designed most of the schools. These groups developed a special level of energy and sense of coownership that made the schools stand out. Professionals had the opportunity to be more directly involved in decision-making. Also key to the success of District 4 was that the New York City School District no longer administered the schools. Instead, the local community school boards governed them.

To Fliegel, this combination of small schools of choice with greater school-based autonomy was a powerful one. It allowed parents and teachers to embrace new ideas even if they couldn't convince *all* their colleagues or *all* the school's parents. As Meier confirmed in her writing, "Creating a different school is possible, only if teachers, parents, and students have time to agree on changes and a choice of whether they want to participate."

Fliegel's presentation inspired me. What he said sounded like a chartered school to me.

With the passage of mandatory open enrollment in May 1988, I thought the Minnesota legislature was probably done with education reform for a while. But now something was becoming clear to me— we had only just begun. Yes, open enrollment is important because it provides public school students access to choice. But what if all the choices are the same? What good is having more access to choice, if there are few choices to access?

As Fliegel so eloquently demonstrated in New York City's District 4, open enrollment choice was only one element necessary to generate new ideas in public education. Equally powerful was the need for autonomy by the parents, teachers, and students who wanted to try something creative and new. If these small, entrepreneurial groups had to convince a whole school board—or even a school principal— of their creative idea, they might have a long wait. School boards and principals have rules, regulations, and budgeting precedents that can't be broken. In fact, one of their top priorities is to uphold the rules—that's their job. Few educators question these rules. Instead, they discuss how they can do things differently within the boundaries of the rules. After all, no one wants to be criticized, and no one wants negative headlines that might result if he or she breaks a rule.

But if we want to create new possibilities, if we want to create real breakthroughs in public education or in public anything, rule number one is, *we have to break the rules*. That's a given. No one at the Itasca Seminar that year was talking about blowing up the public education system and starting over. Speakers were noting that many good things were happening within the system.

But what if we suspended the rules for some small groups of parents, teachers, and students who voluntarily chose to "take the risk," as Shanker suggested, and try something new? This seemed reasonable. No one would force the other parents and colleagues to embrace the ideas of these small groups. But if the ideas generated good results and satisfaction, district schools could use these same ideas. In that way, the small groups could become the "research and development" sector for public education as a whole.

Here's what I and others at that seminar began to ask ourselves: *Could* chartered schools be that research and development sector for public education? Could chartered schools be a way of creating new choices for students and parents, without turning the public school system upside down? A seminar participant put it this way:

> The public education system is like a large boat moving through the ocean. It is hard to change the direction of a big ocean liner. But what if we launch a small boat alongside the big boat to see what might come of a new direction? The small boat doesn't replace the big boat; it moves on its own. If good results are generated, people choose to move from the big boat to the small boat, and the small boat grows in size.

Not only do we have a successful small boat meeting the needs of passengers, but the captain of the big boat may find new ways to serve his customers as well.

Frankly, my head was spinning. What would this system of chartering look like? Seminar participants had only to look at the success of New York City's District 4, with its autonomous schools, to know that good results could come from something like this. Could we build on Minnesota's innovative history of education reform and actually create something like chartered schools as the next logical step?

An Itasca Seminar is not only a great place to learn new ideas, but also a gathering of thoughtful people with whom to talk about them. This new concept of chartered schools interested more than simply me. Other attendees also sat up and took notice. That night at dinner, I sat with a dynamic group of colleagues. The discussion was fast and furious. What might a chartered school look like? How might it be created? Who would authorize it? How would the legislature react?

After the dessert was taken away, a few of us hung around the dinner table to continue the discussion. Among them were Elaine Salinas, program officer of the Urban Coalition; Joe Nathan, then director of Spring Hill Regional Issues Forum; and Barbara Zohn, president of the Minnesota Parent-Teacher Association (PTA). I believe a couple businesspeople were part of the group, but I don't recall who. Our brainstorming continued to flow. Maybe it was the wine!

As a legislator, I most wanted to think about what chartering legislation would look like. Ideas were flying all around me. I took out a pen, reached for a clean napkin, and jotted down the elements we would need to include in such a bill: Who goes to the chartered school? Who decides if a school gets a charter? Who holds those new chartered schools accountable? How do we ensure they are nonsectarian? How are they funded? What if they fail? What if they succeed?

The legislation creating chartered schools was born on a dinner napkin.

Chartering was a win-win all around.

5

The Template: The Citizens League

Creating any legislation from scratch isn't easy. In fact, it's down-right hard. Up to the end of 1988, others had prepared the education reform legislation I'd authored in the legislature. Open enrollment, of course, was an initiative of Governor Rudy Perpich, presented to me in a bill developed by the Minnesota Business Partnership. If I wanted to create legislation on chartered schools, I needed a template.

I found one quickly. To my huge relief, a Citizens League committee formed in February 1988 had been working on some innovative ideas in education. Chartered schools was one of them. They would release their report in December. The big connector in this scenario was Ted Kolderie, senior fellow of the Hubert H.

53

Humphrey Institute of Public Affairs at the University of Minnesota (now called the Humphrey School of Public Affairs). He too had attended the Itasca Seminar. Since 1959, Kolderie had worked in public affairs in the Twin Cities area as a journalist with Minneapolis newspapers. Most recently at the time, he'd served as executive director of the Citizens League. The truth is, the one person most responsible for the emergence and success of chartering is Kolderie. Later chapters will reveal the truth of that bold statement.

The Citizens League, for which Kolderie served as executive director, is a kind of "good government" group almost unique to Minnesota. In 1991, an editorial headline in the *St. Paul Pioneer Press* called the League "one of the state's treasures." The impact of its work on legislative policy was stunning. Prior to its work on chartering, the league recommended several proposals still in effect today in Minnesota: establishment of the Metropolitan Council; enactment of the 1971 Fiscal Disparities Act, a unique tax-based sharing system; the 1971 tax bill which came to be known as the "Minnesota Miracle"; and, yes, open enrollment in public schools.

In Steven Dornfeld's June 17, 1991, column in the *St. Paul Pioneer Press*, he quotes former *Star Tribune* editor and reporter Stephen Alnes as asserting that the "league has been more successful as an instrument of change than any organization in the state. If you want a breakthrough, if you want something different to happen, you don't look to the teacher groups, organized labor, or the political parties. The league is the best vehicle this state has for generating and examining new ideas."

On December 15, 1988, the Citizens League released its report urging the creation of chartered schools in combination with proposals to create "cooperatively managed schools" and to "broaden desegregation efforts." The report was the result of nine months of work by a committee made up of civic leaders and chaired by John Rollwagen. Committee members included Kolderie, vice chair Donn

McLellan, and Louise Sundin of the Minneapolis Federation of Teachers. Jody Hauer staffed the committee. The Citizens League report recommended that the Minnesota legislature do the following:

- Authorize creation of chartered schools by the Minneapolis and St. Paul School Districts in 1989 and by the State Department of Education by 1992. The schools would be open to students from other districts but would be located in Minneapolis or St. Paul, where educational inequities were most apparent. State funding would follow the students. Transportation aid would be provided.

- Allow school boards and teachers' bargaining units in all Minnesota districts to make a choice between (1) negotiating their own terms of management for individual schools; (2) adopting cooperative management of schools; or (3) retaining the current management arrangements.

The report then laid out a series of "elements" of chartered schools that became cornerstones of the legislation when it finally became Minnesota law in 1991. Most of the principles are remarkably central to chartering today:

- Chartered schools must meet specific criteria to establish the schools as "public" schools and to prevent the creation of "elitist" schools.

- Schools that fail to meet criteria within three years or fail to design a plan to meet them are subject to charter revocation.

- Chartered schools must accept students of all academic achievement levels.

- They must meet desegregation guidelines.

- They must not charge fees.

- They must be nonsectarian.

- They must meet accreditation standards.

- Licensed educators must operate chartered schools.

- Students attending chartered schools will be eligible for transportation aid.

- Groups receiving the public school charter can set up their innovative programs in existing schools or in buildings leased for this purpose.

In reviewing the Citizens League report twenty-three years later, I am struck by how fundamental it was to changing the entire nation's longtime, traditional thinking about the delivery of education services. Their rationale included the following points:

- A chartered school is one granted a "charter" by either a school district or the state to be different in the way it delivers education and, within broad guidelines, to be autonomous. It need not be a school building. It may result in several schools in one building. It is the *process* of schooling and *not the building itself* that will differentiate a chartered school from a conventional one.

- The chartering concept recognizes that different children learn in different ways and at different speeds, and teachers and schools should adapt to children's needs rather than require children to adapt to the standard system.

- Doing better necessarily implies the boldness to do things differently.

The report also gives a clue as to why chartered schools happened to arise first in Minnesota out of all the states in the union:

> Most recent efforts at education reform throughout the nation are based on requiring the same system to meet tougher new standards. Minnesota, in contrast, has taken an incentives-and-opportunities approach, giving schools a reason and a way to become better. The state should cling to this "Minnesota difference."

In presenting the report at a press conference, committee chair Rollwagen focused on a great sense of urgency facing Minnesota and the education community. As quoted in the December 16, 1988, *Star Tribune,* Rollwagen said, "If this doesn't work, we face draconian measures . . . because we're reaching a crisis point. . . . We feel chartered schools have the potential to achieve change rapidly." Rollwagen believed that chartered schools would generate in-school camaraderie, enthusiasm, and creativity the present school organizations usually did not allow.

Some in the education reform community, like Joe Nathan, did not think the report went far enough. Although not a member of the task force, Nathan had pushed task force members to espouse the notion of chartering outside the school system and of more flexibility in exchange for greater accountability. Nathan didn't agree with the approach of starting only with schools within Minneapolis and St. Paul school districts.

Nathan also disagreed with some of the requirements, or "elements," set forth by the Citizens League. One such requirement he found worrisome was the need to meet desegregation standards. In his 2011 interview, Nathan explained his point of view: "We had some fabulous schools all over the country that were mostly people of color." He specifically noted Sy Fliegel's Harlem schools.

The response from district administrators to the Citizens League report was to be expected. Robert Ferrera, superintendent of the Minneapolis School District, was quoted in the *Star Tribune* article:

> The concept of chartered schools is not something I'm opposed to if the public schools don't work. But before one says the public school system doesn't work, it has to have the resources it says it needs to fulfill the results the public says it wants. . . . There's nothing magic about chartered schools. There's nothing there that we couldn't do in public schools.

These comments illustrated both the wide gap between points of view as well as the difficulty of the road ahead. On one hand, Rollwagen, the committee chair of the Citizens League and a business executive, saw chartering as a response to a "crisis" in education. On the other hand, Ferrera, the urban school district superintendent, saw it as a solution in search of a problem that didn't exist. According to Ferrera, if the public would only provide the needed financial resources, public schools would be just fine.

As a policymaker who was a product of public schools, but not an educator, my point of view came down somewhere in the middle. This idea for chartered schools wasn't about responding to a "crisis" in education. This wasn't about criticizing the good work that public schools were doing. Instead, it was about stimulating new ways to meet the needs of children and families that the current public schools were simply not meeting. Some kids were falling through the cracks.

For me, chartered schools were about the freedom to become innovative and to create new ways of helping our children learn. They were also about unlocking the creativity of our teachers so they could try new ways of teaching. I was certain that if we unlocked that creativity, all schools in the public system could benefit. To me, chartering was a win-win all around.

*Ted Kolderie is the godfather of chartering
and all that it is today.*

6

Ted Kolderie: Withdrawing the
Exclusive Franchise

To Ted Kolderie—respected newspaper and public television journalist, policy fellow at the Hubert H. Humphrey Institute of the University of Minnesota, former executive director of the Citizens League, and member of the Citizens League committee—chartering was more than simply a win-win. It was key to fundamental reform of the public education system in this country. It was about "withdrawing the exclusive franchise in public education." Only by withdrawing exclusivity could we move beyond public school choice to new public schools. And only the state—the legislature or the governor—could do that.

What does "withdrawing the exclusive franchise" mean? Each of the fifty states sets up its public school system using districts. That is, a district is the only organization offering public education to the schools and children in any assigned geographic area. Thus, public education is a "pattern of territorial exclusive franchises." Kolderie and others believed that an organization with that kind of exclusive franchise would have no reason to change. As Albert Shanker told attendees of the October 1988 Itasca Seminar, "This is a system that can take its customers for granted."

According to Kolderie, this dynamic changes in two steps. First, the state transfers the attendance decision to the student, as Minnesota did with its statewide open enrollment choice. Second, the state makes possible the option of setting up new public schools, sponsored by some public organization other than the district. That's chartering. To Kolderie, the idea of the alternate sponsor—someone other than the district—was absolutely critical to the effort to produce schools operating in new and better ways.

In his July 1990 paper, *The States Will Have to Withdraw the Exclusive,* he states:

> A district fears new schools; even its own. Its interest is entirely in restructuring existing schools: "Help all schools" is the cry. Governors and legislators will need to resist this. They cannot let their options be limited to actions that begin with "re-": Restructuring, revitalizing, reforming, and retraining old institutions is the slowest way to change. There must also be a way to create different and better schools new.
>
> This can happen only if the state opens up the opportunity for some public organization other than the district to start a public school. New sponsors are more important than

new schools, because new sponsors are the key to the appearance of new schools. Innovation almost always moves faster between organizations than within them.

It is critical, too, that the sponsor not own the school. If it did, it would control through process, as the district does now. It should be required to control through performance. Then it will set objectives and measure results. The school must be separate.

The Citizens League report detailed in chapter 5 incorporated many of Kolderie's insights. That wasn't coincidental. In a project known as Public Service Options (PSO), he and the Citizens League had been thinking all through the 1970s about "alternative arrangements" for the public sector. Subsequently, Kolderie and John Cairns, then leader of the Minnesota Business Partnership, created PSO's successor, Public School Incentives. Alternative options for K–12 public schools such as choice and site-based management were part of these efforts.

To know Kolderie is to know someone of extraordinary vision, who often thinks light-years ahead, but still gently prods others along to where he wants them to go. He is accessible, always helpful, always on the phone or meeting with someone who wants to discuss the next idea. He is patient. And most of all, he is humble. He takes no credit for anything. When change for the better occurs, Kolderie credits the power of ideas, not his power as an individual.

Kolderie is someone who would offer me his frequent-flier miles so I could travel somewhere to speak on chartering. Over the years, he contributed generously to support innovation efforts through chartering. Beyond all that, as Beth Hawkins wrote in her August 19, 2011, article for MinnPost.com,

[Kolderie] is a convener of big conversations about big ideas. He writes, he reads, he gets other big thinkers into the same room, tosses a topic at them and then literally records what they come up with. Weeks or months after a Kolderie-led brainstorming session, attendees can expect to receive minutes as a gentle prodding to turn talk into action.

And when Kolderie invited you to a meeting, you attended. No one described this better than Eric Premack, a longtime family friend who Kolderie said he'd known "since he was in short pants." Kolderie drew Premack into discussions about education when Premack was in high school. Premack would eventually become, in his own right, a chartering leader both in California and nationwide.

Premack attended Minneapolis Washburn High School in the early 1980s. Premack was a high school journalist—not surprising, given that his father was Frank Premack, noted *Star Tribune* political reporter and city editor. According to Premack in his 2011 interview:

> The Minneapolis School District was going through a very serious financial retrenchment due to fairly sharp declines in enrollment and other factors. As a high school student, I wrote for the school newspaper . . . and knew Superintendent [Richard] Green and other folks at the school district a little bit. I learned quite a bit about how the school district responded to retrenchment, and often [it] didn't do it very well . . .
>
> Way back then I remember Ted invited us over to his house. . . . [It was] a classic Ted discussion. You get invited over, and you really don't know what he wants to talk about. . . . He was just picking my brain about, what does this look like inside Washburn High School? I rattled on

about all the teachers being bumped and all the young teachers getting fired. I had written an editorial in the high school newspaper about our school becoming "Geriatric High," which didn't go over too well with the faculty. . . .

Sometime later he invited me to a discussion at, I think, Lindquist and Vennum [Law Firm] in downtown Minneapolis. . . . He had assembled the managing partner for that firm, plus the managing partner from . . . one of the group medical clinics, somebody from . . . one of the engineering or architectural firms, and a bunch of forward-thinking educator types he knew—some superintendents, principals, and teachers. In classic form, nobody knew what they were there for.

He put these three firm managers at the head of a [large] conference table. . . . Each of the three firm managers briefly described . . . who they were; what they did within their organization; what the power structure was within their organization; and how they made key financial, strategic, and personnel decisions.

Finally, as the third guy made it partway through [his organization's description], one of the teachers got the light going off in his head and said, "So . . . if we did what you guys are doing, then the principal would work for me, and I could fire him. And I would get to decide how much I get paid, along with my other [teachers]." It was sort of like a flashbulb went off in the room at that point. . . . That's where folks had the "aha moment."

Kolderie would continue to invite Premack to these random meetings, some of them directly focused on charters, some on open enrollment, some related to teacher professional partnerships—a favorite concept for Kolderie—and some related to postsecondary enrollment options.

All of this was going on in the early and mid-1980s, when public school choice legislation was taking root in Minnesota. During one of these discussions, an attendee expressed frustration: "Yes, we have choice now. But if all you have on the shelf is white Wonder bread, how much choice do you really have?"

For Premack, all these different concepts floating around started to gel. "For all I know," he said, "they had already gelled ten years prior in Ted's head." From then on, almost every time Premack returned home from his California college, "Ted would drag me along to at least one meeting." When he finished college, Premack worked as an intern for Kolderie and the Citizens League, and Kolderie invited him to work with a small group on drafting the first chartering legislation.

This is how ideas form: listening . . . engaging . . . listening . . . engaging. That kind of process takes great patience. Kolderie was a master at creating, refining, and redirecting ideas. He never would publicly "own" any ideas, and ways to improve those ideas always presented themselves. He nurtured ideas and connected the dots for others.

In the end, ideas are only ideas. Someone has to implement them. Usually, governors introduce big reform ideas, and legislators pass them. That wasn't the case with chartering. Chartered schools truly came from the citizen grassroots. Legislators simply captured the idea. Legislators don't have the resources governors have to create a bully pulpit and a large constituency to pass a big idea. So, in retrospect, fundamental change like chartering probably shouldn't have happened.

But two things were different in the state of Minnesota in the late '80s. First, Governor Rudy Perpich—the "Education Governor"—had already opened the door to public school choice. Chartering seemed the natural extension of that. I thought the whole concept was an easy sell.

Second, there was Kolderie. A governor doesn't have to boldly lead a new initiative when a state has a thoughtful and credible policy champion like Kolderie who can enroll others. The reason why Kolderie was among the "charter" group of original inductees into the National Charter Schools Hall of Fame in 2007 is simple: Ted Kolderie is the godfather of chartering and all that it is today.

Could the voices of parents, students, business and civic leaders, and entrepreneurial educators overcome expected objections from the education establishment?

7

Creative Writing: The First Chartering Legislation

DECEMBER 1988–JANUARY 1989

The time had come to take the next step with the chartering vision of Ted Kolderie and the Citizens League report. With the report in hand as well as notes from the Itasca Seminar discussions, Kolderie, I, and others sat down with Betsy Rice, Minnesota Senate counsel, in December 1988 and early January 1989. We began to shape what this new concept of chartering and new chartered schools might look like.

Lessons learned from passage of the open enrollment legislation and my own strategic sense guided me toward creating another comprehensive education reform bill, with chartered schools as only one part of it. My reasoning was that if the bill focused only on chartered schools, it might immediately become a lightning rod that would generate opposition. I knew we needed time to sell my colleagues and the public on this exciting new concept.

In January 1989, I introduced in the Minnesota Senate an education reform package that included proposals for mandatory statewide testing, school district surveys, and chartered schools. Mandatory testing, of course, had been part of my 1988 education reform package legislation. While we had successfully passed open enrollment from that bill, neither the house nor senate had passed the testing provisions. The second portion of the new bill, school district surveys, required districts to provide certain uniform data to the department of education so parents would have greater information in exercising open enrollment choices. The third section proposed the creation of chartered schools, with the report by the Citizens League as a template. The bill allowed school boards or the state board of education to grant charters anywhere in the state, not just in the Minneapolis or St. Paul school districts. This differed from the Citizens League's vision, but the group continued to support the proposal.

The coauthors—DFL senators Keith Langseth, Larry Pogemiller, and Donna Peterson, and Republican senator Duane Benson— joined me in introducing the senate education reform package as SF 212 early in the 1989 legislative session. The DFLers all served with me on the senate Education Funding Division, and Benson was the Republican minority leader at the time. DFL representative Ken Nelson, chair of the house Education Finance Division, introduced the house companion education reform bill—HF 1433—on the same day.

The legislation received two hearings in the senate—on March 6 and again on April 4. My sense of the committee discussion was that most people were not taking the chartering idea seriously. They perceived it as a radical departure from the current system, one that definitely needed time to develop. Only the Citizens League and Joe Nathan testified in favor of chartering. And only the Minnesota School Boards Association testified against. Notably, the teacher unions offered no opposition. Actually, most of the testimony regarding my bill was in support for or in opposition to the statewide testing portion, just as had happened the year before.

To at least pass into law some form of the chartering concept, I worked with Senator Randy Peterson, chair of the senate Education Funding Division, and other committee members to narrow the legislation to a chartering pilot program for inclusion in the 1989 omnibus education funding bill. The group agreed to allow two chartered schools: one authorized by the Minneapolis School District and one by Robbinsdale Area Schools, my home school district. Under the pilot program, only after June 30, 1992, could the state board of education grant a charter to an applicant whose application was denied by one of these two school boards.

As I look back now, I understand why teachers didn't oppose this bill and why it didn't create much controversy. The compromise bill required that an application include "evidence of an agreement with all of the bargaining units in the district about employment procedures for the chartered school." The bill also required that teachers in chartered schools be included in the school district's collective bargaining agreement. So, while we had some elements of autonomy in the bill, this pilot program resembled specialized "in-district" schools under contract with the school board, rather than the autonomous chartered schools the legislative drafting group envisioned.

Even this very weak pilot chartering program failed to pass the 1989 house-senate conference committee on the omnibus education funding bill. The house companion bill had been heard only briefly on April 7 and never came to a vote. The house conferees defeated the senate proposal in conference committee.

I learned early on that a conference committee is not the best place to educate legislators on a concept as complex as chartering. In retrospect, waiting another year was a good thing. The pilot proposal, after all, wasn't the kind of chartering concept my coauthors and I had envisioned. Such a compromise might have taken chartering supporters off course in our efforts to develop the true concept.

I was also aware that controversial legislation can take years to pass. During that same 1989 legislative session, I was experiencing a brutal battle as lead author of a living will bill, which had been delayed passage for four years due to the powerful influence of an antiabortion organization. The living will bill finally passed because those before me had worked painstakingly to build a coalition of supporters who became more powerful collectively than the anti-abortion organization.

I wondered if we could ever build that kind of coalition around education reform and chartering. Could the voices of parents, students, business and civic leaders, and entrepreneurial educators overcome expected objections from the education establishment?

It would become a prescient question.

The US public was ready for "tradition-shattering changes" in the policies that govern schooling.

8

Focus on "Change" Becomes Central to Public Conversation

LATE 1989–1990

By their nature, legislative bodies react to public conversation. Initiating or shaping a conversation is harder for legislators than, say, a governor or a university president. The public conversation—at any given time and at both the national and state levels—has enormous impact on the degree of success in generating legislative response.

The national conversation was boiling up on education reform issues in late 1989–1990. I knew our chartered school proposal and even the first results from open enrollment were well ahead of the national response. We needed to let the conversation catch up to us in Minnesota. And soon, it did.

In the September 1989 issue of *Kappan,* the publication of the professional fraternity in education, the results of the "21st Annual Gallup Poll of the Public's Attitudes Toward the Public Schools" were reported to the nation.

The report authors found that the US public was ready for "tradition-shattering changes" in the policies that govern schooling. "The public favors," the report said, "by a 2–1 margin, allowing students and their parents to choose which public schools in their communities the students will attend." The authors found that the idea of parental choice—already state law in at least three states (including Minnesota) and a centerpiece of the Bush administration's education policy—was especially popular among nonwhites and younger adults.

By this time, both President George H. W. Bush and the nation's governors were recognizing the urgency of the public demand for reform in education. Bush invited the nation's governors to an unprecedented Summit on Education held September 27–28, 1989, in Charlottesville, Virginia. There the president and the governors agreed to work together to establish, for the first time in our nation's history, a comprehensive set of national education goals. This was significant in that it signaled Republican acceptance of a greater federal role in education. The plan developed at the summit became the foundation for a report that the National Governors Association would adopt on February 25, 1990. In their report, the governors made the urgency clear:

> Our nation is facing a major crisis in education, one larger and more significant than was realized even a few short years ago. The challenges are substantially greater than those envisioned in *A Nation at Risk.* . . .

All available evidence clearly indicates that an enormous gap exists between current performance levels and those required to secure our future. Despite widespread efforts at reform, the plain fact is that our nation is not more prepared now to meet the challenge than it was a decade ago.

We must also recognize that, with respect to the national goals, our schools are failing. . . . The way students learn in school bears virtually no resemblance to the way they will learn once they are in the workforce.

In their report, the governors emphasized that they were not blaming educators for the failures of the education system. According to the report,

Teachers and administrators are doing the job that has been given to them, not the job that needs to be done. . . . They are working in a system that was invented nearly a century ago, not one redesigned for the next century. . . . We cannot continue to tinker with an educational machine whose fundamental design is defective. More resources may be necessary, but money alone will not stave off continuing failure if the system remains unchanged. Instead, fundamental and dramatic changes in the very design and structure of the education system must be made. . . .

The challenges we face are clear. To achieve the national education goals, we must invent a new education system for the twenty-first century. We must put people and performance first and institutions second.

One of the leading governors on these education initiatives was Democratic governor Bill Clinton of Arkansas. He was serving at that time as chair of the Democratic Governors Association. Under his leadership, Arkansas had become the first state in the country to follow Minnesota's open enrollment plan. Clinton may well have influenced other governors in developing the following collective principles for our nation's public education system. As I read this list today, anyone could entitle it "Principles for Chartered Schools" and create a pretty good fit.

- **The system must provide meaningful choices** to students, parents, and adult learners by recognizing and accommodating their varying learning needs and styles.

- **The system must be performance-oriented**, with an unwavering commitment to achieving results, rather than to maintaining existing procedures, practices, or institutions.

- **The system must be flexible**. Professionals should decide how best to help each individual achieve at high levels, rather than being told what to do and how to do it by distant authorities.

- **The system and those who work in it must be accountable** for the results they achieve. There must be real rewards for high performance and significant consequences for failure.

- **The system must attract and retain talented professionals** and ensure that they receive continued support and professional development.

Among all this conversation and national debate, I and others continued working to pass chartering legislation in the Minnesota Senate. During the 1990 legislative session, chartering was once again included as part of the senate omnibus education funding bill. This time the chartering provisions allowed up to five school districts to grant charters. Once again, the house members in conference committee resisted the chartering provisions and removed them before final passage. The time wasn't yet ripe for chartered schools.

But the national drumbeat for change and for education reform continued to get louder. On June 5, 1990, reporter Kenneth H. Bacon of the *Wall Street Journal* wrote, "Liberals are joining conservatives in calling for an infusion of free-enterprise philosophy that would shake up the nation's school systems and provide more choices for parents and students."

Bacon pointed to AFT president Albert Shanker's proposal to give public schools new freedom to innovate by releasing them from most regulations. He then drew attention to the release that week of a new report from the Brookings Institution (considered a "liberal redoubt," he said) called "Politics, Markets and America's Schools." In this report, Bacon said John Chubb of Brookings and Terry Moe of Stanford University proposed "a new system of public education that eliminates most political and bureaucratic control over the schools and relies instead on indirect control through markets and parental choice."

Closer to home and in a wake-up call to liberals, Wisconsin Democratic representative Polly Williams succeeded in passing a kind of voucher legislation that allowed one thousand children from low-income families in Milwaukee to attend private schools with as much as $2,500 per year in tuition assistance from the state. Republican governor Tommy Thompson of Wisconsin helped push through the plan. The state superintendent of public instruction opposed the new law, and the teacher unions took it to court. But this new, more real threat of private school vouchers stoked the national education reform conversation.

The Minnesota legislature had a bipartisan history of opposing private school vouchers, and I personally opposed them. As defined in national polling questions, vouchers were scholarships funded by public money that enabled students to attend sectarian and nonsectarian private schools. I and most other voucher opponents resisted the diversion of public monies to private and religious schools for at least two reasons: 1) public funding to religious schools was a violation of the constitutional separation of church and state; and 2) private schools were not held to the same standards of accountability as public schools.

I wasn't quite sure how the voucher debate would affect our chartering legislation, but I knew it would be part of it. The voucher conversation was ratcheting up nationwide as the public continued to seek "tradition-shattering" changes. It was becoming clear to me that supporters of the chartering legislation I'd proposed for two years had to distinguish public school charters from private school vouchers at the outset, or we would have no chance of passing it.

In 1990, the Progressive Policy Institute (PPI), a little-known organization based in Washington, DC, joined the national conversation on education reform. President Will Marshall founded PPI in 1989 as a center for policy innovation that would develop alternatives to the "conventional left-right debate." PPI was a project of the center-left Democratic Leadership Council (DLC), which was just coming into its own as the "Third Way" in proposing centrist solutions to complex policy issues. In its publications at the time, PPI described its purpose in part as follows: "The Institute offers a platform to a new generation of progressive thinkers and writers around the country. Through its studies on public enterprise, PPI examines ideas for renewing the public sector by redesigning government along more entrepreneurial and less bureaucratic lines."

Marshall and his colleagues at PPI immediately recognized open enrollment and public school choice as significant alternatives to the "left-right debate." Marshall learned of these alternatives through David Osborne, who had researched innovative policy ideas around the country for his 1988 book, *Laboratories of Democracy*. Osborne discovered Ted Kolderie and Minnesota's public school choice initiative and also wrote about Clinton as an innovative governor. Osborne invited Kolderie to join him for a "reinventing government" panel at the 1990 DLC convention. It was there that Osborne introduced Marshall to Kolderie, who proceeded to sell Marshall on chartering. As Marshall described in an April 2011 interview,

> There was something very fascinating here. Ted was thinking about how to go beyond the public school district choice model to allow you to create schools anywhere. He understood the need to bring innovative schools to where kids live, rather than have kids search for them. His idea was this: what if we withdrew the exclusive franchise of the districts in owning all the public schools in their area? It was a radical reimagining of school, by one of the foremost educational visionaries in our country. . . .
>
> This idea was emblematic of the Third Way, of what PPI could offer to Democrats. Vouchers were in the air. So was privatizing public schools. Ted was way ahead of his time. His idea allowed entrepreneurial people and teachers to create innovative public schools. Ted called it the research and development sector in public education.

Marshall helped Kolderie hone the chartered school vision, and Kolderie then authored one of the first policy papers produced by PPI. Marshall played an editorial role, pushing for clarity for a wide audience. In November 1990, PPI published its policy report—*Beyond Choice to New Public Schools: Withdrawing the Exclusive Franchise in Public Education.* The report was based on Kolderie's original July 1990 paper about chartered schools, but the concept was now more fully developed, as together the two men introduced to a national audience the idea of "withdrawing the exclusive franchise." The executive summary did not mince words in describing the problem to be addressed:

Growing public support for a radically transformed school system stems from the failure of public education to put children first. The education establishment has been full of good intentions and more than willing to spend the public's money. But it has not been willing to change itself in basic ways. Public education has remained a system of big organizations—big schools in big buildings, organized in a traditional, top-down way like the Army or the Postal Service. No matter how unresponsive and ineffective this way of organizing learning has become, the prevailing ideology insists that local school districts must retain their monopoly on providing public schools to the children of the community.

It is time to say this: our system of public education is a bad system. It is terribly inequitable. It does not meet the nation's needs. It exploits teachers' altruism. It hurts kids. Instead of blaming people—administrators, teachers, politicians, parents—we need to fix the system. It is time to organize public education in America on a new basis.

The proposal outlined in this report is designed to introduce the dynamics of choice, competition, and innovation into America's public school system, while at the same time ensuring that new schools serve broad public purposes.

Meanwhile, in Minnesota, I was focused on my own reelection to the Minnesota Senate and was mostly unaware of Kolderie's efforts on the national level. Just as I was recovering from the election, he gave me a copy of the PPI policy report. I skimmed it and filed it away. As a legislative member of the Democratic Leadership Council,

I was pleased to see PPI's support of the chartering idea. But frankly, I had no idea what a significant role that report would play in the future of chartered schools.

I was paying more attention to what was happening in Minnesota. More and more parents and students were participating in the third year of public school open enrollment as well as postsecondary enrollment options—and they were liking the results. Not only students were benefitting, but school systems as well.

Take the Westonka school district, in the western suburbs of Minneapolis. In the fall of 1987, Westonka was in the national news as one of two school districts in Minnesota hit hard by loss of students during the first year of mandatory open enrollment. The superintendent was critical of the new law. That all changed in a couple years. Westonka applied for and was selected for a grant-funded technology project. As stated transparently in its proposal:

> In the past, it was necessary to compete by attracting new residents with school age children to live in the school community. Now, with the advent of Open Enrollment, being competitive also involves maintaining a level of education service so that resident families and their students do not see neighboring school districts as better and open enrolling in them. With much to do both to improve instructional services and the quality image of the Westonka District, technology was envisioned as being the advantage. . . . Technology could be the means of excelling and then competing in the Minnesota open enrollment environment.

When parents and citizens find value in educational opportunity and results like these begin to happen within existing institutions, the perceived objections to system change go away, and a constituency is built. Open enrollment was already building a powerful constituency of families around the state. I was learning that once the genie is out of the bottle, no one can put it back in! The ripples of choice were moving farther and farther away from the state capitol.

The public conversation wasn't just changing on the national level. It was happening right here at home, one family at a time, and legislators were hearing about it.

PART III

The Minnesota Story— Blueprint to Legislative Passage, *Not* Civics 101

I wondered:
Was this the point where we tell the house conferees
that we wanted to lay the bill over for yet another session?
How can we pass a bill
with the name "chartered school"
when it is destined to fail?
Do we pass a bill intended to create chartered schools
that doesn't allow real opportunity for them to be created?
Do we pass a bill that allows critics to say in coming years,
"See, no one really wanted to create any chartered schools"?

It's not about a public school,
but the delivery of public education.

TED KOLDERIE

9

Transforming Ideas into Legislation:
A Painstaking Process

LATE 1990–1991

For many reasons, 1990 was an important election year. DFL governor Rudy Perpich was seeking reelection for a fourth (nonconsecutive) term as governor. All legislators were up for election. Things were quiet on the policy front, and chartering wasn't an election issue. The idea was still largely unknown, and few viewed the concept as likely to become law.

That was the perfect time to step back, reflect, rethink, and start again. At Ted Kolderie's urging, Commissioner of Education Tom Nelson convened a working group to carefully think through the chartering legislation. The group included people from public education and four key communities of color, as well as others interested in improving the system, but not necessarily directly involved in it. Members included, among others, Terry Lydell, a teacher from my senate district; Carol McGee Johnson from the University of Minnesota; Ruth Anne Olson, an education consultant; Kolderie, Curt Johnson, and Peter Vanderpoel of the Citizens League; Verne Johnson, former executive director of the Citizens League; Joe Nathan of the Center for School Change at the Hubert H. Humphrey Institute of the University of Minnesota; Doug Wallace of the state board of education; and Bob Wedl of the Minnesota Department of Education.

This was good news. I had served with DFLer Nelson on the Education Committee during my first term in the senate, when he chaired its influential subgroup, the Education Aids Subcommittee. Both sides of the aisle highly respected him. He'd left behind a strong legacy of support for education when he retired from the senate in 1986. In early 1990, after the departure of former commissioner of education Ruth Randall, Perpich appointed Nelson to serve as commissioner. He was the perfect person to lead the review of the chartering legislation.

By December 1990, a new draft bill emerged from the working group. It focused on the nuts and bolts of implementation, including how chartering would be integrated into a variety of funding formulas, special education mandates, and facilities revenue. The committee recommended that the schools be called "outcome-based schools" rather than "chartered schools" to emphasize an important educational focus of the day. Members believed the focus on outcomes and results would strengthen the legislation and help its passage into law.

The new draft bill also allowed schools to organize under Minnesota law as either nonprofit corporations or cooperatives. Finally, the bill expanded prospective charter sponsors beyond the school district and the state board of education to include higher education institutions. This legislation reflected a shift of philosophy. At the time, Kolderie wrote in a widely distributed memorandum, "With the 'charter school' the state makes it possible for more than one public organization to offer public school on the same piece of ground. Like open enrollment, this changes the traditional givens: it 'un-districts' the system. So it requires a new way of thinking about public education."

Kolderie framed the key elements of the chartered school idea, as summarized here:

- It opens the way for different schools to be created new.

- A variety of organizations—not just the local school board—could organize new schools.

- It is a contract system, not a voucher system.

- A variety of public bodies could sponsor a new school.

- The school gets to trade regulations for results.

- *It's not about a public school, but the delivery of public education.*

That latter point was most fundamental to Kolderie's vision. He tells the story of a conversation with senate counsel Betsy Rice, who drafted the 1991 chartering legislation. After Kolderie described the key components, Rice replied, "These are not public schools."

He responded, "They are part of the state's program of public education."

In her thoughtful way, Rice reflected, looked out the window for a while, and replied "Okay."

If there is one unsung hero in the chartered school story, it is Rice. She went to law school later in life. Her thoughtfulness in shaping the chartering legislation was key to its ultimate success. As a lawyer, I found working with Rice comforting. She raised good questions, and she wasn't afraid to challenge. At my request, she met frequently with Kolderie and others who had ideas and comments about the bill. Being a legislative counsel is a difficult job. But Rice was focused on the ultimate outcome: shaping legislation to express our intent, while anticipating as many issues as possible. An example of this was a memo she sent me on January 22, 1991, raising no less than three pages of questions about the bill:

- Which state statutes are applicable to the chartered schools and which are not?

- Do collective bargaining rights apply?

- What personnel must hold licenses?

- What curriculum is required?

- Is there a minimum number of days the school must provide instruction?

- Can the school sue and be sued?

- Can a school board sponsor existing private schools as outcome-based schools?

- Is a sponsor required to take action when things go wrong at the school?

As I look back at her memo twenty years later, several questions strike me as especially insightful. "Can charter schools offer, perhaps exclusively, adult education, pre-school, community education, etc.?"

she asked. Today there is at least one successful adult-education chartered school in the District of Columbia, and there may be other examples of chartering around the country that go beyond K–12 education. That's the innovation of the chartering process. In another question, she noted that "all school districts receiving less than the state average of general education revenue would receive more money under the bill than current law (since charters receive all state money and no local property taxes). Although I suspect it wouldn't happen, isn't there a financial incentive to convert all of these schools to outcome-based schools?" Now, that's something I had never even thought about. In retrospect, the incentive was clearly there. How interesting that no small school district in Minnesota with property wealth ever took it on. But it was the precursor to the idea of a "charter district," which some parts of the country, such as New Orleans, have partially implemented.

Rice sadly passed away a few years later, but not before she saw the language she drafted in the Minnesota chartering law replicated in dozens of states around the country. Those of us involved in government must never underestimate the importance of insightful, dedicated legislative staff. And Rice was one of the best.

Just as the chartering legislation changed over time, so did the politics and the players. In January 1991, Republican Arne Carlson was inaugurated as governor of Minnesota, after defeating DFL governor Rudy Perpich. Commissioner of Education Tom Nelson resigned, and in his stead, Carlson appointed a surprise choice— Gene Mammenga, the lobbyist for the Minnesota Education Association (MEA). The MEA, one of the state's two teacher unions, had endorsed Carlson over Perpich during the 1990 election.

Just prior to Carlson's inauguration, the Minnesota State Board of Education had endorsed the new chartered school proposal "after lengthy discussion." Doug Wallace, a longtime member of the board and member of Commissioner Nelson's working group, advocated strongly for the board's endorsement. With the change in administration, this endorsement took on more significance than usual. Neither Carlson nor Mammenga supported chartering at the time.

Against this new political backdrop, and with painstaking preparations, the new legislation creating chartered public schools was now ready for prime time.

I had zero confidence that the bill would pass.
I thought it was the longest of long shots.

Representative Becky Kelso

10

The Hearings Begin:
The Players Line Up

March–April 1991

On March 7, 1991, I introduced in the Minnesota Senate SF 630, "a bill authorizing outcome-based schools." I was pleased to have powerful coauthors on the bill, all members of the senate Education Funding Division. DFL coauthors included Senator Greg Dahl, chair of the Education Committee; Senator Ron Dicklich, chair of the Education Funding Division; and Senator Larry Pogemiller. Senator Gen Olson was the Republican on the bill.

When the senate leadership appointed Dicklich of Hibbing as the new chair of the senate Education Funding Division in late November 1990, his firm stand for chartering would become pivotal in the coming conference committee negotiations. In the Minnesota Senate (and Minnesota House of Representatives), the chair of the smaller Education Funding Division is actually more powerful than the chair of the full Education Committee, as the full committee deals primarily with policy, rather than budget, matters.

Though Dicklich had a teaching degree, he had taught only a short time in a community college. Nevertheless, his degree, together with his service on the Education Committee and the Funding Division, made him the "go-to guy" for education for the entire Iron Range, a large area of northern Minnesota that was solidly DFL, solidly union, and dependent on the mining industry. The Iron Range had strong influence in the DFL-controlled legislature, and Iron Rangers were known for their ability to "make deals" and bring home dollars to the Range. Like other areas of the state, the Iron Range was facing declining enrollment in their K–12 schools, and budget cutbacks and closures loomed large.

One such threatened school closure first brought the issue of chartered schools to Dicklich's attention. Gerald Wick, whom Dicklich knew and who was very active in the community, approached Dicklich when the St. Louis County Schools superintendent announced a year in advance that the Meadowlands school would be shut down. Wick said he'd talked to someone in the Twin Cities who told him about chartered schools. So Dicklich immediately asked senate counsel Betsy Rice to fill him in on the chartering legislation that passed the senate in 1989 and 1990. In his 2011 interview, Dicklich confided,

> Now I had an interest. All legislation is local. It only means something if there's somebody in your ear. That

became the tipping point for me that brought me to be—not an advocate—but a strong supporter of charter schools. We could see then that rural schools were going to start to fail because of declining enrollment. I just thought it might be a tool or an option for people to keep their schools. . . . The school is the nucleus of the community. If you lose your schools, it's like losing a major organ. We'd already been losing schools on the Range.

Dicklich's house counterpart—Representative Ken Nelson, chair of the house Education Finance Division—was equally supportive. I sent a copy of the drafted legislation to Nelson, who had been the lead house sponsor with me on the original chartering bill in the two earlier legislative sessions of 1989 and 1990. He, too, had attended the 1988 Itasca Seminar and had conversed with Albert Shanker and Sy Fliegel. He was also aware of the Citizens League's interest in the idea, and one of his constituents—Louise Sundin, head of the Minneapolis Federation of Teachers—was on the Citizens League committee. In his interview, Nelson said,

I did introduce the [1989–1990] bill in the legislature, partly because of the Citizens League interest in it. I authored the charter school bill almost as an aside. I saw it as impor-tant, but it did not rise to the top of my legislative agenda, simply because of the demands of [chairing] the Education Finance [Division]. . . . I put it in, but I didn't push it hard. I didn't make a big deal about it. I don't even know if I had a hearing on it.

Elected in 1972, Nelson was a well-liked legislator from Minne-apolis. He was a member of the full Education Committee the entire time he served and had chaired the influential Education Finance

Division since 1985. Before he ran for the legislature, Nelson was a Lutheran clergyman, not an educator. His first six years of schooling took place in a one-room schoolhouse in Grant County's Delaware Township in west-central Minnesota. For junior and senior high school, he attended Herman, a small rural school. "I always valued education, and just felt [it] was one of the best areas to serve in," Nelson said. "I was always trying to reform and improve education. I saw that as a lifetime commitment." Nelson supported postsecondary enrollment options in 1985 and played a key role in the passage of open enrollment in 1988.

Nelson was a member of several national committees for education lawmakers. In his interview, he explained that

> It was kind of exciting to be part of a change process like that, which I attribute to Perpich's leading. As we went around the country, people had heard about it and . . . it kind of strokes your ego. . . . "You in Minnesota are doing some great stuff. How do you do it?" We became leaders in this realm of opportunity. . . . Charter schools were just sort of a logical step for Minnesota to take.

Nelson always remained supportive of the bill, but when the new, revised chartering bill was ready for introduction in the 1991 legislative session, he chose to ask Representative Becky Kelso, a third-term house member from suburban Shakopee, to be lead sponsor on the bill. Kelso had served as a member of the Shakopee School Board before her election in 1986 to the house. At the end of the second round of conference committee discussions in 1990, Kelso had offered me her support for the legislation.

"I took the bill because I thought it was a good idea," she said in her February 2011 interview. "I would have been for anything that would take away power from the public school establishment—anything short of vouchers, because I feel strongly about the separation of church and state." Kelso acknowledged that "without a doubt," being on the school board affected her opinion.

I was on the school board for six years. I was not a typical school board member. A lot of school board members want to maintain the power of school boards, which [chartering] would have put a small dent into. Not that I thought school boards were terribly powerful. School boards were terribly ineffective against teachers unions. That made me feel like we needed more choice for parents and more student empowerment.

As a legislator, I had so much frustration at what I perceived as a property tax issue. They'd settle the contract and then ask for the money to pay for it in a property tax referendum. Then they would list the cuts that would be made if the voters didn't pass the referendum. They put their school district in that situation by spending the money up front before they had it. I just hated that.

I hated the part that most school board members didn't see it that way. Superintendents do what's easy for superintendents, which is not to have teacher strikes. That made me very cynical. We can't take a strike, so you've already decided you can't take that last step. So, you'd go into horrible negotiating.

I was pleased Kelso would be leading the charge in the house. Capitol insiders considered her a "rising star" on the house Education Finance Division, and she and Nelson would make a powerful team. When asked in her 2011 interview how confident she'd been in getting the bill through the house when she first introduced it, she replied, to my enormous surprise,

> I had *zero* confidence that the bill would pass. I thought it was the longest of long shots. I knew how my party works, and I knew the influence of the teachers unions. Teachers are spread throughout the state, just like the population. They have the influence and the dollars, and I just didn't think they'd let something like this go through. I thought it would take years, perhaps when the Republicans controlled the house. I thought the chances were slim to none.

I'm glad I never asked her the question twenty years ago.

Kelso's coauthors on the bill were strong—they included Nelson, DFL representatives Kathleen Vellenga and Alice Hausman, and Republican representative Charlie Weaver. Elected in 1988, Weaver was an "up-and-comer" on the Republican side. He was already one of the lead Republicans on the Education Committee. According to Weaver in his 2011 interview, he joined the bill because

> I had a great respect for [Kelso]. . . . We were kindred spirits. She was willing to take on the establishment, which I liked. Chartered schools fit within my general view that more opportunity for parents is good, no matter what it is—open enrollment, postsecondary options, chartered schools, vouchers, you name it. I was a prosecutor at the time, so I was seeing every day . . . kids who were dropping out or failing or weren't being helped by our education system, who were ending up in our criminal system. To me, the failure of our education system was personal. I was seeing it every single day in the courthouse.

In another political twist, Weaver was one of few Republicans the two teacher unions endorsed. He explained,

> I think it was partly the recognition they weren't going to beat me. They're pragmatic. Part of it was I had a lot of support from teachers in my district. My campaign manager was a teacher. I had gone to Anoka-Hennepin schools [in my district] . . . so I knew a lot of people among the ranks. I got along well with the union leadership. We didn't agree on everything, but I liked them.

With all the coauthors in place and the players lined up, Kelso and I introduced the new-and-improved version of the chartering legislation into the 1991 legislature. I asked senate counsel Betsy Rice to provide me with an objective summary of the new legislation. This is how she saw it:

> A chartered school, also known as a public outcome-based school, is formed and operated according to a contract between a sponsor and an organization. The focus of the contract and the school is on achievement levels of the students and improving achievement. A sponsor can be a state, regional, or local public board, K–12 or post-secondary, that deals with education. Any individual or group operating under Minnesota law as a cooperative association or nonprofit corporation may contract, for up to three years, with a sponsor. The schools are deregulated and financed with public money. They are site-based managed and outcome-based. The sponsor sets achievement objectives for students in the contract. The school meets the objectives in the best way it sees fit. New and different schools would be created, it is expected, that will better meet stated educational goals.

Building on senate support for the legislation the previous two years, I sought the first hearing on the bill in the Governance and Structures Subcommittee of the senate Education Committee, chaired by Senator Tracy Beckman. At the hearing on March 20, 1991, one of the most effective testifiers was Jim Walker, superintendent of the North Branch School District and 1990 Minnesota Superintendent of the Year. After outlining numerous innovative district initiatives, including an intermediate school run by teachers without a principal, Walker surprised everyone when he acknowledged that "we are still not as responsive to the public as we should be, due to bureaucracy." To chuckles in the room, he shared the dictionary definition of *bureaucracy*: "A system made up of people striving for power; indifferent to human needs or public opinion; lacks initiative or flexibility; defers decisions to superiors; and impedes actions with red tape." He continued:

> I would like to suggest that the school district is a bureaucracy and there is also the bureaucracy of the professional organizations. . . . One of our main ways of being unaccountable in a bureaucracy is by assigning blame to another level. The strength of this charter school bill is that it diffuses bureaucracy very, very quickly.
>
> The problem with the bureaucracy is that the public can't find out who is making the decisions and who is responsible for the decision, and the term we use in North Branch is that we've effectively locked the public out of public education. I think this bill takes a giant step in putting the public back into public education.
>
> There are opportunities with this bill to manage staff, to select staff, to market, to experiment with different delivery systems, to make better use of staff time, and to do flexible scheduling to meet the clients' needs rather than ours. . . .

I strongly suggest that a charter school will make a staff more responsive, will give the employees power to make decisions on what's best for them and what's best for children, and will greatly empower parents. Our district is very excited about this concept.

Walker was followed by Al Jones, a North Branch teacher who taught in the intermediate school run by teachers without a principal. His testimony, responded Senator Greg Dahl, "sent chills down my spine." Jones told the subcommittee the chartering legislation suggested that

Teachers are professionals with tremendous capability. Allow them to take control of the learning environment, and we should expect dramatic change to occur. It's tremendously exciting to think that my colleagues and I could have the opportunity to design our own school with unique programs. Teachers who possess energy, determination, and vision are big winners in a charter-school system.

Students, too, stand to gain tremendously. The charter school system will provide great support for experimentation and development of nontraditional methods of instruction. Where this variety exists, the potential for student success increases dramatically.

Jones also spoke about the excitement of the staff within their existing nontraditional school and their anticipation of becoming a chartered school:

Just the discussion of chartering has caused some very significant changes at North Branch. Classroom teachers in the building where I work have begun to develop truly collegial relationships. Staff lounge discussions now center around education and reform. Special ed teachers are considering how their students' needs can best be met within a restructured school. For the first time in six years, the physical education instructor sees an opportunity to put his health background to use.

The atmosphere in our building is charged with energy—energy that comes from teachers who for the first time feel fully professional. Personally, the past couple months have been very rejuvenating for me. For the first time in many years, I feel I can truly make a difference in very significant ways. By working together with fellow professionals, the potential for change is great.

Finally, Barb Schmidt, a teacher at PEASE (Peers Enjoying A Sober Education) Academy, a school for at-risk youth that operated on a special contract with the Minneapolis School District, told the senate subcommittee that

Youth need this bill. I and the staff people I work with need this bill. Nine of ten students who are labeled "learning disabled" are not learning disabled. . . . 80 percent of them are kinesthetic learners, rather than verbal or auditory. We must vary our approaches to these kids—involve them bodily, tactically. By and large, they are quite successful.

The larger bureaucracy is not set up to meet the needs of these students. We try, but we aren't doing it. Some students will never fit the mainstream school system. . . . They've been subjected to expectations not appropriate for them.

Opponents to the legislation included lobbyist Carl Johnson of the Minnesota School Boards Association. Johnson had served in the house and previously chaired the house Education Committee. Johnson reported on the association's specific concerns about transportation and other logistics, and he said the bill was unnecessary because school districts were already doing things the legislation would allow. He testified that the legislation created "an alternative system of private schools with no rules that is publicly funded."

Cheryl Furrer of the Minnesota Education Association also testified against the bill. Allowing unlicensed public school teachers in the second year of the chartered school was her first concern. She also said, "If funding followed the students, there would be dramatic impact on other programs schools can offer." As I listened, I couldn't help but think: Isn't per-pupil funding *supposed* to follow the student? If it's not following the student, where is it going . . . to a favorite program of the superintendent? What if parents and teachers could decide for themselves what program might be best for their students?

The opponents' testimony was expected, and there were no big surprises. I was relieved that the opposition testimony did not seem to make a big impact on the committee. I was feeling fairly confident that we could include this new chartering legislation in the senate omnibus education funding bill for the third year in a row.

Support in the house was another question.

I was very open to these ideas. Charter schools,
I thought, made sense.

SPEAKER OF THE HOUSE BOB VANASEK

11

Chartering and the House: Below the Radar

MARCH–APRIL 1991

Representative Becky Kelso introduced her house chartering bill (HF 773), companion to my senate bill, on March 11, 1991. She lined up an impressive group of coauthors, including Representative Ken Nelson, chair of the Education Finance Division. To the casual observer, chartering legislation appeared primed to pass the house—at least in some compromised form—for the first time. A *Star Tribune* article dated March 27, 1991, was headlined, "Chartered schools' getting more support." Said the writer, "This year . . . house education committee members are promoting the issue, suggesting that the concept has a good chance of being passed by both chambers."

Not if Representative Bob McEachern had his way. He made no bones about his dislike for chartered schools. And as chair of the house's full Education Committee, he had enormous power to block any education legislation he didn't like.

Elected in 1972, McEachern of Maple Lake was serving his tenth term in the Minnesota House. He had served nearly a decade as chair of the house Education Committee, starting in the early 1980s. His district was primarily rural, so he had a strong following among his rural colleagues. He was a former high school teacher and former head coach of Minneapolis DeLaSalle High School football team. When McEachern passed away in 2008, retired speaker of the house Bob Vanasek called him "one of the most colorful legislators in the last forty years." Other colleagues remembered him as both gruff and fun.

In 1991, McEachern and Nelson shared the education leadership in the house DFL caucus. McEachern chaired the full thirty-two-member house Education Committee, which focused on policy. Nelson chaired the fifteen-member Finance Division, a subgroup of the full Education Committee tasked with appropriating the budget dollars designated for K–12 education. Generally, the allocation of budget dollars in Nelson's division carried more influence in the legislative process than the policy decisions made in McEachern's full committee.

"Bob and I worked well in the caucus, because Bob had a rough edge about him," noted Nelson in 2011. "He could appeal to certain fragments of the caucus, and I had sort of a gentler approach." The two were especially effective in providing more money for education in the house bill than in the senate bill or governor's budget. Nelson observed, "I give him a lot of credit. He would just pound the table . . . in caucus. . . . We delivered a lot of extra money to K–12 education during the years I chaired the Finance [Division]."

In a March 2011 interview, Vanasek described McEachern this way:

> He was the chair of the Education Committee, he was a senior member, he was outspoken, and he could be viewed as being a little intimidating. His vehement opposition made it much more difficult for the [chartering] issue to get widespread support. . . . McEachern had a base of support. On the other hand, Ken Nelson was chair of the Education Finance Division and a senior member. He was much more soft-spoken, much less intimidating.

According to Nelson, McEachern was opposed to the chartering legislation because he was very close to the unions. But Kelso saw it differently, as she explained in an interview:

> [McEachern] thought [chartering] was a stupid idea. . . . I came to respect him as someone who followed his gut. He looked at things from a core set of principles. He was very opposed to vouchers, and he saw charter schools as a form of vouchers. End of story. There was no changing his mind. I didn't spend any time trying to convince him. He was a key person on the house side that was adamantly and inalterably opposed. Everybody knew exactly what he was thinking.

Given his strong opposition to chartering, it was an ironic twist that McEachern himself had his name attached as sponsor of some chartering language in a comprehensive education reform bill he introduced early in the 1991 session. His broad education reform legislation, HF 350, coauthored by Nelson, Kelso, and Vanasek, included chartering language that was quite restrictive—requiring, for example, all chartered schools to honor district collective bargaining agreements. The restrictive provisions may have been included in the comprehensive reform agenda as a strategy to pass a watered-down version of chartering through the house with McEachern's support. That strategy, however, didn't go anywhere.

The teacher unions stopped the chartering provisions of HF 350 at the outset. But while union leaders spoke out aggressively and publicly against chartering, there was no indication they were mobilizing their members around the issue. It appeared that house members were hearing very little from constituent teachers on the issue.

The public comments by union leaders seemed surprisingly strident, against the backdrop of lack of activity among the rank and file at the time. At a house committee hearing on HF 350 in March, Robert Astrup, president of the Minnesota Education Association (MEA), said, "We absolutely disagree with Section 16, or any intent to allow creation of chartered schools." In the April 3, 1991, issue of *Education Week,* Astrup also blasted chartered schools as "a hoax" that could cost "millions of dollars" and "siphon" resources from existing schools. A *Star Tribune* article, dated March 27, 1991, quoted Sandra Peterson, president of the Minnesota Federation of Teachers, as saying chartered schools would drain resources from traditional schools. "It's just vouchers in a disguised form," she said.

The strong language used early in the 1991 session by leaders of both teacher unions appeared as if they were trying to "one-up" each other. As Ted Kolderie noted in one of his memos, "There's what some people call 'a war' going on in Minnesota between the two unions, and it's not a time either can afford to be seen as anything but militant in defense of teachers rights." Chartering was apparently becoming a target in that war. It appeared the war was being fought at the grass tops, not among the grassroots.

So by the time Kelso introduced her chartering bill in the house on March 11, 1991, chartering proponents—and opponents—felt certain nothing about chartering could ever pass the house Education Committee. With the early public outcry by union leaders against chartering, opponents were confident that the war against chartering had already been won. Nevertheless, Kelso sought an informational hearing on her bill to educate the members about the idea. McEachern set the hearing for April 10.

The last thing Kelso wanted was for McEachern to call for a vote at the hearing. She knew if he did so, the bill would be defeated. She decided to plan for an informational hearing, and if worst came to worst, she'd withdraw her bill from the agenda. As Peter Vanderpoel wrote to Kolderie on March 27, "Becky says she doesn't (or can't) quite believe that [McEachern] would actually kill the bill . . . although she clearly is not at all certain at this point about his intentions. He does know that she does not have illusions about passing it (or attempting to pass it)."

Kelso's bill did make it to hearing in McEachern's committee. It was the sixth of six bills heard in a two-hour period. In her February 2011 interview, Kelso said:

> The hearing did not make much of an impression on me. I think the predictable people said the predictable things. There was never a lot of interest in charter schools on the house side. The interest groups were very low key. The whole establishment was opposed to the idea, but not stirred up about it. My feel was that the teachers never got riled up about this. . . . My cynical suspicion was that someone pretty important somewhere along the line told them [not to worry because] it wasn't going to happen.

Although the hearing was cut short before all could testify, the record includes written testimony in support of the chartering legislation from someone who would later become a state representative and chair of the house Education Finance Division herself. Mindy Greiling, then school board chair of Roseville Area Schools, offered the following testimony to the house and later to the senate:

> From my perspective as a school board member, I support applying for charters from either the [Minnesota State] Board of Education or the local board. Reluctant school boards and unions may be more willing to seriously discuss charters locally if the opportunity to short-circuit them is available.
>
> I encourage you to give every consideration to liberating willing schools. I believe that enabling charter schools to exist would also provide a catalyst for real change within the system that would benefit all students, and I urge you to vote for HF 773.

The house hearing only confirmed what Kelso already knew: Chartering hadn't made a big impact in the house for the third year in a row. But maybe not making an impact would turn out to be a plus. In her February 2011 interview she said,

> It was crystal clear to me, from whenever I decided to get involved in this, that the only hope for this was to have it come out of the senate omnibus bill in the conference committee.
>
> [However,] the fact that it wasn't dealt with real strenuously in the house—in other words, [it] didn't get people riled up—was probably a plus. If it would have been in the house [omnibus education] finance bill, the [opposition] would have been extremely nervous, because it would have been in [the bills of both houses]. That would have given

them lots of advance notice. . . . There would have been a lot of time for action against it.

Kelso was now counting on the senate chartering bill making it to the house-senate conference committee and that there would be three votes in favor of chartering among the five house conferees. The power of appointing those conferees rested with the most powerful person in the Minnesota House of Representatives—the speaker of the house. Kelso had no idea what Vanasek was thinking about chartered schools. "I don't remember ever talking to him about it," said Kelso. "Education was not his thing . . . not his focus in any way, shape, or form."

Well, maybe not a visible focus anyway. Vanasek, elected to the house in 1972, was speaker of the house from the summer of 1987 through the 1991 legislative session. He supported both postsecondary enrollment options and open enrollment when they were controversial in the house. Vanasek was also aware of chartering because Kolderie talked with him about it. In a March 2011 interview, Vanasek said, "I was very open to these ideas. Charter schools, I thought, made sense." He continued:

> With charter schools, what appealed to me about it was a way to get around all the bureaucracy or all the rules in place. What I liked about the idea was the entrepreneurship—that you could have teachers in the lead of how best to come up with a program to educate students, rather than . . . the traditional structure. I was very interested in those kinds of reforms.
>
> In the 1991 session, I had a proposal of my own that would have restricted education financing in a way so that the focus would be on the school building—not the district, but the school building. You'd have teachers, parents and administrators set the main goals for that building [i.e., English as a

second language in an urban area, or more foreign languages in a rural area]. You'd be held accountable for meeting the goals. If they met the goal, there would be financial reward for everybody in the building—the janitors, principals, and teachers. If they didn't meet the goals, there would be sanctions, including and leading up to that building being declared educationally bankrupt by the department of education.

We also called for finding a way for teachers for whom the occupation didn't fit . . . to guide them out of teaching, but do it in a nonadversarial way, so you didn't have the unions lining up right away to support the teacher.

My proposal was opposed by the superintendents, the principals, the teachers—just about everybody. So I knew I was on the right track! My caucus didn't even want me to introduce the bill. I finally said, "I'm going to introduce the bill." But I had to do it as an individual member, not representing the position of the DFL caucus.

As I reflect on all these events twenty years later, I realize chartering proponents were fortunate on two counts: First, the forces against chartering, particularly in the house, didn't take the legislation seriously, based on how it had been defeated the previous two years. As before, they did not expect chartering would ever pass a house-senate conference committee. Second, and unknown to almost everyone, the speaker of the house was already predisposed to passage of the chartering legislation. That would later prove pivotal in the passage of chartering into law.

This was the situation in the house as I worked the bill through senate hearings in March and April of 1991. Unions may not have been "riled up" on the house side. But they were starting to work overtime on the senate side.

Gov. Rudy Perpich jokes around with his fellow Croatian, Sen. Ember
Reichgott, during a bill-signing ceremony.

Gov. Rudy Perpich meets the press.

Gov. Rudy Perpich, Sen. Bill Luther, Rep. Ann Rest, and Sen. Ember Reichgott greet young constituents in the governor's reception room.

Ted Kolderie, the key visionary behind chartering.

John Rollwagen, CEO of Cray Research and chair of Citizens League committee that produced chartered schools proposal.

Joe Nathan, founder, Center for School Change.

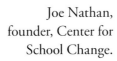

Curt Johnson, executive director, Citizens League.

Sen. Randy Peterson, chair of Education Funding Division 1987–1990, provided critical support for passage of open enrollment legislation in 1988.

Sen. Tom Nelson, chair of senate Education Aids Subcommittee 1983–1986, worked with Rep. Connie Levi to pass postsecondary enrollment options in 1985. In 1990, as commissioner of education, Nelson convened a working group to revise chartering legislation for the 1991 legislative session.

Sen. Ember Reichgott, DFL-New Hope, chief sponsor of senate chartering legislation.

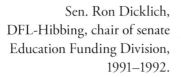

Sen. Ron Dicklich, DFL-Hibbing, chair of senate Education Funding Division, 1991–1992.

Sen. Gen Olson, R-Minnetrista, conference committee member.

Sen. Greg Dahl, DFL-
Ham Lake, chair of senate
Education Committee.

Betsy Rice, Senate Counsel to
Education Committee.

Sen. Gary DeCramer, DFL-Ghent,
conference committee member.

Sen. Sandra Pappas, DFL-St. Paul,
conference committee member.

Hearing of house Education Finance Division.

Speaker of the House Robert Vanasek confers with Reps. Nelson and
McEachern on the house floor.

Rep. Ken Nelson,
DFL-Minneapolis, chair
of house Education
Finance Division.

Rep. Jerry Bauerly, DFL-
Sauk Rapids, conference
committee member.

Rep. Bob McEachern, DFL-Maple Lake,
chair of house Education Committee.

Rep. Becky Kelso, DFL-Shakopee, chief sponsor of house chartering legislation.

Rep. Gary Schafer, R-Gibbon, conference committee member.

Rep. Charlie Weaver, R-Anoka, bill coauthor.

Conference committee co-chairs: Rep. Ken Nelson and Sen. Ron Dicklich.

House conferees (L to R): Reps. Schafer, Kelso, Bauerly, McEachern.

Conference committee members at work.

CIVICS 101

Bill Introduction
(*Bills are the same*)

Committee
Hearings

Floor
Action

Senate

Charter Bill → Subcommittee → Committee → Full Senate

House

Charter Bill → Subcommittee → Committee → Full House

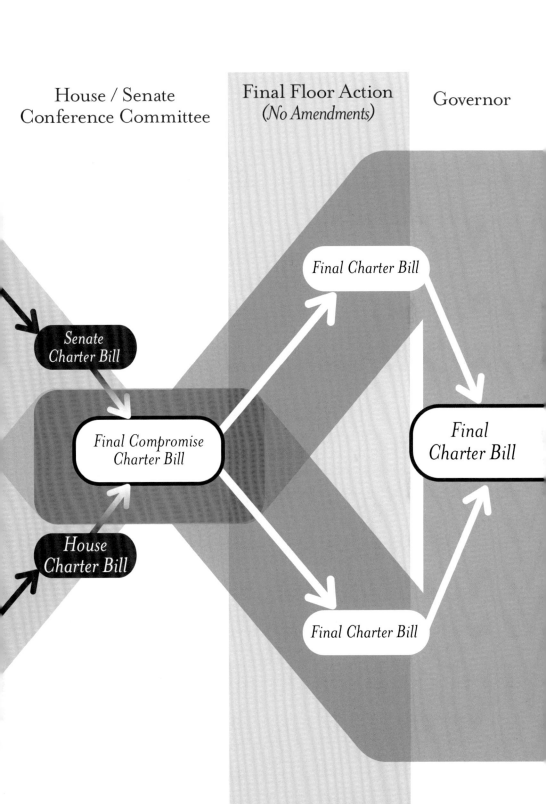

House / Senate
Conference Committee

Final Floor Action
(*No Amendments*)

Governor

*Senate
Charter Bill*

Final Charter Bill

*Final Compromise
Charter Bill*

*Final
Charter Bill*

*House
Charter Bill*

Final Charter Bill

1991 CHARTERING

BILL INTRODUCTION	COMMITTEE HEARINGS	FLOOR ACTION
March 7: Senate File 630 March 11: House File 773	March – April	May

SENATE

(SOEFB) Sen. Education Committee Chair: Sen. Greg Dahl, DFL

Senate (SOEFB)

(SOEFB) Education Funding Division Chair: Sen. Ron Dicklich, DFL

S.F. 630 • Sponsor: Sen. Ember Reichgott, DFL

Governance & Structures Subcommittee Chair: Sen. Tracy Beckman, DFL

HOUSE

H.F. 773 • Sponsor: Rep. Becky Kelso, DFL

House Education Committee Chair: Rep. Bob McEachern, DFL

HEARING: NO ACTION

(HOEFB) House Education Committee

House of Representatives (HOEFB)

(HOEFB) House Education Finance Division Chair: Rep. Ken Nelson, DFL

KEY
Omnibus Education Funding Bill (OEFB)

SOEFB = Senate Bill: Charters Included

HOEFB = House Bill: Charters NOT Included

Final Funding Bill: Charter Compromise Included

LEGISLATION

FINAL
Funding Bill

Members: Dicklich,
Dahl, DeCramer,
Pappas (DFL); Olson (R)

FINAL Funding Bill
Charter Compromise

Signed by Governor
Arne Carlson (R)
FINAL Funding Bill

Members:
Nelson, McEachern,
Bauerly, Kelso (DFL);
Schafer (R)

FINAL
Funding Bill

Motion to send back
to Conference Committee
(Failed 60/64)

The leadership of the American Federation of Teachers (AFT) spoke to employees of the Minneapolis School District at the Metrodome around 1989: (L to R) Louise Sundin, AFT vice president and president of Minneapolis Federation of Teachers; Albert Shanker, AFT president; and Sandra Peterson, AFT vice president and president of Minnesota Federation of Teachers.

This bill is very dangerous to public education if passed in its present form.

BARRY NOACK

12

The Unions Rise Up

MARCH–APRIL 1991

By now, I was totally aware that my longtime political allies and friends in the teacher unions had significant objections to the chartering legislation I was sponsoring to improve public education. The two key union leaders carrying the message were my constituents. One was even my own ninth-grade social studies teacher, Barry Noack. The situation was awkward. Painful.

I have always been a proud product of public education. I had attended the Robbinsdale District 281 schools from the fifth grade on and especially loved my three years at Robbinsdale Senior High School from 1967 to 1970. I had great respect for my teachers, and several of my favorites made a huge impact on my life.

I didn't know much about unions while I was growing up in suburban Robbinsdale. My parents were in retail sales, working for local department or jewelry stores. I remember how little a major department store paid my mother as a buyer, let alone as a salesclerk when she phased down toward retirement. In her last working years, I think she made minimum wage, despite decades of high-level retailing experience. She once told me that things might have been different if retail stores had unions.

I first became aware of unions as a political entity when, at the age of nineteen, I became involved in my local DFL Party. To me, the word *Democrat* was always synonymous with *labor*. I thought all states had a DFL party, not just a Democratic Party. Many people I served with on the local party's central committee were teachers or other union members. My state representative, Lyndon Carlson, was a teacher and longtime union member. Unions were allies in the causes I felt strongly about, including education.

When I ran for the Minnesota Senate in 1982 to fill the seat vacated by Senator Hubert H. Humphrey III, his first advice was to seek the support of the local Robbinsdale teacher union. I knew unions brought powerful resources to politics—both financial contributions and volunteer help. But to me, seeking the endorsement of the Robbinsdale Federation of Teachers (RFT) went far beyond that. These were *my* teachers. These were the people who'd helped shape my values as I grew up in our community.

I wore their union endorsement as a badge of honor during my campaign as I knocked on doors with RFT teachers, some of whom had taught me in the classroom. With DFL and union endorsement, I won election to the Minnesota Senate on my first try at the age of twenty-nine, just twelve years after graduating from high school. I was thrilled to represent the senate district where I'd grown up. Because of the importance of public education in my personal life and in the quality of life of my suburban district, I quickly sought and received appointment to the senate Education Committee. I would serve on this committee for all eighteen years of my state senate career.

One of those RFT friends and supporters who knocked on doors with me during my state senate campaigns of 1982, 1986, and 1990 was Sandra Peterson. Peterson was my constituent and served as president of the RFT for ten years from 1976 to 1987. Her peers considered her a strong and capable union leader, so it was no surprise that she was recruited to lead the state union, the Minnesota Federation of Teachers (MFT). She ran against and defeated the incumbent state president in 1987 and wasn't afraid to make tough decisions, including restructuring the leadership staff. Like Louise Sundin, the leader of the Minneapolis Federation of Teachers, both served as vice presidents of the American Federation of Teachers, led by president Albert Shanker.

Like Sundin, Peterson was a change agent. As she said in a 2011 interview, "My time with the MFT and Education Minnesota [the successor union] was filled with change and new visions and new ways of doing things." This is a bold statement, and it is true. Peterson began working in the early 1990s with Robert Astrup, president of the competing teacher union, the Minnesota Education Association (MEA), to merge the two teacher organizations. They had to overcome great animosity built over many years of battling each other in local elections for union representation. As Peterson told it,

> We spent tons of money . . . thousands of dollars on these elections every other year to see who's going to be the bargaining representative. . . . We said terrible things about each other. The reason we did merge was so we could focus

on profession and schools and kids, rather than fighting each other. We could have one organization that could represent all the teachers and education personnel.

The merger, finally completed eight years later in 1998, was an extraordinary accomplishment, the first such merger in the nation. I have great respect for people who are willing to take on—and successfully accomplish—difficult challenges. During the battles with the unions over chartering, I had viewed the union leaders as resisters of change. I saw them as protectors of the status quo. Many chartering supporters saw them the same way. But nothing is ever black and white. I realize now Peterson and Sundin were reformers in their own right—well ahead of many of their union peers.

Another key union leader in this story is Barry Noack, the RFT executive secretary, who was not only my former teacher, but also a good friend. Noack, like Peterson, had supported and volunteered for my campaigns. I felt fortunate to have such strong relationships with the teachers in my district.

For the most part, my senate voting record and the teacher unions' positions were in sync. For years, I was a strong advocate for funding for suburban schools. When I sponsored open enrollment legislation in 1988, the union representatives had shared some concerns about the impact it might have on our school district. But they did not hold strong objections. Open enrollment was more an issue for the Minnesota School Boards Association than for the teacher unions.

I don't think my local union friends took the chartering legislation seriously in 1989 and 1990. I do remember talking about it with Peterson. She and I both participated in the 1988 Itasca Seminar where Shanker broached the topic. Peterson attended Itasca along with Sundin. As AFT vice presidents, they had special interest in Shanker's comments, because they would be part of the team to deliver on his reforms.

Three years had passed between that seminar and the 1991 senate deliberations on the chartering bill. Only then did I begin to hear significant concerns from the unions. I was probably naïve, but the strong opposition took me by surprise. After all, Shanker, their national president, had introduced the concept to me. For me, chartering was all about empowering teachers—giving them the authority to take leadership as professionals by spearheading and forming new chartered schools. I felt it was an option for entrepreneurial teachers to break away from the system—the status quo—and try something new.

In March 1991, I began a series of meetings with Noack and other teacher union representatives. I figured we could find common ground for compromise. We had plenty of issues to work on, and we still had time in the legislative session for crafting amendments. I especially wanted to find compromise with the MFT, as that was the main bargaining unit for my Robbinsdale teachers. I didn't have much connection with the MEA, which represented locals in many rural areas.

Our discussions started out cordially enough. On March 22, two days after the first hearing on my bill, I led a meeting of union representatives and chartering supporters, which included Kelso. Union members present at that meeting were Noack, Sundin, and Rose Hermodson representing the MFT; and Cheryl Furrer and another representative from the MEA. While I disagreed with many of their objections, I was committed to searching for some middle ground. I thought if they could perhaps achieve some visible "victory," they might remain, at the very least, neutral on the bill. It was important for both sides that the MFT be responsible for some visible changes. They could report back their success to their membership, and I could point out to my colleagues that I had addressed some of the union concerns during the legislative process.

The list of original MFT objections to the legislation was not extensive. The first point, said Noack, was to eliminate any chartering sponsors other than the local school board. The March 20, 1991, RFT *Collective Bargaining Bulletin* confirmed this point. It printed the following paragraph:

> On March 22 Barry Noack of the RFT and representatives of the MFT, MEA and the School Board Association will meet with Reichgott in an attempt to limit sponsorship of charter schools to K–12 schools, intermediate districts, cooperative districts, or joint powers districts. Noack said, "This bill is very dangerous to public education if passed in its present form."

The second key concern to the MFT was a provision allowing unlicensed teachers to work in a chartered school in the second year of operation. Third was a series of issues protecting teacher seniority and collective bargaining rights. The relative importance of the third concern was brought home in several ways. A March 19, 1991, letter from Noack concluded that the RFT would oppose any bill "which permits sponsors of charter schools to *contract out teaching services to agencies or groups which are not part of the teachers' bargaining unit.*" (Italics added.)

Sundin underscored these concerns in her August 2011 interview. Regarding teacher licensing, she explained that

> Unions were involved [in the discussions around chartering], and although lip service was given to their concerns when the bills were written, most aspects of the legislation provided little protection for workers. As we recall, it was a major fight to require licensed teachers, and to this day, charters are weak on having licensed staff provide the education.

The requirement that they have a licensed teacher in each area of instruction is monitored [only] if reported, and many times abuses occur. In particular, the licensed teacher isn't doing the actual instruction, but is supervising staff doing the instruction.

Regarding collective bargaining rights, Sundin explained the following, reemphasizing Shanker's original vision of chartering:

Shanker created the [chartering] concept as a way for teachers and parents to start schools where they have a better program or methodology and where the teachers are leading the effort and remain within the union. When Minnesota's proposed language in the law was weak on union support and excluded teachers from tenure protection, he was not supportive. . . . Collective bargaining, tenure protection, and licensure were all strong positions for Shanker in order to prevent the victimization of teachers that has happened in many charters.

Supporters of charter schools in Minnesota never understood this concept, and to this day, teacher employees can be fired at will, have no tenure protections, and if they try to unionize, they are usually dismissed. It has caused teacher "churning" [or turnover] at charters. Profit became the motive for many charter creators.

When asked what the unions most feared from the chartering legislation, Sundin replied,

The lack of quality education of students in many charters was a main concern. It was the fact that we were losing students out of the public schools, which we felt were better [than chartered schools]. The charters were sold on the fact that they would do so much better a job with the same kids. It's mostly that they may be able to do as good, but they aren't doing any better.

Peterson expressed the union fears in this way:

> We did oppose [chartering]. The organization opposed it. Teachers opposed it. They were afraid of [chartered schools] taking away the money and students out of the school district. . . . If [you lose] too many students, you lose staff. If you lose too much staff, you might lose programs, depending on the size of the school.
>
> We had plenty of choices. You didn't need to start charter schools. That was one of the things we said very often. We have postsecondary [options]. We have open enrollment. We've got all these things happening. We can have charter schools within districts, but we don't need to expand it like everybody's proposing.

According to Sundin, privatization was also a fear.

> I know, technically, they are [public schools], but back then, that was not accepted [by teachers]. It felt like a step to privatization, I think. It just felt like, if you could allow families to escape the public school system for a public charter . . . the next step would say, "Here's a voucher, and you can go to a private or a religious school."

With the unions voicing their objections during the meetings in March 1991, I began to see more clearly the heart of union opposition. The union leaders did not want chartered schools to collectively organize outside the protection of the district teachers' bargaining agreement, as proposed in my bill. However, I knew I couldn't accommodate this objection if I and the chartering working group were to preserve the fundamental autonomy of chartered schools.

The discussions at the March 22 meeting were not easy ones, but we kept at them. I thought we were making progress. I was looking for any areas of compromise. I was grateful we had a good discussion about potential charter sponsors, particularly the state board of education. During the meeting, Doug Wallace, a state board member, spoke of the need for outside pressure from an alternate sponsor to leverage the district bureaucracy. That argument appeared to resonate with Noack, who said, according to meeting notes: "You've sold me. But if the state board is in, we should give them the resources to do it right." I indicated I might be willing to give up postsecondary and other charter sponsors, as long as we could keep the state board of education as a sponsor.

I was ready to confirm that and several other compromises to the union representatives at our next meeting scheduled for April 5, 1991. Noack was out of town, so Peterson attended with other representatives and presented on his behalf a letter he wrote on March 28. The letter was a complete surprise to me. It made clear that the state board of education as a sponsor was unacceptable to the unions. Only the local school boards were acceptable.

Now I was seriously concerned. Our discussions had taken a 180-degree turn. At this new meeting, the unions were pretty clear they were not interested in helping me improve the bill. The discussion kept coming back to the basic objections: "Public schools can do this now" and "This is not the way to help public education." In her August 2011 interview, Sundin remembered these meetings.

We kept reiterating our concerns about union issues— bargaining rights, tenure protections, and licensure. We were accused of being blockers of reform. We just didn't accept that accusation. We—the Minneapolis Federation of Teachers—were farther out in front of reform nationally than almost any other local in the country. There was also some pressure by state and local leaders around the country that we shouldn't be opening this [chartering] door either.

Regarding the state board of education as a sponsor, Sundin responded, "We didn't have a lot of faith in the state board. The state board [was abolished by the legislature] not so long after that, and it is kind of amazing that nobody's missed them." Peterson saw it this way: "We always felt [sponsorship] should reside at the district level and the school district should have the responsibility, not the state. That was a cop-out. If [the charter] couldn't get their school district, they shouldn't do it."

To say I was disappointed at this turn of events is an understatement. At the end of the meeting, I told the group I was not going to give in on the basics and that the senate would likely pass the bill. I would be willing, however, to propose some changes to the legislation as a result of our meetings.

But we needed to make those decisions immediately. At the fast-approaching April 16 hearing, we would need to present the amended language for the omnibus education funding bill. Kolderie, Peter Vanderpoel, I, and others met with senate counsel Betsy Rice the next day to develop the draft amendment. After hearing the MFT concerns and after discussion with senate colleagues and staff, I agreed to some changes, most significantly the following:

1. I would take out all postsecondary institutions as prospective sponsors, while maintaining only local school boards and the Minnesota State Board of Education.

2. I would require that all teachers be licensed, thus removing a provision that allowed unlicensed teachers to teach under certain circumstances.

That was as far as I could go without compromising the necessary independence for chartered schools. I offered no changes to address the union's collective bargaining concerns, except to make clear that teachers in chartered schools could choose to organize in the way they saw fit, including staying within the umbrella of their district collective bargaining agreement. I knew, however, that this amendment was not going to be enough to gain union support or even neutralize their position.

I thought back to a comment a union leader made to me following the senate subcommittee hearing: "You should back off chartered schools—for your own protection." I was irritated. But I wasn't intimidated. I angrily scribbled a note (still in my files) to Senator Greg Dahl, "That just makes me even more committed to it!"

The threat behind the union leader's words was becoming real. With or without union support, there was no turning back.

*The time had come to publicly break
from my union friends.*

13

The Unions:
Breaking Up Is Hard to Do

April is a unique month in the legislative calendar. Days at the capitol are long, intense, and without break. Legislative deadlines for budget and policy bills make legislators feel as if everything is happening at once. They try to be in three places at the same time. Emotions run high. Lobbyists and other members of the public feel locked out of decisions being made behind closed doors. Everyone craves sleep.

In other words, April is a grumpy time at the legislature.

In my optimistic—albeit naïve—way, I had hoped the

compromises I was making to the chartering legislation would bring some relief to the unions. They didn't need to love it. But I knew their outright opposition could greatly complicate the path to successful passage of the bill Representative Becky Kelso and I were shepherding through the legislature.

In this critical time, I heard from people on all sides of the battle. Shortly after the April 5 meeting, I received the following letter from Tom Nelson, the former DFL senator and education commissioner who was then working at the University of Minnesota:

Dear Ember,

I wanted to send you this short note on the meeting we had last Friday on the Charter School bill. I believe you handled this meeting extremely well. This bill is the ONE piece of education legislation this session that has the potential to make a real difference. For that to happen, the Senate bill needs to stay together without a great deal of changes. The House bill on charter schools will not create the same environment for change.

It is tough to disagree with friends, but their issues, on this bill, are ones of protectionism and not what is best for children. I understand the position they are in, but that does not make it right.

Hang in there! This one will be viewed as major change down the road.

Sincerely, Tom

I also received the following memo from Ted Kolderie:

A person friendly to the bill talked the other day with Sandra Peterson. He reports: The MFT just may want to come out with something, if it can meet their concerns. These are with the "Senate bill," specifically:

- The provisions for teacher-leave don't protect seniority.

- It would permit unlicensed teachers in the schools.

- It sounds like the Tesseract [private, for-profit] school.

- These schools drain off resources that would otherwise go to reducing class size and to increasing teacher salaries.

This is amazing. It's worth checking with Betsy [Rice], but Sandra probably misunderstands the leave provisions of the bill, probably misreads the licensing provision (at least in the current draft), and apparently does not understand that you have ruled out for-profit operators. The point about "draining off resources that could otherwise go to salaries" speaks for itself.

My friend told Sandra: "This [bill] is the ultimate opportunity for teachers to get professional status."

Things were also heating up outside the walls of the capitol. In a March 25 memo, Kolderie wrote me: "The MEA clearly does not accept it. The state office has put out the word to the local leadership to tell their legislators, over the Easter recess, to defeat SF 630." Similarly, in an April 15, 1991, *Legislative Update* widely distributed by the Minnesota School Boards Association (MSBA), lobbyist Carl Johnson wrote the following about the chartering bill:

It is being advanced as an extension of open enrollment and site-based management. It could also be perceived as an extension of the homeschool—in the other direction. All money, including capital expenditure and formula allowance, go with the student. The district must provide transportation. This is a terrible concept. It could be much improved if only school boards could do the chartering or be the sponsor. One district—North Branch—is experimenting with a similar concept. Please share your feelings on this one with your legislators. The concept of chartered schools will be a part of the Omnibus bill, unless we can prevent this idea from being established as state policy.

For their part, the MFT and RFT were still working with me on the public front. The April 16, 1991, RFT *Collective Bargaining Bulletin* reported our progress as follows:

> In the last Collective Bargaining Bulletin, there was a brief report on a charter school bill, SF 630, introduced by Sen. Ember Reichgott. The RFT Executive Council voted to oppose the bill in its current form and asked Executive Secretary Noack to lobby against the bill unless substantially modified.
>
> The bill, as currently drafted, allows boards of K–12, intermediate districts, joint powers groups, University of Minnesota, any State College (4 year, community, or technical), and the Minn. Board of Education to sponsor a charter school.
>
> A charter school might consist of a small number of teachers wishing to operate their own school free of the rules and bureaucracy found in many school systems. "This concept by itself is not bad," said Noack, "but should the legislature allow boards other than K–12 or intermediary school districts to sponsor charter schools, permit them to hire unlicensed teachers, and send to these schools the per pupil funding normally allocated to their home and school

district, it will be seriously tampering with the public school system as we currently know it in this country."

Reichgott met recently with Noack and other interested parties and promised to revise SF 630. The MFT and most education organizations oppose SF 630 as currently drafted. A hearing on the bill is scheduled for April 16.

By now, other legislators and I were hearing quite a bit about the "charter school bill." What was most frustrating was that I was hearing "facts" about the bill that were untrue. Not only were some objections misinformed, but the language was also ratcheting up. The Minnesota Education Association (MEA), especially, was rallying its troops with a four-page document entitled *Why MEA Opposes Chartered Schools* (see Appendix II). The document called the proposal, among other things, "insulting," "a costly hoax," "more bureaucracy," "lax standards," and "elitist." It claimed children would be "guinea pigs." Of all the objections, one totally floored me:

Open door to vouchers

Finally, chartered schools provide an open door to vouchers. The ability to procure funds could mean that leaders of private schools would seek charters to obtain public money for their particular institutions—under the guise of a chartered school.

Vouchers? From me? You've got to be kidding. I had always opposed them. Yet, of all the issues raised, I knew this could be the most politically damaging. We needed to make crystal clear that chartered schools were *public* schools, not *private* schools. Like all public schools, they would be tuition free and open to all students—first come, first served. Ironically, though, this voucher discussion may have helped reframe the education reform discussion just enough to help clinch passage of chartering legislation. Vouchers were now a topic of raging national debate. Parents were demanding that legislators improve our public education system. In Minnesota, we were on the brink of offering a new kind of public school choice that seemed far more acceptable than opening the door to private school vouchers.

By mid-April, the chartering proposal was being debated on multiple fronts and taking on a life of its own at the capitol and in legislators' districts. This forced me to be on the defensive. I spent a good part of my days calming fears among senate colleagues and setting the record straight about what the chartering bill actually was meant to do. With so many objections being circulated, I knew no amount of negotiation with the unions would make the legislation acceptable to them.

Sundin affirmed this in her August 2011 interview. She felt the compromises I had made in the legislation regarding licensed teachers and removal of postsecondary sponsors were not enough. She added,

> And I don't know [what would] have been enough, frankly. . . . I don't know that [Reichgott] could have gone far enough to ever get support for it at that time. The unions realized that [any amendments] would only be temporary, and that once we went down this road, the issue would continue to be amended to undermine traditional districts.

We were now at another strategic fork in the legislative road. Could we even pass chartering legislation through a senate and house dominated by union-supported DFL majorities if the teacher unions were fully mobilized against it? I sought counsel with supportive senate and house colleagues. We agreed we *could* pass it—and we should. Frankly, the myths being generated by union opposition were as disturbing to my colleagues as they were to me. Some colleagues were downright angry.

We did not anticipate a problem passing the legislation as part of the senate omnibus education funding bill, as most senators had already voted for chartered schools twice before. An informational hearing on Kelso's chartering bill in the house Education Committee had just taken place. Kelso would not push to include any part of it in the house omnibus education funding bill carried by Representative Ken Nelson, as her attempts to move it would likely end in defeat.

Once the two omnibus education funding bills would meet in conference committee, we could work to assure the necessary three votes from each legislative body to adopt the chartering language into the final bill. While the conferees would likely adopt additional amendments and compromises to obtain house support, I was hopeful the fundamentals would stay intact. Once the chartering language was part of the final omnibus education funding bill, no amendments could be offered on either the house or senate floor. Any final vote in the house would not be on chartered schools, per se, but in support of or against the entire omnibus education funding bill with much-needed revenues for education. No one could remember a time when a legislative body had rejected an omnibus education funding bill.

The time had come to publicly break from my union friends. My supportive colleagues and I saw a pathway to passage, but it wasn't going to be easy.

The next few weeks were going to be miserable.

Minnesota teachers saw charters as threatening to all,
not empowering for some.

14

The Conference Committee:
Ground Zero

CONFERENCE COMMITTEE, MID-MAY 1991

In the bicameral system, conference committees wield a lot of power. Conferees can change the course and impact of an issue in a single vote. That's why some, particularly proponents of unicameral legislatures, have called the conference committee "The Third House."

An omnibus funding bill, whether it be for education, human services, environment, economic development, or any other area, is also known as an appropriations or budget bill. The top leaders of the house and senate negotiate the amount of the state budget that can be spent in each omnibus funding bill. Once that amount is set, conferees negotiate how they wish to spend the allotted funds.

When drafted, omnibus funding bills can exceed four hundred pages. They can include hundreds or even thousands of provisions for review, which include specific appropriation line items and related policy changes. (Chartering would be a related policy change in the education omnibus funding bill.) Many provisions will be different between the house and senate, reflecting the distinct funding and policy priorities of the legislative bodies. The task of the conferees is to painstakingly review the differences and hammer out a final compromise for the overall bill. They can propose numerous amendments to either the house or senate positions to ensure the compromise will be acceptable to a majority of members from both houses.

Usually, the legislative leaders allot a minimum of a week or ten days near the end of the legislative session for funding conference committees to do their work. It is hard work. Some of the conference committees' work is done in public, but often the house and senate funding chairs meet in private to narrow the issues and provide an outline to their common goal. The final week of a conference committee is an arduous time, with meetings often occurring day and night and throughout the weekends. Conferees may work two or three nights in a row with little sleep.

Despite this intense responsibility, legislators prize an appointment to a major funding conference committee. Five members from each house negotiate the omnibus funding bills. The house and senate funding division chairs work as co-chairs of the conference committee. Each serves as author of his or her respective funding bill and recommends favored appointees for the four other conferees. These appointees generally reflect the partisan balance of each house. In 1991, that meant each co-chair would generally recommend three DFL members and one Republican.

In 1991, I served as chair of the Property Tax Division of the senate Tax Committee and would therefore serve on the tax conference committee. Since senators are generally appointed to just one budget-related conference committee, I would not have a seat on the omnibus education funding conference committee. In my view, that was fine. I was too close to the chartering issue, and my colleagues could make the case for chartering just as well as I during conference committee discussions. I knew I would be kept in the loop on any proposed changes to the chartering provisions.

For any conference committee, the appointments don't just happen by accident. I couldn't have been more pleased with the appointed members of the 1991 omnibus education funding bill conference committee. The co-chairs were, of course, the funding division chairs: Senator Ron Dicklich of Hibbing and Representative Ken Nelson of south Minneapolis. Dicklich continued to be steadfast in his support of chartered schools. Indeed, the bill would not have gotten as far as it did without his support. And Nelson had been involved in the charter issue with me for three years.

As expected, the other four senate conferees were solid in their support of chartering. They were DFLers Senator Greg Dahl of Ham Lake, chair of the Education Committee who had been, coincidentally, my classmate at St. Olaf College; Senator Gary DeCramer from rural Ghent; and Senator Sandra Pappas from the St. Paul district surrounding the capitol. Pappas' interest in chartered schools reflected the concerns of the urban coalitions and communities of color, who saw opportunity with these new autonomous schools. The final senate member was Republican Senator Gen Olson of suburban Minnetrista. Olson was a leading Republican member of the Education Committee, and we knew each other well as first-termers in the senate class of 1982. Beginning in 1988, she'd been a solid bipartisan partner on the chartering bill. Indeed, as both Olson and I have often recounted, the chartering legislation would not have become law without strong bipartisan support.

On the house side, the fate of chartering legislation in conference committee would be determined by one person: the speaker of the house, who had sole power to appoint house conferees. In addition to co-chair Nelson, Representative Becky Kelso, the author of the house chartering legislation, was appointed conferee. The two other DFL house conferees did not support chartering. They were Representative Bob McEachern and Representative Jerry Bauerly, an assistant majority leader from Sauk Rapids. Bauerly served as vice chair of the Education Finance Division, and according to Vanasek, was a "rising star and one of the newer members who had a lot of influence over the other members." The fifth house conferee was Republican representative Gary Schafer from Gibbon. In his March 2011 interview, Vanasek explained that Schafer represented the "deciding vote" for chartering. Schafer supported chartering. This was not a coincidence!

With Kelso, Schafer, and Nelson as chair, the three house votes needed to finally adopt the chartering provisions from the senate bill into the conference committee report seemed, for the first time, very real.

Even before the ten conferees met for the first time in early May 1991, opponents within the education community mobilized. Their mission was to kill the chartering bill by quashing it in the conference committee for the third year in a row. Failing that, they would attempt to weaken the senate legislation by amending it. Outside the capitol, opponents were even approaching those who supported charters. On May 3, 1991, Ted Kolderie wrote me:

> We've had a kind of funny thing happen. Two teachers who've been supporters of the bill have now told me that they've had Minneapolis school people ask them about it.
>
> In one case it was an administrator saying to Barb Schmidt, "I hear you gave some testimony on charter

schools." In the other case it was a Minneapolis school board member saying to one of the interested teachers (Launa Ellison), "I saw your name on a list of people supporting charter schools." The list came to her from the school boards association.

Opponents were organizing quickly and aggressively on multiple levels. In the first week of May, the Minnesota Federation of Teachers (MFT) sent a flyer to all its school-building representatives. In short order, a supporter gave me a copy. The flyer included a list of the names and phone numbers of the ten conference committee members and read:

We're concerned and you should be, too.

There is legislation that could:

- jeopardize seniority rights as well as salaries and benefits

- establish charter schools which would not be required to operate under the same rules and regulations as public schools

- subtract dollars from public school districts' general funds

- allow unlicensed personnel to take positions that currently require a teaching license

We need you to act today!
Call Members of the Conference Committee
and tell them to vote "No!" on the charter school bill.

Unknown to me, Terry Lydell, a teacher at Robbinsdale Cooper High School in my district and a supporter of the chartering legislation, crafted a response to the conferees. He shared a copy with me dated May 11, 1991:

> Attached is a copy of a flyer sent to all Mn. Federation of Teachers building representatives. It contains some misleading information and one outright lie. I am bringing this to your attention because I believe that you as a legislator should know what measures are being taken to influence your vote on the charter school issue.
>
> Before I detail the issues, I feel that you should know four things:
>
> 1. I am a member of the Federation of Teachers and the MEA.
>
> 2. I served on the writing team that helped draft the charter school bill so I am familiar with the paradigm, concept, and language.
>
> 3. I am a classroom teacher in a program for "drop-out" students.
>
> 4. I support a charter school bill.

Lydell then responded in detail to each of the MFT's concerns about seniority, waiver of rules and regulations, loss of dollars, and unlicensed teachers. To the last point, he was especially bold in taking on the union leadership:

> This very simply is not true. The charter bill calls for licensed teachers—period.
>
> When I discussed this item with [an MFT representative], she said she knew that Senator Reichgott had dropped the unlicensed provision from the bill but "[the conferees] might put it in . . ." MIGHT. The flyer doesn't say MIGHT.

This statement misleads the reader on an issue that is extremely important to education professionals. In my opinion, that is unethical. It is a breach of faith for the MFT Executive Board to mislead the membership. That issue becomes more complex when its results are visited upon you as a legislator as you go about trying to do the right thing.

Coincidentally, at the same time the MFT flyer was generating discussion, president Albert Shanker of the American Federation of Teachers (AFT) came back to Minnesota to speak at a St. Paul meeting of AFT and national school board members. The meeting was about the new school-district-initiated Saturn School of Tomorrow, a "break-the-mold" school in St. Paul. Kolderie attended Shanker's informal discussion on May 9 and sent me these notes quoting Shanker's conversation:

> And I'm convinced that we in education, too, are not going to do the hard things needed to change the schools unless we have to. Unless there are consequences. Something has to be at stake. There is, in other fields. Your organization could fail. People in these fields dislike change, too. But they have to do it. We in education don't. Because for us, nothing is at stake. If our kids do brilliantly, nothing good happens. And if we don't push, we can count on remaining popular with our colleagues.
>
> We have got to deal with this question of consequences for adults. Educators simply are not going to take the risks of change, against the pressures of everyday popular feelings, unless they have to. We do need something to happen that is truly revolutionary.
>
> When a teacher in the audience asked, "How does that happen?" Shanker replied,

I'm not an optimist. I don't expect unions to come out for incentives and rewards. I can do it, because I'm retirement age. But we're not going to have what we have now much longer. It doesn't work, and everybody knows it doesn't work.

A lot of educators don't think they are affected. . . . [They] think they're not threatened by the pressures that are building. They're dead wrong.

In another coincidence, Nelson had his own contact with the AFT president during this time. In his 2011 interview, Nelson related this story:

When we got into the debate about charter schools [in conference committee], the Minnesota Federation of Teachers was against it and made it very clear they were against it. I would say, "Well, Shanker supports this, you know." McEachern would challenge that and get upset about that.

So . . . I went and called Shanker. I happened to get him on the phone right before he was leaving on a trip. I said, "Hey, we've launched this charter school idea based on your idea. . . . But . . . your local unions out here are beating up on us. What's going on?"

As Nelson recalls, Shanker said, "Well, the structure of the AFT is to kind of let the locals decide their own destiny." Nelson added that Shanker said he "still remained convinced that it [was] a viable experiment, [but he] left it at that. The locals had their own freedom and their own point of view on things like this."

I didn't know back in 1991 about Nelson's conversation with Shanker. But at the time, I did reflect on the stark contrast between the language of the local MFT flyer and Kolderie's notes from the national AFT president, all happening the same week. Shanker was right. In Minnesota, educators were resisting the risks of change. And the conferees were certainly hearing about it.

This dissonance was awkward for the state union leaders, too. As MFT president Sandra Peterson said in her September 2011 interview:

> The states were very independent. Even though Shanker was up there talking about all this stuff, he'd throw the ideas out to see which ones would stick . . . But each state had their own leadership and would make their own decisions. And they were not buying . . . charter schools.
>
> Shanker was such a strong leader. . . . Everybody on the [AFT board] certainly expressed their opinions and concerns about charter schools. [Minnesota chartering supporters] took the concept of Shanker's charter school and ran with it in a different way. There are some schools that are probably carrying out what he was thinking about, but they're outside the district. I think we should be doing this inside school districts. . . .
>
> Our members were very threatened. We had votes against charter schools. . . . That's why, even though [we] might support Shanker's forward thinking, and Ember, who said, "This is to avoid vouchers," we lobbied her a lot about not doing this.

How ironic. My original motivation for pursuing chartering legislation was to empower teachers. Back in 1988 and again three years later, Shanker's comments affirmed this as a laudable goal. But in Minnesota, teachers saw charters as threatening to all, not empowering for some. And they were aggressively pushing back. How could we ever break through the great fear being generated among their colleagues?

I once read this acronym definition of *fear*: False Evidence Appearing Real. There is nothing harder to overcome than FEAR.

You get what you can, and then you get what you want.

REPRESENTATIVE BECKY KELSO

15

The Decision Revisited: "Pigs Get Fed, and Hogs Get Slaughtered"

MAY 10–17, 1991

This was the third year the senate had passed chartering legislation, and it was the third year of debating chartering in conference committee. Finally, in May 1991, we seemed to have the necessary votes—five senate conferees and three house conferees—to adopt the chartering language as originally intended. But more likely, the language would be compromised in some way.

As long as a provision is in either the house bill or the senate bill, it is "in play" for amendment and final passage. Compromise in a conference committee can take many forms. Sometimes compromise means the creation of a "package deal," in which each house gets its top policy or budget priorities by accepting the top priorities of the other house. And sometimes compromise means finding an acceptable middle ground on a particular provision between the positions of the two houses.

If chartered schools were to have the autonomy necessary to succeed, only a little middle ground was left on its provisions. At least that was the view of chartering supporters. As bill author, I had already yielded to two top-priority requests made by the teacher unions: eliminating postsecondary institutions as sponsors and ensuring that all teachers in chartered schools would be licensed. Of course, more compromises were possible, as supportive house conferees still had to ensure the provisions could pass the house even after they were accepted in committee. But I was not anticipating compromises on the fundamental features of the bill. To me, the most important features were the following:

1. Allowing a separate bargaining unit for teachers in a chartered school.

2. Having the Minnesota State Board of Education serve as an alternative sponsor to the local district school board.

Without the alternative of the state board as a sponsor, a local school board would have no incentive to approve a chartered school, even if a community strongly supported a new school. In my view, it meant Minnesota would have no chartered schools. Some education groups maintained that a school sponsored by any entity other than a school board would not be a "public" school. My response? The issue depended on whether the school would follow the three principles of public education:

1. That it be nonselective.

2. That it not charge tuition.

3. That it be accountable to public authority for public objectives.

As Ted Kolderie wrote around this time,

> What's giving way . . . is the old notion that the character of the purpose is defined by the character of the agent. Many if not most systems already operate on a different principle. Nobody, for example, would define a road as a private road because it's built by a private contractor. A road is a public road if there is a public decision to build it, if the public sets the specifications, if it is paid for with public funds, and if it is open to the public for travel. In this as in so many things education has simply been slow to follow: continuing to insist that public education is and is only the traditional public school.

By now, the general opposition against the chartering bill had grown to a fever pitch within the teacher unions and other education groups. The pressure was enormous on all house DFLers, most of whom the teacher unions had backed in the election six months before. The unions were now urging house members to tell their conferees to reject the chartering bill.

And I suspected no one was feeling the pressure more than Representative Ken Nelson. He was the key legislator who would shape any amendments to the chartering language in the conference committee. He also seemed to be the number-one union target— and for good reason. Nelson had been instrumental in getting the chartering legislation to this point; he had authored the early legislation in the house in 1989 and 1990. But I speculated that as the unions became more sharply aggressive, he had to listen. He was, after all, the chair of the house Education Finance Division, and his

DFL caucus members were counting on him to make the right choices on their behalf for policy *and* politics. If unions were displeased, they could adversely affect how much financial and volunteer support union members would provide the caucus and its individual candidates in the 1992 election.

I also understood what politics Nelson could personally face. He was a legislator from south Minneapolis, a liberal DFL stronghold. The real threat to an incumbent in such a district is a strong opponent for DFL party endorsement. Unions, of course, were often key to winning DFL endorsement and party primaries. A union-backed opponent against Nelson in the next election was a real possibility. While he was well respected in his district and at the capitol and could likely overcome such a threat, the battle could get emotionally brutal. No candidate looks forward to that.

In her 2011 interview, Louise Sundin confirmed that the unions were in conversations with Nelson about chartering. When asked whether the unions threatened to back another DFL opponent in the next election, she replied, "Oh, no. We wouldn't threaten out loud. We were in the background, grooming somebody else for the spot." The MFT had begun talking with DFL representative Myron Orfield, who had been elected in 1990 in a neighboring legislative district. After redistricting lines were drawn from the 1990 census, Nelson and Orfield ended up in the same legislative district for the 1992 election cycle. In a 2011 phone call, Orfield confirmed he would have run against Nelson in the DFL primary election.

Sundin acknowledged that the union pressure on Nelson was significant "because, of course, we knew Ken pretty well. Being a Minneapolis legislator, we interacted with him a lot and expected a lot. I think we just thought he'd gone a bridge too far." On his end, Nelson recalled in his interview how close he was to the teacher unions and how they aggressively opposed chartering:

Not only did Louise Sundin live in my district, but so did [MFT] lobbyist Rose Hermodson. Rose was particularly active in my campaign. She had chaired one of the precincts and always got literature out very diligently. . . . When you're chair of the Finance [Division], you get the union's attention. I delivered as much as I could for urban districts and for K–12.

One of Nelson's most difficult encounters with the unions was when Representative Bob McEachern brought Hermodson to a private meeting with some conferees during final negotiations. Nelson explained,

We were meeting in one of the rooms at the capitol. It was not a large meeting room, and I don't know how public it was, or if this was just an effort between house and senate to knock heads again and come to agreement. But what McEachern did . . . was bring in Rose Hermodson to . . . speak against [chartering] to house and senate conferees. [It was] totally inappropriate to have a lobbyist come into a conference committee like that. . . . I think it was one of those meetings where you try to get things focused apart from the public eye. . . . [It] really put pressure on me because she was not only the lobbyist for MFT but active in my district.

I knew none of this at the time. I speculated Nelson was getting union pressure, but I was unaware of the detailed negotiations. Here's another significant factor unknown to me and everyone else: Nelson had made the decision in 1990 to not seek reelection at the end of his two-year term, but he would not announce his retirement until the spring of 1992. Here's how he put it in his interview:

The next two years were going to be my last. That would wrap up twenty years. Reapportionment was coming up. By that time, I was tired of campaigning—ten races. I just wanted to try something else. I received a Bush Fellowship and was able to go to Harvard for some graduate work.

In some ways, it might have given me more freedom to act [in support of chartering], because I wasn't going to run in '92. If I had decided to run again, the unions would have had more influence on me. . . . I suppose I have to honestly say that. On the other hand, it kind of angered me the way they took me on, and that made me a little bit stubborn. . . . [I thought,] I'm going to see that this gets passed—the charter school bill. All I've done for the teachers over the years, and then they turn on me over one issue. I was a little upset with that. I thought that was unfair.

For Nelson, seeing that the chartering bill got passed meant making some compromises. It wasn't long before I was hearing from Kolderie and others that Nelson was considering making a significant amendment to the legislation before he would support it in the conference committee. I heard he was in conversation with the unions, his colleagues, and others. No one knew what amendment he would propose, but we all knew it would likely be the final legislation. MFT President Sandra Peterson recalled working with Nelson on the amendment:

Ken was very good to work with, because he would try to find places to compromise. He was really looking at reform in kind of a bigger picture. . . . I do think we tried to modify the language the best we could so that it would at least be a little bit of salvo to our members, who were so concerned. . . .

These were our friends who were working on this—you try to work with your friends. Even though we didn't like everything, we were trying to work with them and get the best deal.

With compromise in the wings, the question now became "What's critical and what's not?" for successful chartered schools. Chartering supporters went into action to devise compromise amendments that would not totally undermine the legislation. As Kolderie wrote in his May 11, 1991, memo to me:

What's Critical

Everybody—and this includes emphatically the teachers who are so interested in the idea getting enacted—agrees on these:

1. The State Board, as alternate sponsor. (The only one that counts.) The up-front exemption from the rules.

2. The separate bargaining unit for teachers.

The "Killer Amendment"

At some point someone will surely offer to let a provision with the "charter schools" title go through if the authors will agree (a) to limit the sponsor to the local board and (b) to agree that no significant number of charters could be issued.
That isn't worth having.

I couldn't agree more. Yet I had to step back and give Nelson the space he needed. All I could do was offer ideas through colleagues and through Kolderie. Three main compromises seemed to be under discussion. The first was to limit the total number of charters granted by all sponsors. I thought something between ten and twenty-five would be a reasonable cap to allow diversity geographically and in curriculum.

The second area of compromise was a "right of first refusal." Charter organizers would first work with the local school board to come to an agreement. If an agreement was not possible, the charter applicants would have the right to look elsewhere for a sponsor. To me, this was superior to another proposal in which charter applicants would first have to be "turned down" by the local school board before they could approach another sponsor. As Kolderie described in his May 11 memo:

> Nothing would come of putting the organizers of a school in the position of having to take to the State Board a proposal with a big stamp on the cover: REJECTED BY THE LOCAL BOARD.
>
> When someone gets the right of first refusal, they don't get the right to dictate the terms of the agreement. They get a chance to meet your terms before you make the deal with somebody else.

The third main area of compromise seemed to be bubbling up from the teacher unions. They wanted teachers to be "in charge" of a chartered school. At the time, I wasn't sure what that meant, though it would later become an important point.

By now, I had to accept that some significant changes would be made to the fundamentals of the senate chartering bill. I want to be honest here: letting go of the original vision of chartered schools wasn't easy for me. The road to passage had been long, and the end seemed so close. I was already deeply disappointed. Moreover, I was angry with the leadership of the teacher unions. What disturbed me most were the mistruths they were circulating about the legislation and my supportive colleagues.

To the unions, we were now *union busters, voucher-lovers,* and *anti–public education.* We would destroy public education as we know it. We would drain scarce dollars from already struggling school districts—never mind that those dollars would instead directly follow the individual student the public funding was supposed to support. Forgotten in all this, it seemed, were the new opportunities we could create for students, their families, their communities, and, yes, even teachers.

The teacher unions were equally disappointed in how the compromise was playing out. According to Sundin in her 2011 interview,

> There was not much interest in interacting with Kolderie and the other reformers because . . . there was no compromise with them and they didn't really understand or support union teachers' issues. . . . They didn't seem to be willing to go far enough in their compromise to allow . . . collective bargaining and to protect teachers in charter schools. They'd tinker around the edges, but they didn't seem willing to go, obviously, as far as we wanted them to go. . . .

And the unions were not happy with me, personally. As Sundin said,

> Barry [Noack] and Robbinsdale [Federation of Teachers] weren't happy about Ember's role but wanted to try to maintain a civil relationship because she was their senator. The state MFT as a whole did not want to support Senator

Reichgott, and this carried over into later races. There was very little support for her within the state MFT . . . primarily because of her role in pushing charter legislation. Members did not trust [her] nor feel that [she] in any way understood unionism.

I think there was a kind of a feeling—and I might be reading too much into this—that she was kind of a "limousine liberal" from the 'burbs and not enough of a hardcore, blue-collar unionist from the city or the [Iron] Range.

MFT president Peterson, my constituent, had this to say in her interview:

We were upset with Ember in particular. I can tell you that . . . because she was the leading force on this. It was hard for me, because she was from our district and I supported her as a legislator and continued to support her. But we were very frustrated with her. There was no moving on this. . . .

Ember was [like], "This is the way it's going to be." [Sandy tapped her finger against the table for emphasis.] She certainly tried to work with people, but she was definitely the leader here. Ember could influence, and she did. I didn't like everything she was doing, but I learned a long time ago that you separate what you're doing over here in policy. You try to do the best you can. I've never let that stand in the way of supporting Ember [in later races]. . . . People are going to promote things, and I think it's sad if you let that get in the way.

Obviously, it wasn't an easy time. Tensions were building and relationships were strained. As I waited to hear the elements of Nelson's amendment, I had an uneasy feeling in the pit of my stomach. I don't remember who finally told me. I don't think it was Nelson himself. I just remember my reaction: I burst into tears. To me, the battle was over.

Nelson was drafting an amendment with three elements:

1. A chartered school must be approved by *both* the local school district and the Minnesota State Board of Education. There were no alternate sponsors.

2. Only eight chartered schools would be allowed in the entire state; a single school board could approve no more than two.

3. Only licensed teachers could form and operate a chartered school. A majority of the chartered school's board of directors would have to be licensed teachers employed at the school.

I was stunned. Never, in my worst scenarios, did I imagine that a chartered school would need *double* approval—by both the local school district and the state board. Never did I imagine that *only* teachers could start a chartered school. What about parents? As an attorney, I couldn't fathom how a board made up of a majority of teachers could govern a school. Not only did that limit the size of the board and limit outside financial and other expertise, but it was also, in my view as an attorney, an outright conflict of interest.

Nelson, of course, had a different view about the amendment, as related in his 2011 interview.

> It wasn't to kill it. It was actually to keep it alive. And I think it really helped to keep it alive. . . . I thought the one amendment with the teachers in charge was a good one. It was the original Shanker vision. But also, why not? It just seemed to me teachers knew best. We limited it to eight schools, and I thought that was enough for a trial run. And

approval by the local board and the state board—we knew the state board would do it. . . . And then the local board— you didn't want the local board fighting everything. . . . I felt, "Let's get their approval, in hopes they wouldn't stop [a charter application]."

Some key chartering supporters in the legislature saw Nelson's amendment as progress. Senator Ron Dicklich had put chartered schools on the line long ago as a "must-have" in his negotiations. The Meadowlands school, detailed in chapter 10, continued to be his motivation. In his 2011 interview, Dicklich said, "The house was going to fight me to the end. I had a number of things I wanted. I told Bob McEachern . . . and Ken Nelson, who was favorable to charter schools, 'Here are six things I want. Give me six things you want and call me, because we're not meeting again until I get those six things.'"

So when Nelson came to Dicklich with his proposed amend- ment, here's what Dicklich thought:

To me, that showed there was movement—that they were going to accept this thing. He wouldn't have brought that to me without checking with his people, because he had to have three votes for it. That showed me they were going to take our charter school [language].

Ken said to just limit it to eight. I thought about it. So I pretended I went and talked to members, [but] I didn't. If they said "no," then what [was] I going to do? I remember Ember questioning it, and I said, "Ember, do you want this thing or not? Three years you've been here. . . . If you don't make it this year, you'll probably never make it. Things only have a shelf life. Let's get it. We'll go after more in future years."

Dicklich also liked the "go slow" approach of the amendment.

[I] just wanted to get charter schools started. I was interested in one. I wasn't going to hold this thing up and have them stalemate it, because I wasn't willing to just take eight schools. That's my feeling. Let's look and see how things are. Let's not do something that may be detrimental to kids and their education. It kind of goes along with my philosophy.

Dicklich added, "Pigs get fed, and hogs get slaughtered."

Representative Becky Kelso also supported the compromise amendment. "To me, the narrowing was not a bad thing," she said in 2011. "I thought it was a reasonable way to start. You get what you can, and then you get what you want."

As for me, all I knew was, *this was it*—either this amendment or nothing. But it was, indeed, as Kolderie had written me, a "Killer Amendment." With just days left in the session, no more options remained. Kolderie, the Citizens League working group, and other chartering supporters hated the amendment just as much as I did, but we had nowhere else to turn for help.

I wondered: Was this the point where we tell the house conferees that we wanted to lay the bill over for yet another session? How can we pass a bill with the name "chartered school" when it is destined to fail? Do we pass a bill intended to create chartered schools that doesn't allow real opportunity for them to be created? Do we pass a bill that allows critics to say in coming years, "See, no one really wanted to create any chartered schools"?

In eighteen years as a state legislator, I made thousands of split-second decisions. None would ever have the impact of this one. Instinctively, I decided we had to take the amendment and go with it. I knew this legislation would get harder to pass, not easier. The unions were now at full roar. Some of my colleagues had been viciously attacked. With a heavy heart, I wrote a short note to my five senate colleagues on the conference committee:

Dear Colleagues—

You've been great. I really appreciate your strong and heartfelt support.

Ken's "comfort level" [amendment] is being drafted. It includes:

- Double approval

- Eight pilots, up to two by one district

- Only licensed teachers can create the charter school.

If you can change anything, try to change the last one—so other educators, parents, etc. can form the charter school and hire licensed teachers. That's how our bill reads now.

Thanks,

Ember

As I watched the final action of the conference committee from the audience, I was completely drained. Nelson presented his amendment. The amendment was adopted on divided vote: three senators and three house members voted in favor. (Two of five senators were absent; their votes weren't needed.) Chartered schools had been the last provision to be resolved, so the conference committee's meetings were over.

I didn't want to stick around because I knew my emotions were out of control. I stood up and walked out of the hearing room, into the hallway, talking to no one. It was in the hallway that I heard one teacher union lobbyist say confidently to the other, "Don't worry—we have the votes to kill it on the house floor."

As meaningless as the amended bill seemed to me, I couldn't believe the teacher unions were still pulling out the stops. The next battleground was now the 134 members of the Minnesota House of Representatives: 79 of them were DFLers, 55 Republicans. We had one day. *No one* would bet on the outcome.

If chartering wasn't going to happen that year,
it probably was not going to happen.

SPEAKER OF THE HOUSE BOB VANASEK

16

Passed by "An Absolute Hair"

MAY 18–20, 1991, HOUSE AND SENATE FINAL VOTES

The 1991 education omnibus funding bill, which included the chartering provision, was on its way toward final vote, but there were many obstacles yet to overcome—especially in the house. An omnibus funding bill can prove to be the toughest of votes for a legislator. It is filled with hundreds of provisions—some you support, some you don't. In the end, you must balance the pros and the cons and cast one vote on the whole bill as a package. This gets even more complicated after conferees make hundreds of amendments and compromises, and the final bill looks much different than when it first passed your legislative body.

Generally, each party holds a caucus before voting on the conference committee report of a major bill. Sometimes the caucus leaders take votes to determine a party's collective position on a bill. I expected that when the house DFL caucused on the omnibus education funding bill, there would be robust debate among chartering supporters Representatives Becky Kelso and Ken Nelson and chartering opponents Representatives Bob McEachern and Jerry Bauerly. The speaker of the house makes a big difference in the outcome of a caucus and the fate of legislation, especially when the caucus is divided. That happened in 1991. Speaker Bob Vanasek recalled in his 2011 interview:

> My recollection on the charter schools was that it was deeply divisive in our [DFL] caucus. . . . The leadership in the caucus on education issues was divided. Voices were getting raised. . . . It was heated. . . . And because those four folks . . . had a lot of respect in the caucus, it made it hard to know what to do. I sided with the reformers.

Vanasek never called the caucus to vote on the issue. Vanasek explained his decision:

> If the caucus takes a position, there's an expectation that all members should vote for the position. . . . [But in this case], the differences were for the most part really heartfelt. People either believed this was a good idea or this was really going to hurt public education.
>
> We just sort of left it where it was. . . . There would be several Republicans who would vote for [the final bill], so we didn't need all the Democrats. I'm only interested in getting enough votes to pass the bill. I'm not going to try to force

somebody to vote against their conscience or a legitimate position, unless you really have to.

When the house took up the conference committee report on Saturday, May 18, I watched the debate on television from my senate office. I knew the greatest threat would be a motion to send the omnibus education funding bill report back to the conference committee, rather than take the final vote on it. Usually, this procedural move is used to make a political point by the minority, because sending an omnibus budget bill back days before session end is rarely successful. But for this bill in May 1991, all bets were off.

I wondered which DFLer opposed to chartered schools would rise against party protocol to make the motion. I thought McEachern might do this. He had chosen not to sign the conference committee report the night before. To my surprise, the motion did not come from a DFLer. Instead, three Republicans—Representatives Sally Olsen, Ron Abrams, and Jerry Knickerbocker from the western suburbs of Minneapolis—did so.

A listener hearing the motion debate on the house floor would not have thought chartering was much of an issue at all. The most emotional debate was about highly controversial changes to education funding formulas. The new "equity" funding formula created "winners" and "losers" around the state, and legislators were keenly aware of the impact. The formula most adversely affected the three Republicans' St. Louis Park school district. They never even mentioned chartered schools in their passionate motion to send the bill back.

The powerful combination of differing forces in the house did not bode well for the bill. We desperately needed Republican support. And now Republicans were as split as DFLers. It was shaping up to be a perfect storm. I knew the vote on the motion would determine whether chartered schools would become a reality. If the bill went back, I had little doubt the conference committee would remove chartering altogether.

During the house debate, members lined up on both sides of the bill. Nelson, the bill's chief author, was also the bill's chief defender:

> We can be proud of this bill for financial reasons and for a fair distribution of dollars, and we can be proud of it in terms of the number of state education initiatives and reform initiatives.
>
> On the motion [to send the bill back], we have been negotiating as much as we can with the Senate. They are very adamant on several of those provisions [including chartering] in both the MEA and MFT letter. . . . We did our best to modify those. The Senate wants those much stronger; they've traditionally wanted those much stronger. In previous negotiation sessions, we've always beat those back, we weren't able to do so this time. Consequently they are here in a very, very limited manner . . .
>
> We went to the Senate earlier today to talk about the possibility of going back to the conference committee even before we signed the conference report. Stonewall resistance. They absolutely would not even talk about any of those items. . . .
>
> I beg of you to resist this motion and to get on with the action on the bill. I hope there we'll get a positive motion to pass this bill out, because it is the best we're gonna do this legislative session.

Republican representative Charlie Weaver, a coauthor of the original house chartering bill, gave a spirited defense of the bill. Representing a school district with low property wealth, he mostly spoke to his support of the funding formula. But at the end of his comments, Weaver touched on the chartering issue.

I know you are getting a lot of heat from the teaching organizations. The MEA and MFT both endorsed me last time. I'm telling you this is bad policy to send this back. . . . I encourage you to take a look at the language in the bill. This does not open the door for any kind of dangerous charter school where there is a group of crazies teaching our kids. This is tough, tough language. I would again ask you, if you are looking for fairness for all kids, not just the privileged; if you are for outcome-based education; if you are for increased parental empowerment; please vote against Representative Olsen's misguided effort.

DFL representative Mary Murphy, a union supporter from a district just south of Duluth, was the first chartering opponent to focus on the issue:

I'm going to support this motion. . . . There are people from eight different school districts in my legislative district, and they're scared about the money. . . . They want to do new things, and do progressive things, and do outcome-based education. . . . We are trying to address the needs of *all* the kids. . . . [But] I don't believe that with the limited amount of money that the budget this year provides we can afford to adopt several new initiatives that have the potential of draining that money away from our schools. I have supported alternative education, I have supported all the new initiatives continued in this bill, but I can't continue to support all of them this year.

Murphy had apparently intended to be the DFLer to make the motion to return the bill to conference committee. But the Republicans had trumped her motion. Now both parties were vying to send the bill back. My heart sank farther when McEachern next rose to speak:

> I encourage you to support the . . . Olsen motion. . . . You all received a letter from the teachers unions saying they can't support the bill. There are only about two or three little points in the bill that they're not supporting, so if we can get back to a conference committee, we can clear those up. We've been threatened by the gentleman over in the senate, [Dicklich] that he'll [hold the bill]. Well, we've had those before since I've been here, and we have always gotten a bill out, so don't be threatened by that.

Shortly thereafter, Vanasek called for the vote. It didn't take long before he closed the roll, even though only 124 votes out of 134 had been cast. The final vote: sixty votes in favor of and sixty-four votes against sending the bill back to conference. As I watched the vote on television, I let out a long breath. I didn't realize I had been holding it. A mere three-vote switch would have sent the entire bill back. A mere three votes would have ended the hope of chartered schools. Possibly forever. As Kelso said later, "It passed by an absolute hair."

I now had a strong indication the speaker was on our side. The speaker had the advantage because only he could see the cumulative tally of votes cast for and against the motion. Knowing he had the votes to defeat the motion, Vanasek moved quickly to close the roll. Indeed, he personally registered a red vote against the motion. I was grateful.

The breakdown of the vote was fascinating. Clearly, multiple issues were playing out. In the end, the financial equity issue may have helped take just enough heat out of the chartering debate. Overall, 56 percent of the minority Republican representatives voted to keep the bill moving toward final passage. Only 42 percent of the majority DFL representatives voted to keep it moving forward. Think about that: in a body where DFLers had a strong majority, only 42 percent kept the bill moving. The breakdown was as follows:

	DFLers	Republicans	Total
Voting for motion	42	18	60
Voting against motion	33	31	64
Not voting	4	6	10
Total	79 (59% of 134)	55 (41% of 134)	134

I knew then the house would likely pass the bill. It took only sixty-eight votes to pass a bill, and ten members had not yet voted on the motion. In addition, as the debate on final passage continued, I could see that some who had initially voted to return the bill to committee were now planning to vote for the bill. One such member was Republican representative Dean Hartle of Owatonna. He had been concerned that the language in the bill wasn't clear enough regarding the limit of eight chartered schools statewide. Nelson clarified the point on the house audio recording, and when the vote on final passage of the bill was taken, Hartle voted in favor of it.

The final vote was eighty-five to forty-five for final passage—well over the sixty-eight votes needed. Again, the final vote defied predictability. And once again, Republicans had provided the margin for adoption of the bill:

	DFLers	Republicans	Total
Voting for final passage	52	33	85
Voting against final passage	25	20	45
Not voting	2	2	4
Total	79	55	134

The battle had been won on the house floor. It was now clear that the bill, with chartering included, would become law.

With much less ado, the vote on the omnibus education funding bill of the conference committee came to the Minnesota Senate on the last day of session—Monday, May 20. I don't remember much debate on the senate floor about chartering. (Unfortunately, the audiotape has not been archived.) No senators made a motion to send the bill back to conference committee.

I was grateful for the two days between the house vote on Saturday and the senate vote on Monday to wrap my head around what happened. My emotions went from deep disappointment, to anger, to a sense of shame that I had failed. I had one last opportunity to speak publicly on the senate floor on Monday about chartering and all that had happened since the legislation left the senate a month earlier. I knew my colleagues would support the modified legislation, no matter what. So I prepared my remarks not for them, but for the public, including a direct message to the teacher unions:

> It has been most unfortunate that the opponents to this [chartering] proposal, modified as it is, have flooded legislators with misinformation about this proposal. They claim that this would jeopardize the seniority rights and salaries and benefits of teachers. They neglect to tell you that charter schools are voluntary and only those teachers who wish to participate will do so.
>
> Opponents fear that charter schools will not operate under the same rules and regulations as other public schools. My response is, amen. Aren't we all trying to remove state mandates from education and other areas? How many teachers have you known who have burned out over many years because they fought the system and lost? Frustrated teachers are leaving the profession because they can't express

themselves and teach as they would like, because there is too much bureaucracy and too much resistance. In the end, both teachers and students lose.

Opponents say this would subtract dollars from public school district general funds. That will happen no more than any other choice program that we've established so far. If a student leaves a school for a better opportunity, isn't this a healthy reallocation of our state dollars?

Opponents state that unlicensed personnel will be allowed to teach. This is absolutely false, as the bill clearly states. I changed the legislation to accommodate the concerns in this area raised by teachers. Yet even after the legislation was changed, legislators were told differently.

And finally, perhaps the biggest issue of all: Chartered schools are a new kind of *public* school. They are not private schools. No tuition can be charged. All learners who apply must be considered on a first-come, first-serve basis, or by lot. The bill clearly prohibits the use of dollars for any sectarian or religious schools. Yet the opponents tell you otherwise.

Members of the senate, you deserve better than this.

Members, we've heard these fears before. They are the same horror stories we heard when this legislature passed open enrollment and postsecondary options. Today we point with pride to the success of these programs and the students who have achieved in them. I expect no less of the charter school proposal.

[It is not possible to have] "too many" options for kids or teachers. Please vote to make chartered schools a reality.

The final roll call vote on HF 700, the education omnibus funding bill, spoke for itself. It was a bipartisan vote of fifty-six yeas and eleven nays. Those voting nay included three Republicans and eight DFLers.

	DFLers	Republicans	Total
Voting for final passage	38	18	56
Voting against final passage	8	3	11
Not voting	0	0	0
Total	46	21	67

Ironically, one of those voting against the final bill was Republican senator Gen Olson, a strong supporter of chartering who had played a major role in its passage. But according to Senator Ron Dicklich, conference committee co-chair, Olson tipped her final vote because of the house refusal to accept a provision allowing parental involvement in a health curriculum matter.

The bill had passed both houses. To the teacher unions, the battle was lost, but the war was just starting. Ted Kolderie remembers a union lobbyist leaving the senate balcony after the final vote. "We'll take care of this this summer," she told him with anger in her voice.

The bill was now in the hands of Republican governor Arne Carlson and his commissioner of education and former MEA lobbyist Gene Mammenga. Neither looked too kindly on the chartering idea.

Had legislators passed the bill on its own, Carlson may well have vetoed it. But since the chartering language was tucked inside the huge budget bill and did not require an appropriation subject to a line-item veto, I knew we were relatively safe.

And yet chartering supporters like Kolderie, Pete Vanderpoel, Curt Johnson, Joe Nathan, and I were deeply disappointed. All of us believed the compromises in the final bill would severely limit the creation of any new chartered schools at all. In stark contrast, the house supporters felt differently. "I thought it was spectacular," said Kelso, in her 2011 interview. "I thought the fact that it went through was unbelievable. I thought the fact that it was so narrow and yet still made it—it was really a long shot. The chances were so slim. It's a miracle that it passed."

On one point, everyone was unanimous. "They say timing is everything," said Vanasek. "Issues can have their time. And if it doesn't happen, that time can come and go—and sometimes go for a long time. If chartering wasn't going to happen that year, it probably was not going to happen."

Was the resulting legislation even worth it?
Had I made the right decision to go through with the
severely compromised chartering legislation?

17

The Morning After

MAY 21–JUNE 5, 1991

Imagine running a thirty-day marathon at top speed and with few breaks, little sleep, new decisions to be made every few minutes on multiple issues, and angry constituents and lobbyists clamoring for your attention. Then imagine everything coming to a dead stop.

At the stroke of midnight at the end of May 20, 1991, the legislative session was over. Done.

There was the usual partying at the end of the legislative session. I wasn't up for it. I woke the following day after sleeping nearly twelve straight hours. Even at the relatively young age of thirty-seven, I was a physical and emotional mess. I felt battered and bruised after riding an emotional roller coaster for nearly a month. Returning so abruptly to "normal" life was disorientating. I couldn't recall what normal felt like.

Typically, I would look forward to my work as part-time contract counsel with Carlson Companies/Radisson Hotels for the rest of the year. And for senators, this would be our only summer off between the campaigns of the 1990 and 1992 election years. The senate usually has four-year terms, but due to redistricting, one two-year term occurs each decade. So enjoying the short and beautiful Minnesota summer was especially important that year.

I felt a certain loneliness as I returned to my suburban home where I lived alone. So much was going through my head, and I had no one with whom to talk or share. Second-guessing everything once you see the light of day is so easy. What could I have done differently in sponsoring the chartering legislation? How much had I sacrificed in relationships with colleagues and friends? Had I let down the dedicated group of supporters who first had the vision to develop the chartering idea? Was the resulting legislation even worth it? Had I made the right decision to go through with the severely compromised chartering legislation?

Even with a solid night of sleep, I could not help but be bitterly disappointed with the outcome. The legislation would serve so few students and teachers. Moreover, could just eight schools even be successful under the severe restrictions? The impact seemed so minimal for such intensive efforts over three long years. I was tired and, frankly, deflated.

During that very emotional time, I received a note from Ted Kolderie. It meant a great deal to me.

> Even as it came out of conference, the law has a lot of promise. I can't begin to tell you how much I admire what you and Becky did, this past six months. In the time I've been

around I've seen some very good things done, but never against
that kind of opposition. Perpich got a smaller part of his choice
legislation than you got of the new-schools legislation the first
time around . . . and he was the governor for heaven's sake!

I needed that encouragement. I knew the debate about chartering wasn't over. The unions had made it clear they would seek
repeal of the chartering law in the 1992 legislative session. Their
stand, as spelled out later in the *Minnesota Federation of Teachers
News* of December 1991, didn't leave room for any doubt. The
bulletin said, "MFT will seek the repeal of legislation authorizing
charter (outcome-based) schools passed in the 1991 session and will
oppose any similar alternatives that establish schools outside of the
public system and fund them with public monies."

Even AFT president Albert Shanker, who had originally proposed
the idea of charter schools at the Itasca Seminar three years before,
was clearly opposed. In May, Kolderie sent Shanker the MFT flyer
denouncing Minnesota's chartering bill, suggesting Shanker might
want to weigh in on the debate. Shanker didn't reply until August 2:

Dear Ted:

Sorry for the delay in responding, but I am not surprised
by the MFT's flyers against Minnesota's charter school bill.
I, too, was disappointed with the way the bill came out.

For one, teachers have to give up most of their rights in
order to teach in one of these schools—hardly an incentive. I
also understand that, although they could still be in the
retirement system, they would have to pay both the employee
and employer costs—again, not an incentive. Second, I wish
the architects of the bill had worked out the collective
bargaining issues with the teachers unions. While I understand the potential contradiction between adhering to a

particular district's collective bargaining contract and starting off a school fresh, telling unions that they, in effect, would have to begin from scratch in organizing teachers and then bargain at the school level is not a particularly thoughtful solution. It's certainly not an approach designed to make friends, and, as you saw, it didn't. . . .

This Minnesota bill seems to be traveling to other states. I still see the baby in it, but the bath water has covered it up. Could it still be shaped up?

Sincerely,

Al

What a turnaround from Shanker's comments three years before. There seemed to be a disconnect here. After all, no one was forcing teachers to enter chartered schools or change their benefits. And why would Shanker consider holding back those teachers who wanted to take on something new in their professional life?

I didn't know Shanker personally. What I did know is that sponsoring chartering had strained my personal relationships with teacher unions and their leaders on the state and local level. This was made clear after John Kostouros penned a column about the 1991 education legislation in the July issue of *Minnesota Law and Politics*. Kostouros had written that there were "bad feelings" between legislators and teacher unions. Barry Noack of the Robbinsdale Federation of Teachers responded to Kostouros and copied me. His letter addressed me specifically:

> Though she has demonstrated a commitment to improving public education by promoting several good programs, such as Success by Six and Early Childhood Education, she is not positively supporting school reform with her Charter School Amendments.

From the Federation's point of view, we had input into this piece of legislation only after Sen. Reichgott and her educational advisors had drafted a very onerous version. Once it was clear we were prepared to testify against the Charter School bill in committee hearings, Reichgott invited us to meet with her advisors on this issue.

The final draft, which passed as part of the School Finance Bill, was substantially modified as a result of our early political work in the Senate and the resistance of several House members on the Conference Committee.

It is our understanding Reichgott informed the conferees that "this is only the beginning" and that she intends to return next session to strengthen the bill with additional provisions desired by her educational advisors.

As you imply in your article, it is most unfortunate that proponents of improved public education such as Sen. Reichgott, Joe Nathan, Ken Nelson, and MFT leaders like Sandra Peterson, Louise Sundin, Marcia Averbook, and myself do not work together more constructively to improve the public schools.

Hopefully, your article may serve as a catalyst for this to happen. Once bills are drafted and sent to committees, the power battles begin. This was the position we found ourselves in too often during the 1991 session.

As I reflect back on my strained relationship with the union leaders, I now believe I could have involved them earlier in the discussions about the chartering legislation. In the end, I still don't think we could have reached an agreement on the fundamentals of chartering. I do think, however, that chartering supporters would have been in a better place if I had been less interested in persuading union members of my point of view and more interested in actively listening to their concerns. People can disagree and still feel heard. I didn't do well on that score.

I came to that realization years later, after focusing on my personal leadership growth once I left the legislature. I realize now that as a relatively young lawyer and legislator, I was more about advocating and less about generous listening. The most successful legislators—particularly legislative leaders—can accomplish both of those goals. Perhaps if I had approached the conversations with a more open mind, we could have developed that final compromise together, allowing the unions to share in the ownership of chartering. And perhaps if I had been curious enough to learn more about the history and rationale for unionism, it would have been less "Us versus Them."

As it turns out, I wasn't the only one reflecting on all that had happened. As Sandra Peterson said in her 2011 interview,

> I think I was a bit torn, because I felt the reality was that we were going to have some form of a charter school. And because Shanker had even proposed them, I was a bit intrigued. . . . But I also wanted to control it. I wanted to find ways that the union could work with it and that the union could find some safeguards, if it was going to move.

These perspectives have come with time. But I was still in an uncomfortable emotional place when I received a note dated June 6, 1991, from former senator John Brandl, a well-respected colleague who had retired from the state senate the year before. Even today, I treasure this note. Despite my self-doubt, it comforted me with its assurance that something good would come of the chartering legislation.

> Dear Ember,
>   This is to tell you of my admiration for your leadership on the charter schools issue. Your intelligence and industry

have always stood out in the legislature. And this year, on this issue, your courage and toughness saved what in years to come will be recognized as the beginnings of one of the major breakthroughs on education policy in our time.

Best Regards,

John

On June 4, 1991, Governor Arne Carlson signed the omnibus education funding bill. Chartered schools were now law in Minnesota. But was that law nothing more than eight chartered schools that didn't have the independence to be successful? Or was it, as Brandl predicted, the beginning of a major breakthrough in education?

As I sat at home recovering from the intensity of the legislative session, I had no idea chartering was already a part of the national conversation about education reform. Two developments—from two different points on the political spectrum—would take us in the direction of Brandl's prediction.

PART IV

From Idea to National Movement

Durenberger saw this bill as a way to
"break the logjam" on school choice.
He was trying to educate people that chartered schools
was a middle position.
Chartering was something that could accomplish
the objectives of vouchers,
but still be within public education and earn the
support of Democrats.
It would be a bipartisan strategy for improving
public education.
That's the central message here.

Jon Schroeder

Could public chartered schools—
public school choice—become a powerful alternative to
private school vouchers in the national debate?

18

Charters Explode onto the
National Scene

MAY–JUNE 1991

Two days after the Minnesota Senate vote, Republican president
George H. W. Bush and his education secretary, Lamar Alexander,
were coincidentally scheduled to visit Minnesota on May 22, 1991.
They were launching the president's new education initiative, the
America 2000 Excellence in Education Act, at the Saturn School of
Tomorrow in St. Paul.

That same day, Senator David Durenberger entered a statement in the record of the US Senate noting the president's visit and lauding the Minnesota legislature for passing the chartering law. Durenberger made a lengthy point about the Minnesota tradition of bipartisanship in education reform. He noted the bipartisan authors of the legislation—Representatives Becky Kelso, Ken Nelson, and Charlie Weaver, and Senator Gen Olson and myself—along with the civic leadership of the Citizens League and individuals such as Ted Kolderie and Joe Nathan.

As a member of the US Senate Committee on Labor and Human Resources, which considered education legislation, Durenberger issued an additional statement on May 23, upon Senate introduction of the America 2000 act. He titled the statement "Redefining Public Education" and spoke about Minnesota's chartering legislation:

> Mr. President, at the very heart of Minnesota's leadership on educational reform is a strong belief that choice and choices should remain within public education.
>
> But, one big lesson in what Minnesota is now doing—a lesson that we can learn from in Washington—is that we must begin to redefine what constitutes a "public school."
>
> And, we must begin to understand the important difference between the traditional values and assets of "American public education" and what we have traditionally defined as the "American public school."
>
> This distinction is an important principle behind new "chartered schools" legislation adopted by the Minnesota House and Senate earlier this week. . . .
>
> I believe the Minnesota chartered schools proposal offers important lessons to those of us who will now pick up President Bush's challenge to craft legislation implementing his America 2000 initiative.

To help advance this discussion, I intend to introduce legislation modeled after the Minnesota chartered schools proposal and look forward to working with my colleagues in both the Senate and Administration to help shape the legislation we finally approve.

At the time, I didn't realize the importance of Durenberger's statement. Not only had he elevated chartering to the national stage, but as a moderate Republican, he was also astutely laying out a centrist political pathway between the Bush administration's private school voucher proposals and many Democrats' steadfast opposition to any school choice. Durenberger was creating a fresh conversation with the Bush administration about a new kind of "public school choice." This would help establish a middle ground where public school choice and chartering could be sustained politically.

With this happening in the US Senate, I was beginning to see that the legislation we had worked so hard to pass in Minnesota might not be meaningless after all. Governor Carlson hadn't even signed our chartering legislation yet, and already a US senator was committed to introducing national legislation modeled on our state law. Durenberger would prove to be a champion for the chartering cause on the national level.

What came next was even more surprising: immediate national support from another side of the political spectrum—my own. On June 5, 1991, the day after Governor Arne Carlson signed the chartering bill into law, the center-left Democratic Leadership Council (DLC) issued a press release titled, "DLC Legislators Architects of Bold New School Choice Legislation." This development was enormously important, as it reframed the national debate and rallied chartering support from Democrats, even in the face of union opposition. The release announced our passage of chartering legislation in Minnesota, noting it was authored by two members of the

DLC—Kelso and myself. The press release quoted the DLC chairman as saying,

> DLC members are offering new choices to Americans across the country. The initiative of State Senator Reichgott and State Representative Kelso in Minnesota is a great example of DLC leaders on the cutting edge of the issues that matter to people. Public school choice is a progressive approach to our country's education policy. As Democrats, we know the solutions to many of the country's problems can be solved with quality education for our young people.

The chairman of the DLC was a little-known governor who coincidentally had been the first governor to model Minnesota's open enrollment law in his own state. He was *already* a firm supporter of chartering, as I would learn years later. He was Arkansas governor Bill Clinton.

Now the word about chartering and public school choice was spreading quickly across the nation. The Center for Choice of the US Department of Education quickly endorsed the plan, issuing in part this statement: "Choice, after all, is as much about empowering educators to create improved and distinctive schools as it is about empowering parents to choose from among those schools."

On June 24, 1991, the *Washington Times* published a column by Donald Lambro, chief political correspondent, that put "Minnesota's daring new plan" of chartering squarely in the middle of the national debate. He wrote:

> School choice is this year's hottest educational reform movement and an idea that is likely to become a key political battleground in the 1992 elections.

It is an issue that President Bush and his party have locked onto with their domestic radar screens, though there is strong support as well from some conservative-to-moderate Democrats seeking to change their party's message. Yet it is an issue with grass-roots appeal that cuts across virtually every political, economic and racial boundary in America.

After citing Minnesota's public school choice history and noting that twenty-eight thousand students throughout the state were currently participating in interdistrict choice programs, he wrote:

Notably, Minnesota's decision to push school choice into new, uncharted territory was also strongly supported by a significant segment of the Democratic Party—the politically centrist Democratic Leadership Council and its grass-roots supporters. And therein lies the movement's potential for expansion and political acceptance.

Lambro went on to describe recent polling data showing strong public support for education tax credits or vouchers for tuition at public or private schools. He also noted that Representative Polly William's voucher program for inner city Milwaukee schoolchildren had received an "impressive" range of national endorsements, but had been given the "cold shoulder by her party's liberal, labor-dominated establishment." He concluded:

Nevertheless, Minnesota's bold new choice plan gives a much-needed political boost to the emerging school-choice movement. Finally, the suffocating, anti-competitive monopoly in American education is being broken—not in Washington but in our state legislatures.

The article, I admit, made me somewhat uncomfortable because it mentioned both chartering and private school vouchers as similar examples of school choice. Nevertheless, I was aware of the tremendous opportunity this national conversation provided—first and foremost, for our efforts back in Minnesota. Our chartering legislation was fragile: The house vote had been exceedingly close, the teacher unions already threatened to repeal it in the next legislative session, and it would take time to build a supportive constituency. Given these realities, I knew a national strategy was our best chance to sustain the fledgling chartering opportunity. Repealing would be much harder if we could build support from opinion makers, journalists, national policymakers, and national organizations.

But even looking beyond our Minnesota borders, the national conversation about chartering was exciting. Could public chartered schools—public school choice—become a powerful alternative to private school vouchers at a time when parents around the country were calling for major education reforms and more choice? Most Democrats shared my opposition to vouchers, but they had little else to answer the public's call for education reform. Could chartering be that new idea to bring innovation to public education, while fending off private school vouchers in Congress and state legislatures?

Governor Bill Clinton had figured that out long ago.

Nine months—nine whole months—before Minnesota passed the chartering legislation into law, Clinton was out on the road to nearly half the states, promoting chartering as a "New Democrat Idea."

19

The Rise of the "New Democrat"— Governor Bill Clinton

Sometime in the late 1980s, I joined the Minnesota chapter of the Democratic Leadership Council (DLC). So did Representative Becky Kelso. To me, the DLC stood for innovation, new ideas, and a different way—though still within our basic Democratic principles—of approaching problem solving. I liked that. The DLC immediately supported Minnesota's open enrollment plan and endorsed the expansion of public school choice. That's all I needed to sign on. I knew the DLC, however, did not represent the mainstream of Minnesota DFL politics. Minnesota had a tradition of being a very progressive and liberal Democratic state. Our longtime governor, Iron Ranger Rudy Perpich, was a populist. Unions were very strong, and most DFLers sought union endorsements immediately upon announcing their candidacy for any office.

Minnesota DFLers had done well during the 1980s. We were firmly in control of both houses of the legislature, as well as the governorship. On the national front, however, things were not going so well for Democrats. The party was bruised and battered. With the defeat of Governor Michael Dukakis in 1988, Democrats lost a presidential election we thought we would win. In fact, Democrats lost five out of six presidential elections between Lyndon Johnson's victory in 1964 and Bill Clinton's victory in 1992.

It was out of those years of frustration that the Democratic Leadership Council had emerged. It formed in 1985, when a group of young, generally moderate or center-left Democratic Congress members joined forces with a group of innovative Democratic governors. They stood for a "Third Way," an alternative to the two-tiered approach of liberalism and conservatism that no longer worked. The founder and CEO of the DLC was Al From. He had been in Democratic politics for a long time, eventually "running" the US House Democratic Caucus.

In an interview in April 2011, From said, "We decided if we didn't change what our party was about and start figuring out modern ways to achieve traditional Democratic goals with new ideas, we would cease to be a national party." The DLC's "New Democrat" philosophy would eventually define DLC chairman and Arkansas governor Bill Clinton's candidacy for the White House. In a 2005 speech, From described it this way:

> Clinton's New Democrat philosophy is the modernization of liberalism. It is a modern day formula for activist

government: progressive policies that create opportunity for all, not just an entitled few; mainstream values like work, family, responsibility, and community; and practical, non-bureaucratic solutions to governing. It reconnects the Democratic Party with its first principles and grandest traditions by offering new and innovative ways to further them.

In April 1989, after the Dukakis defeat, From began recruiting Clinton to be chairman of the DLC. He recalled,

> Clinton was absolutely the most talented political leader I had ever come across. At DLC conferences he set the room on fire. What made Clinton stand out was not just his political charisma, but also his passion for the issues—his ability to make even the most complex policy idea easily understandable to ordinary citizens. He believed that the ideas were so important . . . that if we got those right and got the message right, all the politics would fall into place.

When Clinton assumed the DLC leadership in March 1990, "We basically agreed that we would create a different agenda," said From. As described in chapter 8, Will Marshall and his colleagues at the Progressive Policy Institute (PPI), a DLC think tank, immediately recognized open enrollment and public school choice as a significant education alternative to the "left-right" debate. He and Ted Kolderie launched discussions during the summer of 1990 of the next idea—chartering. Their discussions brought about the publication of the November 1990 PPI policy report authored by Kolderie: *Beyond Choice to New Public Schools: Withdrawing the Exclusive Franchise in Public Education.*

Kolderie and Marshall were working on the report in September 1990, when From and Clinton began their journey to take the new

DLC agenda "on the road" to nearly half the states. Said From, "We went around the country and tested the ideas that would become the DLC agenda. Charter schools was often a subject [Clinton] raised. The Ted Kolderie paper wound up being really important."

Clinton was an education reformer, but he did not immediately embrace the chartering idea. After Minnesota passed open enroll-ment, he had implemented the same legislation in Arkansas—after battling the Arkansas Education Association union. So Clinton knew being a chartering frontrunner was not without risk. In his April 2011 interview, Marshall related the following story about how Clinton finally "warmed" to chartering:

> Governor Clinton and Al From were on the road honing and refining the New Democratic message. Clinton was getting a lot of criticism that the DLC was divisive, combative, causing disharmony and disunity in the party. Teachers were expressing anxiety about chartering.
>
> I remember talking on the phone with him, somewhere on the road. He had been getting pushback and blowback and wanted to know why we were so keen on chartering. I explained why it was a potential alternative between the "More Money Dem" crowd and conservatives, who saw public education as a hopeless bureaucracy to bypass with vouchers. We had a vigorous conversation. . . . It got a little heated. I was arguing the Third Way; he accused me of being willing to poke a stick in the eye of liberal interests and being unduly provocative of groups with whom he had good rela-tionships, which he wanted to keep.
>
> I said we needed to champion reform, not just funding. He had been called a reformer in [David] Osborne's book, *Laboratories of Democracy.* So I told him, we either reform the public school system or conservatives would get the upper

hand. He understood that. He found a way to wrap his mind around it and be comfortable with it. He knew ideas were powerful—ideas like national service. . . . [Like national service, chartering] included a core logic that ordinary people found attractive. So he warmed to the idea of chartering and weaved it into his repertoire.

Clinton never wavered after that. As From remembered, "We went to Mississippi in 1990 or 1991. We arrived very late for an event. . . . We wound up missing the event. Clinton came in and just did a press conference. With all the education people and the teachers unions in the back of the press conference, he did his deal on charter schools." In another instance, From recalled, "I remember going to Los Angeles in 1991, and we were at a dinner that Warren Beatty, Annette Bening, and Patricia Duff had put together. The first question was, 'You're not for charter schools, are you?' And Clinton said, 'Yes, I am, and you should be, too, and here's why.'"

As I write this history twenty years later, nothing astonishes me more than this: Nine months—nine whole months—before Minnesota passed the chartering legislation into law, Clinton was out on the road to nearly half the states, promoting chartering as a "New Democrat Idea." I knew none of this at the time. Moreover, I don't think Kolderie knew it either. Clinton, From, and Marshall took a visionary idea from Kolderie's PPI paper and began a national discussion. Unbelievable. What a leap of faith!

Clinton and From officially rolled out the DLC agenda at their national convention in Cleveland on May 5–7, 1991. The convention included more than a thousand Democrats from all fifty states, including delegates from twenty-two DLC state organizations. By this time, the DLC included over six hundred federal, state, and local elected officials.

On May 6, Clinton presented his keynote speech, which Clinton later said was one of the best and most important he ever gave. In that speech, he laid out the themes that would become signatures of his eventual presidential run: opportunity, responsibility, and community. From recalled, "A big part of that speech was choice— about giving people more choices to do things. Charter schools was one of the four or five big ideas that we did in Cleveland that defined the agenda." Specifically, Clinton said this about choice:

> We should be for more choices. . . . Choice is not a code word for elitism or racism. We are living in a world when all of us want choices . . . even 60 channels on cable television. . . .
>
> With appropriate protections against discrimination based on race or income, we can provide our people more choices: child care vouchers, public school choice options, job training programs, and choices for the elderly . . . to let them have more choices to stay independent and stay at home . . .

Following Clinton's keynote speech, the convention passed "The New American Choice Resolution" with the following language for "Making Public Education Work":

> [States] and communities must commit to restructuring educational systems, pushing more decision-making down to the school level to principals and teachers on the firing line, while increasing accountability by districts and states, with rewards for schools which are succeeding and consequences for those which are not. States should develop public school choice plans, with protection against discrimination based on race, religion, and poverty; *should consider giving entities other than school districts the opportunity to operate*

public schools; and should develop alternative public schools. . . . We support ways to encourage shared decision making among parents, teachers, government, and citizens of the community. [Italics added.]

The DLC agenda would shape Clinton's presidential campaign in 1992. In his interview, From noted:

> One of the remarkable things about the 1992 campaign is that most of the ideas we ran on came from outside Washington. . . . The Ted Kolderie paper was critical in the charter school thing. Most of the things we were looking at were things that weren't really being debated in Washington . . . These ideas changed the whole course of Democratic politics. That is why it was so important that you had a Democrat that would [lead] it. Otherwise, with chartering, the teachers unions would not have let anything happen. This was really important.

The presentation of "The New American Choice Resolutions" at the DLC National Convention in Cleveland was not without controversy. Later, on November 10, 2005, From would give a speech to the eleventh Presidential Conference at Hofstra University, where he would say:

> The New Choice resolutions broke new ground, calling for ideas like national service, an expanded Earned Income Tax Credit, welfare reform, charter schools. . . . and reinventing government. Those ideas may not seem radical or even particularly bold today, but in 1991, they provoked plenty of controversy. Jesse Jackson protested outside the convention hall. So did other Democratic interest groups. A rival group of

liberals led by Senator Howard Metzenbaum of Ohio, called
the Coalition for Democratic Values, met in Des Moines that
same weekend, arguing that Democrats should reject Clinton,
the DLC, and the New Democrat approach.

You'd think I would have been aware of all this conversation
about chartering at the national level. But we were in the middle of
the crucial conference committee negotiations, and the unions were
rising up quickly and powerfully. Would the knowledge that one
thousand center-left Democrats had passed a resolution supporting
chartering have helped—or hurt—our cause in Minnesota? Even
today, I'm not sure. All I can say now is that I'm glad I made the decision to go forward with the compromised chartering legislation.
According to Marshall in his 2011 interview, the fact that chartering—in any form—began in Minnesota was key:

> It was so important that it started in Minnesota with
> Upper Midwest progressives and then went on to another
> progressive state like California. It could not have started in
> the south with a difficult racial history. I talked with the
> Dems in my home state of Virginia, and they were not
> convinced. . . . They saw [chartered schools] as segregation
> academies.

The chartering concept was already on its way. Clinton, our most
powerful supporter, was leading the charge. It wouldn't be long
before Clinton would have key support from another centrist.
Minnesota Republican senator David Durenberger was about to
introduce chartering legislation into the US Senate.

*Durenberger . . . was trying to educate people that
chartered schools was a middle position.*

Jon Schroeder

20

The Republican Pragmatist—
US Senator David Durenberger

July–August 1991

Chartering had indeed moved quickly to the national scene. Even
Congress began paying attention—to my great surprise. Delivery of
public education was historically viewed as a state function. A federal
role in education was unclear, at best. If chartering were to become
federal legislation—or even if the federal government were to have
impact on state policy—we needed a congressional champion to take
on this difficult challenge. We needed an independent lawmaker who

loved to develop new policy ideas, often without regard to traditional boundaries of party doctrine.

David Durenberger, Minnesota's senior US senator, fit the bill perfectly. Coincidentally, his passion for health care had put him in a key position to shape an education issue like chartering. He was a member of the Senate Labor Committee, chaired by Senator Ted Kennedy, which oversaw health issues as well as education. Being on the labor committee also allowed Durenberger to serve on the influential House-Senate education conference committees.

More importantly, Durenberger was a product of the same reformist roots that generated the chartering idea. He was chair of the Citizens League Public Service Options (PSO) project prior to his election to the Senate in 1978. The project had a great impact on Durenberger. So did Ted Kolderie, who was then executive director of the Citizens League and who became Durenberger's close advisor on education reform and other system-reform issues. The PSO project contended that public problems should not necessarily lead exclusively to government-run programs. Instead, the government should buy results from whoever could best provide the services.

For Durenberger, it got him to think about "financing choices" rather than "financing the institutions that deliver the choices." In an August 2011 interview, Durenberger said, "That whole concept of changing the role of government was very, very important. It was so unique as a way of thinking about public service that I'd have to work to find somebody that could understand it in Washington. It was a little bit difficult." Durenberger credited this new concept to Kolderie. "I think that was [Kolderie's] biggest gift. He just put his finger on where it's at in changing the role of government. It's as current today as it was then and it's just as important."

Since the 1980s, Durenberger and his staff had been closely following Minnesota's public school choice and chartering initiatives. Finding people who understood those ideas was difficult too.

When Minnesota ushered in open enrollment in the mid-1980s, Durenberger struggled to convince his colleagues that public education students should have choices beyond their "neighborhood" schools.

> In Washington these education experts didn't get this. . . . [They] couldn't understand this, because public education meant the neighborhood school. We put all of our regulations against the neighborhood school. . . .
>
> They were having trouble trying to figure out why we just don't improve the neighborhood school. I would say, the way you improve it is to give kids and their families a choice of which neighborhood school they want to go to."

Durenberger also believed that creating competition among public schools would be helpful to teachers.

> Teachers are the only ones [who] don't get to decide what education is. They get trained up in various higher education institutions and get graduate degrees, and they get out and teach. But they don't control the product. They have no responsibility for the product. . . . They don't get rewarded
> . . . .
>
> I always made a point when teachers came to lobby me. . . . "Before I answer your question you've got to tell me . . . the last time you can remember waking up in the morning and you couldn't wait to get to school." In all my years of experience, I never got an answer to that. I never had someone volunteer, "It was last Tuesday, it was last Wednesday, it was three weeks ago, it was ten years ago." Not one person said, "Dave, I've got to tell you how much I love this profession." I [was] trying to be helpful. I [was] trying to find a way.

Durenberger was convinced teachers wanted reform such as chartering, despite what the teacher unions contended:

> I think we make assumptions about the strength of the teachers unions and their ability to always reflect the will of the majority. . . . There just has to be a market out there among people who choose education as a career to do something other than the two-step every two years. "I got promoted regardless. All I've got to do is get a few more credits."

After Minnesota passed chartering legislation in May 1991, Durenberger thought it was time to push public school choice to the national level. He saw chartering as a means to an end. He thought introducing competition and choice via chartering would provide a "stamp of approval from the feds" on the need to reform elementary and secondary education on the state level. Said Durenberger, "I was a believer in 'let a thousand flowers bloom.' Let's see what each state does. Let's see how it evolves."

Durenberger had help in this effort from Jon Schroeder, the senator's director of policy development and a self-described "home-state policy wonk." Working out of Durenberger's Minnesota office, Schroeder came from the same reformist roots as Durenberger. Hired by Kolderie, he was a Citizens League staffer from 1972 to 1977 and had worked with Durenberger and the PSO project. Durenberger had asked Schroeder to keep an eye out for "good Minnesota ideas to take to Washington."

Schroeder and Durenberger agreed that chartering was one of those good ideas, but they needed to figure out the best way to bring it to the nation's capitol. Schroeder was sensitive to the limited role the federal government played in financing and delivering public education. He knew Durenberger's initial goal would be to educate his colleagues and others around the country about this new chartering policy innovation in his home state. That meant introducing a bill.

As Schroeder said in an April 2011 interview, "When you're a legislator—at the state level, but particularly true in Washington—if you have an idea you want to promote, you have to have a bill. That's the currency; that's the stuff they do. They are in the business of passing bills." A bill would open the door to cosponsors, statements in the *Congressional Record,* hearings, and press conferences. But most of all, it would create a bully pulpit where they could invest time in the issue, talk with people, and build support for the idea in Minnesota and around the country.

Introducing a federal bill would also provide leverage for those states wishing to pass their own chartering policies. Back in 1991, this wasn't a traditional approach for Congress. But Durenberger and Schroeder felt each state could pass its own legislation if Congress and the presidential administration endorsed chartering. Most importantly, Schroeder felt states could pass chartering legislation if they could count on start-up money in addition to funding once the chartered schools were up and operating. As the key initiator of the idea, he explained in his 2011 interview,

> What we came up with was the start-up grant program . . . the start-up funding. That's what we heard from charter school people—people who were starting to develop proposals. This was the biggest problem. In Minnesota's law, there was no money for planning and developing proposals. There was no capital money from the state for even things like desks and computers or remodeling costs.

Schroeder crafted brilliantly strategic legislation for Durenberger to introduce. Under the bill, the federal government offered grants to states that passed chartering laws. These states' departments of education would, in turn, give start-up grants to approved charter proposals. The grants could be used for planning, start-up costs, equipment purchase, and minor renovations. If a state department of education chose not to apply for grants, then the authorizers of chartered schools in that state could directly apply for grants to the US Department of Education. The bill would authorize $50 million in grants.

Schroeder and Durenberger based much of their chartering legislation on Minnesota's law—with the hope of making a federal standard to help shape other states' laws. "We were intending to have states model their laws after Minnesota, which, except for the cap on schools and the district-only chartering, we considered a strong law," said Schroeder. Those two weaknesses were left out of the Durenberger bill. Chartering was or would soon be making its way into legislatures across the country. In September 1991, Republican governor John Engler would include chartering in a comprehensive education reform package he proposed to the Michigan legislature. Legislators and education reformers in a number of other states— including Massachusetts, Florida, Wisconsin, and Tennessee—were actively discussing chartering. That summer and fall of 1991, the public debate about chartering and vouchers would especially heat up in California. City leaders in Baltimore, Philadelphia, Detroit, and Chicago would engage in chartering discussion in 1992.

With legislation now drafted, Durenberger moved quickly to introduce the legislation on July 31, 1991, into the US Senate as the "Public School Redefinition Act of 1991." In Durenberger's press release, he focused on the bill's three goals, as summarized here.

- **Create more choices:** "States like Minnesota . . . are now moving to the next stage of education reform by encouraging more choices. My legislation puts the federal government squarely behind states that want to take that next step."

- **End the exclusive franchise for local school boards to deliver public education:** "We would never accept a situation in which A&P [an East Coast supermarket chain] had an exclusive franchise to operate every grocery store in Washington, D.C."

- **Redefine public education:** "Public education shouldn't be defined by who owns the building or who hires the teachers. It should be defined by outcomes, by the Constitution, by who pays, who must be accepted as students, and who can't be excluded." [Subheads added.]

More interesting to me, however, was Durenberger's official statement about the bill on the Senate floor, in which he took aim at the politics of education reform head-on. In his statement, he said his legislation addressed the concerns people had about the initiatives President George H. W. Bush and Education Secretary Lamar Alexander offered. He was referring, of course, to their steadfast support of private school choice and federal funding to support private schools. Durenberger said this of his chartering legislation:

> And it points all of us toward a new, more effective, and politically achievable definition of American public education. I say that in part because of the difficulty some of us in Washington seem to be having in breaking some traditional barriers to reform that states like Minnesota seem to have long ago put behind them.
>
> The old debates about public and private school choice don't have to stand in the way of fundamental reforms if we're willing to redefine public education. And getting past that barrier has made all the difference in removing partisanship from this debate in a state like Minnesota where Democrats—in both the governor's office and the

legislature—have been our biggest champions of choice and reform.

Here was the face of Durenberger the pragmatist. He was looking for an alternative to education reform that was politically possible. Said Schroeder in his interview,

> Durenberger saw this bill as a way to "break the logjam" on school choice. He was trying to educate people that chartered schools was a middle position. Chartering was something that could accomplish the objectives of vouchers, but still be within public education and earn the support of Democrats. It would be a bipartisan strategy for improving public education. That's the central message here—other than that vouchers were never going to pass.
>
> This was pure Durenberger. [He resisted] these polarizing positions of making the whole national government's role in education dependent on consensus around an issue that they would never agree on. The voucher amendment got only thirty-five votes in the US Senate and eighty votes in the US House.

The issue was simple for Durenberger: "I was always wedded to the notion that the charter school reform was something that needed to take place *inside* public education," he said in his interview. "[It] was our notion that [chartering] would create competition between schools, rather than between private education and public education. Simply putting publics in competition with privates wasn't going to do it."

For this strategy to work, Durenberger knew his legislation needed to be bipartisan. At that time, Democrats controlled both houses of Congress. He needed a Democratic coauthor for the bill.

One likely prospect was Senator Joe Lieberman from Connecticut, a leader in the Democratic Leadership Council (DLC). Lieberman and his staff were aware of the chartering idea. In 1991, Connecticut legislators had hotly debated chartered schools, and ultimately, the state legislature created a task force to study the concept and bring back a report by January 1992.

After Durenberger invited Lieberman to cosponsor, the DLC moved into action behind the bill. The DLC asked me to call Lieberman's staff to respond to questions and provide comfort that chartering originated as a Democratic initiative. In early August 1991, Lieberman signed on as the lead Democratic sponsor of Durenberger's chartering bill. I couldn't have been more pleased that a prominent Democrat had signed onto the bill. Later in September, the DLC arranged a meeting so I could personally thank Lieberman and share the story of chartering in Minnesota.

Allow me a personal aside to this happy story: I had no inkling at the time that Lieberman's involvement in this groundbreaking national platform for education reform might rise up in my own political career years later. In appreciation for his leadership on chartering, I offered my visible support for Lieberman when he later sought both the US vice presidency and presidency. But then he switched party allegiance from Democrat to Independent in 2006, just as I was running in a DFL primary for Congress in a liberal urban district. The blogger world and my opponents tied me early on to Lieberman's policies. My past support for Lieberman and my long-time support of chartering were very unpopular in the district and were two factors that contributed to my primary defeat.

However, back in 1991 (and yet still today), I was deeply grateful for Lieberman's critical bipartisan support for Durenberger's chartering legislation. The fate of this legislation still remained to be seen. Whether it would pass the US Congress that year or in years later was not pivotal. What was most important was that it created a platform for the national discussion around chartering, public school choice, and even private school vouchers. *That* debate was just getting started.

In my view, chartering gives incentive to strengthen our public schools. Private school vouchers give incentive to abandon them.

21

Chartering: Not "Voucher Lite"

It didn't take long for policymakers and chartering proponents to position public chartered schools as an alternative to private school vouchers. As detailed in chapter 27, that became most apparent in California in the summer and fall of 1991, when chartering was introduced as a positive education reform measure to counter voucher advocates mobilizing to put a voucher initiative on the ballot in the fall of 1992.

As chartering proponents focused on positioning charters as an alternative to vouchers, chartering opponents focused on tying the two together. An August 7, 1991, article in the *Los Angeles Times* noted that the two major teacher unions in Minnesota "vigorously opposed the charter school plan," quoting a key reason from Minnesota Federation of Teachers (MFT) lobbyist Rose Hermodson: "Here we are using public money to fund quasi-private schools."

With the politics of education reform rapidly heating up in the national conversation, I used every visible opportunity I could to make the distinction between private school vouchers and chartering. I have always opposed public funding to private K–12 schools, so it struck a chord with me when opponents constantly referred to chartering as disguised private school vouchers or "voucher lite." In my view, while both private school vouchers and chartered schools offer more choices for families and parents, the similarities end there. Chartering gives incentive to strengthen our public schools. Private school vouchers give incentive to abandon them. It was important for me and other proponents to act quickly to make clear distinctions between chartering and vouchers.

I entered the public debate by writing several commentaries for local and national media sources, focusing on four elements of quality public education that chartering could accomplish better than private school vouchers: innovation, accountability, competition, and inclusiveness. This kind of comparative approach was important to the rise of chartering and to the nation's understanding and acceptance of public school choice. I summarize my key comparisons here:

- **Innovation:** Chartering provides an opportunity for parents and teachers to design a new school—design a whole new structure or approach to learning. Vouchers do not create new schools; they support existing schools. Chartering offers a research and development sector of public education. The innovations don't just benefit the few. They benefit the many. The innovations easily transfer to other schools because the ground rules are the same—they all deliver public education. In short, chartered schools give innovation an opportunity to thrive, and the entire public school system can benefit as a result.

- **Accountability:** While many public school rules and regulations are waived for public chartered schools, the schools are still held accountable for performance. An authorizer and a chartered school board negotiate performance outcomes they expect from teachers and students. If these outcomes are not achieved, the school can—and will be—closed. This is more accountability than most school boards require of their district public schools. In contrast, private schools neither abide by state regulations nor are required to commit to performance standards or outcomes. In 1995, US Secretary of Education Richard Riley summarized the difference this way: "Vouchers pull enormous public resources from one system that is accountable to one that is not."

- **Competition:** Vouchers cannot provide true competition. How can one system that is accountable to the public compete with one that is not? But as US Senator David Durenberger noted, chartered schools stimulate competition within the public school system. A Minnesota superintendent told me three years after passage of the chartering law, "I'm never going to be able to make the changes we need in this school district until we have a charter school operating across the street." For that superintendent, direct and visible competition was important to reduce staff resistance to proposed changes. In some cases, just the prospect of a new chartered school in a district can bring about desired change.

- **Inclusiveness:** By definition, chartered public schools
  must serve all students on a first-come, first-served basis
  and cannot charge tuition. But even with vouchers,
  finances will still prohibit access to private school for many
  families. Some private schools charge well over $7,000 per
  year. Few voucher proposals meet even half of that.
  Families receiving vouchers must still raise the remainder
  of the tuition.

The commentaries were good opportunities to shape the differences between vouchers and chartering, but I needed to do more. That was why I participated in the "America 2000 Daily Conference Call" with US Secretary of Education Lamar Alexander on November 4, 1991. Wisconsin Democratic representative Polly Williams, who pioneered the Milwaukee voucher program, was the secretary's other guest. Alexander described us as "two of the nation's leading education innovators."

If anyone had suggested a year before that I would be on a nationwide conference call with the secretary of education from the Bush administration, I would have laughed. I wasn't a Republican. Education wasn't my leading issue at the legislature. I wasn't an educator. I didn't even have children. But I did want to take every opportunity I could to promote chartering and distinguish it from vouchers.

After Williams detailed progress in the second year of the Milwaukee voucher program, Alexander gave me an opportunity to talk about expansion of public school choice through chartering. To contrast Williams and the voucher concept, I intentionally emphasized the public education elements of chartering.

I was pleased when Alexander described Minnesota's chartering legislation as a chance to create "innovative schools" that would give "teachers an opportunity to contract with their local school boards to create brand new schools. . . . I know of no other state that's done anything quite like that." He went on to focus on chartering's impact on teachers within the public education system. He said,

> President Bush has talked about a new generation of American schools, and this sounds right up that alley. It sounds like it would give teams of teachers [the chance] to do what many teachers must dream of doing, which is take their knowledge and start from scratch and create a new school. . . . It sounds like [chartering answers] the question that many teachers sometimes say, which is, we hear all this talk about reform and where is our place in all this reform?

Even as the national debate swirled around public and private school choice, the most important test was yet to come—right here in Minnesota. The time had come for teachers and parents to step forward and make the concept of chartering a reality. It was time to create chartered schools.

That evening, the Winona School Board voted five to two to authorize Bluffview as a chartered school. It was the first school board in the nation to approve a charter.

22

Starting Chartered Schools: "Electric Expectations"

FALL 1991

By September 1991, the Minnesota Department of Education reported interest from some forty groups around the state that wanted to learn more about submitting charter applications. Earlier, in June 1991, Joe Nathan and others had organized two meetings at the Hubert H. Humphrey Institute of Public Affairs at the University of Minnesota to review resources available to chartering proponents interested in using the new law. Passing a law is one thing; interpreting it and implementing it is another. I always believed the hardest part was in the latter—in starting the schools. In the June 25, 1991, *Minnesota Journal*, Curt Johnson, then head of the Citizens League, described the first of these meetings:

> In mid-June about 40 people gathered in late afternoon in a room at the Humphrey Institute. They were frustrated but dedicated teachers, a principal ready to leave the safety of the system for the uncertainties of helping to birth a chartered school, a superintendent who said his board is ready to help teachers who want to form these schools, an attorney who spread early confidence that technical barriers are not insurmountable, a marketing expert who encouraged the group to think like entrepreneurs, and the director of a major program with resources to apply to new ventures—a roomful of people who want to start schools and people who want to help them.
>
> There was the subtle current of electric expectations—the fears and uncertainties stirring around in a mixture of visions and promise. It is the stuff of which movements are made.

The group raised numerous questions that needed answers. Questions such as: Could teachers presently teaching approach a school board other than the one where they are employed? How will the Minnesota Department of Education "rank order" the eight schools that may be established—by date of approval or date they open for students? What start-up funding might be available for the planning process? What if school boards resisted, en masse? Representative Becky Kelso reminded the group that the chartering provision "passed by an absolute hair." According to Ted Kolderie's notes, Kelso told the group, "Nothing else could have passed. If school boards obstruct its implementation, they will be building the case for the legislature taking them out of it. But I have real hopes the boards will respond well."

Everyone present in these meetings knew they had to establish good, quality chartered schools. They were all aware that the future success of chartering depended on creating quality. Nathan, who founded the Center for School Change at the Humphrey Institute that year, stepped forward to help. He explained in his 2011 interview:

> We used a lot of the research and a lot of the experience of the alternative schools to say, "Here are the things you need to think through." There was a lot of experience with the alternative schools of the '60s and '70s—some of them successful, some of them not successful.
>
> The Center for School Change was able to get some money from the Minneapolis and St. Paul Foundations and from TCF [then Twin City Federal]. We were able to hire a person whose full-time job was to try to help people . . . start new kinds of charters. We helped people set up a series of rural options—some of them schools within schools, some of them charters.

Most of us who'd supported chartering thought that North Branch superintendent James Walker, an attendee of the Humphrey Institute meeting who had publicly advocated for the legislation, would lead the movement by establishing one of the first chartered schools in his district. To my disappointment, he informed me by letter on August 13, 1991, that their proposal would be delayed. He explained the delay with these words: "It is the intent to keep our provisional request for a charter school in place, but it is clear that there are too many questions that need clarification prior to implementation. The teachers and I have agreed to try to work through these issues during the 1991–1992 school year so we can charter in 1992–93."

The chartering legislation had become law in June 1991. But it would take until November and December for the first two chartered school applications to be presented to the local and state boards. Frankly, the schools were not what chartering supporters expected. We anticipated that teachers and parents would spawn, design, and run *new* schools. But the first two applications came from *existing* schools. One was from a private Montessori school requesting charter status, and the other was from a small rural school that would otherwise be closed due to declining enrollment.

Transforming private schools into public schools and saving small rural schools wasn't exactly what we had in mind when we passed chartering legislation. Kelso responded to this point in a November 18, 1991, article by Mary Jane Smetanka in the *Star Tribune*: "Certainly schools that already have a base are going to be the first applicants. I would be very alarmed if we had charter school proposals put together hastily. . . . Starting a charter school is a whole lot of work." Kelso expanded on these remarks in an article by the same reporter in the winter 1992 edition of *Agenda*:

> My intent was that the law would be very broad. It would not exclude any of these kinds of options. I don't want to say that I'm disappointed in these kinds of charter schools. What we would hope to see in time is groups of people who have new ideas in education, who start from ground zero to build a new school. But I accept that that will take a good deal of time.

The first school to be granted a charter was Bluffview Montessori School in Winona, a city in the southeastern tip of Minnesota. At that time, Bluffview was a preschool-to-grade-six private school with seventy students. On November 18, 1991, Bluffview director Michael Dorer presented to the Winona School Board a proposal for becoming a kindergarten-to-grade-six chartered school. He argued that the Montessori option should not be limited to the wealthy. He presented a petition that included nearly 1,200 signatures from people in Winona who supported Bluffview's move to become a chartered school.

I joined Dorer and several Montessori parents at the hearing. As described in the *Winona Daily News,* we "defended the proposal for one and one-half hours before a packed Jefferson Elementary School auditorium audience." Dorer stated his clear understanding that as a chartered school, they must accept all applicants for whom they had room. He also confirmed the school would move from its present quarters in a Catholic church to affirm its nonsectarian nature.

That evening, the Winona School Board voted five to two to authorize Bluffview as a chartered school. It was the first school board in the nation to approve a charter. What was even more stunning is that the board approved the school over the objection of superintendent Ronald McIntire. He told the board that Winona schools, which had about 4,900 students, would lose approximately $90,000 in state funds if the Montessori school met its enrollment projections for thirty-four new students. McIntire also questioned the premise of the chartering law: "If the legislature wants to fix the system, why not give all schools in Minnesota the chance to function without the 1,600 mandates that are on the books?" he asked. Not an unreasonable question, in my view.

Stuart Miller, who had a child in the Bluffview preschool and was chairman of the Winona school board, supported the charter plan. As reported in *Star Tribune* articles from November 18 and 19, 1991, he said, "I think the benefits outweigh the risks. The whole point should be what's best for children, not what's best for the School

District or the Montessori school." He also said the argument that the district would lose money was specious. "If we lose students to the charter school, we don't have to expend the revenues to serve those students. . . . I think we gain a new way of delivering the public school to people and we give them choice."

For me, it was a watershed moment. It was pure joy to personally observe the first approval of a chartered school in the nation. Dorer and the Bluffview teachers were ecstatic. The energy of the teaching team, their vision for the future, and their deep commitment to the students they served moved me. The support from the community also moved me. At long last, I had seen evidence that the compromised chartering legislation might still impact children's lives. November 18, 1991, was one of the most meaningful days of my eighteen years in the Minnesota Senate.

The proposal moved quickly to the Minnesota Board of Education, where Bluffview Montessori Charter School was approved on December 10, 1991. In a letter to Miller confirming the approval, Thomas Lindquist, president of the board of education, wrote, "This was an historic moment for both Winona and the State Board because Bluffview is the first charter request to be presented and approved."

On January 7, 1992, on the heels of this approval, US Senator David Durenberger traveled to Bluffview to hear firsthand the realities of starting a new chartered school, including the need for start-up funding. He told reporters he was expecting his chartering legislation to be considered as "the first item on the Senate's agenda" when Congress reconvened January 21 and that he was working with Senator Ted Kennedy to make sure chartered schools like Bluffview would qualify for the proposed grants built into his legislation. Ironically, the Bluffview approval also threw fuel on the political fire about chartering and vouchers. According to reporter Lynn Olson in the January 15, 1992, issue of *Education Week,* chartering opponents portrayed Bluffview as a "modified voucher plan" and "proof that the legislation would open the door to further privatization of education."

Around this same time in early January 1992, a second chartered school proposal was pending before the Minnesota Board of Education. This application came from Toivola-Meadowlands, a K–12 school serving several communities in northeastern Minnesota. As described in chapter 10, this tiny rural school was the main concern of Senator Ron Dicklich, chair of the senate Education Funding Division. The Meadowlands school was scheduled to be closed at the end of the 1991–1992 school year due to declining enrollment. Dicklich never wavered in his support for the chartering legislation because he wanted to find a way to keep this particular school open. Making Toivola-Meadowlands a chartered school was the only way the school could survive.

The Toivola-Meadowlands proposal was for a multi-age, multi-activity classroom—an "open school" that would focus on environmental and agricultural themes. At that time, the school had 165 students in northeastern Minnesota. Dick Raich, a parent working with others on behalf of the school, reported that seventeen committees of teachers, parents, students, and community members were designing "a new, much more progressive, entrepreneurial curriculum" for the school, which would include foreign language for elementary students, a strengthened outcome-based reading program, and integration of classes in different subjects, all built on students' interests.

Once the local school board had granted the charter, the next step was to receive approval from the Minnesota State Board of Education. But that was anything but routine. The nine members of the state board were divided. Some resisted because the application was put forth only to keep a district school alive that would otherwise be closed. Four members were in favor, and five opposed, including the chairman.

Enter Dicklich, the consummate Iron Range dealmaker. He met with the state board chair, telling him he was there to lobby for Toivola-Meadowlands. After the chairman expressed his concerns with the school's application, Dicklich asked him, "Don't you have that request in at the legislature for $300,000?" The chairman said, yes, it was funding for a really important state board project. Replied Dicklich, "This is really important to me. We'll see how important that is." As Dicklich concluded the story, "The chairman changed his mind and would vote for the charter school. So that's how they got their school!" The school opened on September 7, 1993, for 190 students in grades K–12.

In her 2011 interview, Minnesota Federation of Teachers president Sandra Peterson recalled her concern about Toivola-Meadowlands and the example it set: "As time went on, we saw charter schools sometimes used for the wrong purposes. . . . That's when I get dismayed, because that isn't the purpose. . . . The charters were also to be models of good curriculum and something different. It wasn't to avoid consolidation . . . I think that's a real issue."

Local school boards and the state board of education had now approved two of the eight schools allowed by the new chartering law. But the road was getting very bumpy for others.

It appears from these poll results that any attempt to temper or repeal reform efforts such as charter schools may not be viewed favorably by the public.

23

The Unexpected Ally—
US Senator Ted Kennedy

Once Senator David Durenberger introduced in late July his US Senate legislation to establish start-up grants for chartered schools, I didn't hear about it for a while. Things move slowly in Washington. But unbeknownst to me and most others, much was happening behind the scenes in the nation's capitol. By January, chartering would receive an important boost from an unexpected ally.

The America 2000 Excellence in Education Act, the major

education initiative proposed by President George H. W. Bush and Education Secretary Lamar Alexander, had been introduced on May 23, 1991, as S2 in the US Senate. Senator Ted Kennedy of Massachusetts, chair of the Senate Labor Committee, was lead sponsor of the S2 version to be considered on the floor of the Senate on January 24, 1992. Beginning in August, Durenberger and Senator Joe Lieberman set out to insert language into S2 based on the bill they introduced to authorize federal funds to support chartered schools.

This breathing room from August 1991 to January 1992 allowed Durenberger to build awareness as both a public and a private messenger. That is, it gave him time to work with Kennedy. The two had always worked well together, and they were social friends in the sense that Durenberger visited Kennedy's home a number of times. In his 2011 interview, Durenberger described their relationship this way: "Guys like Ted Kennedy who are always legislating—a better way of doing this, a better way of doing that—are always looking for Republicans, someone like me, who is not only smart and willing to work with them . . . but has a constituency. . . . Getting things done is where it's all at, not the politics." Jon Schroeder described the respect between the senators, who were both on the Senate Labor Committee, in his April 2011 interview:

> Kennedy was a good chairman, very attentive, listened to witnesses. When Durenberger would ask a question, I could just tell intuitively, watching Kennedy, how hard he was listening to Durenberger's question and the setup to his question. Maybe he didn't even agree with the road he was going down. But he really did listen and felt he learned a lot. I've heard Durenberger say the same thing about Kennedy . . . that Kennedy was a very effective legislator. . . . He really worked hard.

Whether it was the power of the Durenberger-Kennedy relationship or the power of the chartering idea—or both—Kennedy agreed to include the chartering concept from Durenberger and Lieberman's bill as a provision in S2. The new provision would allow states to use a portion of the block grant authorized under S2 to help establish new public schools. But because the legislation wasn't explicit that chartered schools were eligible as these new schools, Durenberger entered into a colloquy with Kennedy on the Senate floor on January 24, 1992. A colloquy is a process that establishes legislative intent in the *Congressional Record* when clarification is needed about an issue.

During that colloquy, Kennedy first read verbatim the criteria that defined chartered schools as public schools under Minnesota law. He then confirmed, "With these understandings, it is my intention that chartered or 'outcome-based' schools as defined by Minnesota law will be eligible for funding under [this provision]." Next, the senators discussed a new definition of *public school* as "a public school that operates under the authority of a state education agency or local education agency" and confirmed that a chartered school, as defined in Minnesota law, met the definition. The senators concluded:

> **Durenberger:** I want to thank the Senator for his willingness to add language to S2 authorizing start-up funding for Minnesota's chartered schools, an important innovation in education reform that I trust will soon emerge in other states, as well.
>
> **Kennedy:** I would like to thank the Senator for his efforts to expand the number and diversity of public school choices available in his and other states and for his leadership nationally in helping to improve the quality of education for all Americans.

S2 and its chartering provision would have a long road ahead. However, I cannot overstate the significance of this colloquy exchange between Durenberger and Kennedy. It had tremendous impact on the chartering movement across the nation. According to Schroeder,

> It was evidence that charter schools were starting to be known. Also, it was really important to establish that charter schools were public schools, even though they might not be directly under school districts, as we've always defined public schools. . . . To get Kennedy to say that and that it was his intent that they would be eligible as new public schools . . . was important.
>
> It wasn't an automatic thing for Kennedy to do, because particularly the National Education Association was pretty strongly opposed to charter schools—particularly chartered schools that weren't authorized by school districts. And Kennedy was close to them and did a lot of heavy lifting for the teachers unions over the years. So for him to legitimize this [was significant].

The importance of Kennedy acknowledging and supporting chartering in his legislation—and what it meant for our Minnesota legislation—wasn't lost on me. In Minnesota, Kennedy's liberal politics were golden. On February 21, 1992, I sent a memo to all my Minnesota legislative colleagues summarizing the chartering activity in Congress. I attached the colloquy for all to read. I emphasized that start-up funds could be available in the future on the federal level.

That memo followed my February 7, 1992, memo to key DFL colleagues and legislative leaders that included data from a Harris Poll on education reform, published in the winter 1992 issue of *Agenda*, a national education magazine. The poll's headline read, "The Public Takes Reform to Heart," and its key finding was this:

"The latest in a series of original surveys . . . finds the American public playing for keeps when it comes to education reform—and suggests that the state of the schools will be a central issue in the 1992 elections." The following are poll results for some of the key reform issues related to chartering:

Poll Question	Favor	Oppose
Giving individual schools much more authority over their teaching and spending decisions?	68%	29%
Giving teachers a greater decision-making power over what is taught and how it is taught?	74	24
Freeing schools from tight regulations?	58	37
Making individual schools accountable for how well they educate their students?	93	6
Emphasizing actual student performance in learning rather than learning how to score well on tests?	91	7

Finally, in rating the president, Congress, and political parties, the pollster had these observations about the public's response:

Politically, it appears that President Bush is far from gaining high marks for being "the education president" [36 percent Satisfactory; 62 percent Unsatisfactory]. By the same token, however, he comes off better than Congress [19 percent Satisfactory; 79 percent Unsatisfactory]. This advantage is tempered by the 10-point lead the Democrats have [40 percent to 30 percent] in credibility in being seen as better able to improve the quality of education in America.

With the poll results attached, I ended my memo to DFL leaders: "As you know, Minnesota has been at the national forefront with its past emphasis on choice and new focus on chartered schools. It appears from these poll results that any attempt to temper or repeal reform efforts such as chartered schools may not be viewed favorably by the public."

I had a reason for writing both these memos to my colleagues: I was well aware that in the 1992 legislative session, which had started January 6, some members of the Minnesota House of Representatives would attempt to repeal the chartering legislation. And frankly, I was well aware of how difficult it was for teachers and parents to form chartered schools. As Representative Becky Kelso had described the climate in *Education Week* on January 15, 1992, "It's generating more discussion sooner than I expected. And it's every bit as controversial as I had feared."

It was surprising to see how far chartering had progressed on the national level just six months after passage of the Minnesota legislation. But that progress was necessary for those of us in Minnesota fighting to sustain the law and for those charter applicants working to get their schools approved. It gave us "cover" and hope. The road ahead would be both rocky and lonely.

Some local school boards are unwilling to relinquish power for school experiments out of their control.

STAR TRIBUNE EDITORIAL

24

Chartered Schools:
The Bleeding Edge of Change

FEBRUARY–APRIL 1992

The controversy around chartering was starting to get ugly. After relatively smooth sailing for the first two chartered schools, the next seven charter applicants ran into opposition from local school boards for a wide variety of reasons. Perhaps some of the charter proposals needed more work. But local school board rejection of seven out of seven? "I'm afraid there is a trend developing here," observed Representative Becky Kelso in the *Star Tribune* on March 16, 1992.

For the applicants, these school board rejections were nothing less than heartbreaking. I had the opportunity to work with Griff Wigley and other parents who brought a proposal for Cannon Valley Middle School (CVMS) before the Northfield School Board, in the city where I attended college. In my view, this proposal was one of the "purest" to date because it created a new and innovative school. Both Kelso and I thought the proposal was "exceptionally good." So did the Blandin Foundation, a philanthropic organization supporting rural Minnesota, which selected CVMS as one of twenty finalists for funding out of eighty-four applicants.

The CVMS application proposed an ungraded program for one hundred eleven- to fifteen-year-olds. It was centered on the idea that students can solve community problems while learning. The approach would develop the intellectual, emotional, physical, social, aesthetic, and spiritual capabilities of the whole person. Developed by a local group of teachers and parents, the group first presented the application to the Northfield school board on November 25, 1991. The proposal was subsequently featured in numerous public forums and school board hearings. Both Kelso and I attended at least one of these gatherings to answer questions about the chartering law.

In the end, our informational hearing was for naught. The Northfield school board, on the recommendation of superintendent Charles Kyte, voted five to two on February 24, 1992, not to sponsor the school. Some of the parents involved in the CVMS proposal had started a private elementary school—Prairie Creek Community School—in Northfield ten years before after trying unsuccessfully to set up an alternative in-district program. According to Wigley, that perception of private-school elitism was hard to shake, even though the CVMS proposal aimed at assuring equal access to all students. As Mary Jane Smetanka reported on March 16, 1992, in the *Star Tribune*:

"We had all been involved in starting a school before, and they knew they weren't dealing with fly-by-night folks," said Griff Wigley, one of the parents who planned the charter. "But it brought up a lot of tension in the community. . . . We were seen as a group of Prairie Creek people trying to start a private school with public money."

As many as 175 people attended public hearings on the issue. Much of the discussion centered on money. Many people, who remembered the decade-long budget crisis that ended just three years ago, were frightened that the school district could lose up to $300,000 in state aid if 100 students switched to the new school.

Superintendent Charles Kyte, whom many credit with stabilizing the district's finances, opposed the charter. His main concerns were philosophical. Taxpayers in public schools have a voice in school governance through school board members, he said, but charter schools "disenfranchise" taxpayers because only teachers and parents are represented on school boards.

Kyte also said he was concerned that the charter school would create a "separate public school experience" that would become elitist, because only certain kinds of students would be interested in the school. Wigley said the charter group proposed that the regular and charter middle schools be equally promoted as choices. "The system we have now is elitist, because only people who can afford to move, pay tuition or transfer out have a choice," he said.

Before the charter surfaced, the district and Wigley's group had discussed starting a similar program in the regular middle school. The failed charter has killed that plan, Kyte said. "The staff at the middle school was quite threatened by this. . . . The implied message was that something was wrong with the middle school," he said. "The bridges have been burned for the time being."

It was hard to read this kind of comment. Chartering is about choices, not about making any school's approach right or wrong. And how can chartering "disenfranchise taxpayers" when the parents and teachers of the chartered school are taxpayers as well? Most importantly, in chartering, the money directly follows the child. Isn't that the greatest accountability of all?

My heart went out to Griff and the other parents who had worked so hard to make this dream a reality for their children and the community. These were proven entrepreneurs who wanted to make a difference. And they were stopped in their tracks with no other option open for them. On April 16, 1992, Wigley wrote the following memo to chartering supporters:

> If misery loves company, I guess we're all feeling a bit better these days, as we watch nearly all the charter proposals bite the dust. It's taken us a while to recover, not only from the disappointment of the 5–2 board "no" vote, but just from the grueling pace we'd all been keeping in the final weeks leading up to it.
>
> We met formally as a provisional board last week, and have decided to disband for the time being. None of us had much inclination to shop around for a sponsorship outside of Northfield, as we felt that it would just create more divisiveness in the community. I did approach Supt. Kyte about whether he'd be open to our proposing a site-based managed alternative school within the district. As you may have seen in the [Star Tribune] article a few weeks ago, his answer was that we "burned our bridges."

One thing we did reach consensus on before we disbanded, however: we will work to help pass an amendment to the law to make it possible for another publicly accountable body to sponsor a charter school, should a charter sponsorship be denied by a local board. . . .

On another positive note, a "rescind charter schools" amendment proposed recently at the DFL Rice County convention was soundly defeated. I think we'll have more public support next time around, especially if we can muster the energy to keep the issue in the public eye.

The difficult Northfield experience was becoming the norm for chartered school applicants. On February 21, 1992, I attended a St. Cloud community forum of parents and educators in which the participants discussed Joan Riedl's proposal for a chartered school. A six-page article in *Teacher Magazine*, a national publication, had recently featured Riedl's innovative teaching methods. The article, entitled "Daring to be Different," was a glowing account of Riedl's growth as an educator and of her "Choices" learning approach, which combined learning stations, hands-on problem-solving activities, and advanced technology.

But then on March 24, the school board decided—without even taking a vote—to reject Riedl's proposal. On April 14, Dana Schroeder, editor of the *Minnesota Journal*, reported that according to St. Cloud superintendent Ron Jandura, the board turned down the proposal because "it is not convinced that the existing system stifles innovation and creativity." All I could think was, *excuse me?*

In the same *Minnesota Journal*, Schroeder reported about a chartered school proposal in Emily, Minnesota, that was also rejected. Schroeder quoted Bruce Grossman, superintendent of the Crosby-Ironton school district, as saying, "If it didn't have a financial impact in Crosby-Ironton, we'd have nothing against it. . . . We'd be skeptical of the quality of education though. It's hard for me to grasp that what occurs up there could be better than the program offered in the elementary school in Crosby."

Another heartbreaking rejection was dealt to the teachers who sought to turn their successful Area Learning Center (ALC) in the suburban Mounds View school district into a chartered school. ALC served some of the north suburbs' most challenging young people ages sixteen to twenty-one, who had a variety of academic and social issues such as drug use, abuse, or pregnancy. Of these students, 80 percent were over sixteen, so they didn't even have to go to school. ALC staff wanted to do things differently in order to reach these students, many of whom had dropped out of traditional schools. They proposed a chartered school.

Peggy Hunter of the Minnesota Department of Education called the proposal "outstanding." According to local news stories, however, the district administration thought that accepting the ALC proposal would set a precedent "we can't live with for the district as a whole." The superintendent recommended against the change to chartered school. In early April 1992, the Mounds View school board defeated the proposal with a four-to-three vote.

Ted Kolderie couldn't help but point out the contradictions in the rejections. The Northfield school board rejected the CVMS proposal because it was new and untried and risky—because it would take away kids from the existing school and create financial problems for the district. The Mounds View school board rejected the ALC proposal for opposite reasons. It wasn't new or risky, and if anything, there would have been a positive financial impact—some were students who would not otherwise be in school. It was as if the board felt ALC was doing a fine job in its current status, and no changes were needed. Charter applicants couldn't win.

To make matters even worse, one of the previously approved chartered schools was now under threat. The Winona Education

Association, the local teacher union, was threatening to file a grievance if the Winona School District signed the contract with Bluffview Montessori Charter School. The union contended it was a "subcontract" to an outside group for educational services. The union's contract forbade such subcontracts. While this contention was eventually rejected in the legal process, it wasn't the only setback. In July 1992, the Winona School Board rejected the proposed charter contract. The contract had to be rewritten because two of the three teachers who sponsored it—Michael and Rose Dorer—were no longer with the school. The rejection delayed the opening of the school until fall 1993.

Yes, the road to change is indeed a rocky one. As one charter applicant said, "We are truly on the *bleeding edge* of change." Clearly, there was an inherent conflict in asking local school boards to authorize chartered schools, when the boards stood to lose from such proposals. As Hunter noted in the January 15, 1992, *Education Week*, "That's sort of like putting the fox in charge of the chickens."

An editorial in the *Star Tribune* on March 21, 1992, nailed the issue:

> Half-measures abound in public school reform. And a half-measure is what Minnesota got when the Legislature enacted a charter school law last year. Now the predicted problems are materializing: some local school boards are unwilling to relinquish power for school experiments out of their control. The Legislature should amend the law to allow charters to be granted through the State Board of Education as well as the local district.

One silver lining brightened the clouds of the rejections: In Forest Lake, just the prospect of a chartered school in a district brought about change. A group of families had been working for a

Montessori alternative within their district for over two years. "Too much money for teachers, equipment, and transportation," the superintendent told them. Then the group presented a Montessori charter proposal on March 16, 1992, to the school board. It was enough to make the superintendent overcome his previous objections to a K–3 Montessori in-district alternative. The families got their school—it didn't matter what kind. But it wouldn't have happened without the pressure of a chartered school option.

With only two of the first nine charter proposals passing through their respective school board gatekeepers, it became clearer than ever that we needed to seek an amendment in 1993 for an alternative sponsor or an appeal to the Minnesota State Board of Education. But first, we needed to keep the chartering legislation alive in the 1992 session. On April 2, DFL Representative Bob McEachern offered an amendment to the 1992 omnibus education funding bill to repeal chartered schools. His amendment was defeated by a floor vote of sixty to sixty-nine in the house.

To me, McEachern's amendment was never a serious threat because the senate would never have supported repeal. But the voting breakdown was a concern. The following table shows the vote in 1991 for the motion to send the funding bill—with the chartering legislation—back to conference committee, as it compares to the vote in 1992 for McEachern's amendment to repeal chartering. Of course, different factors affected each year's vote. The 1992 vote was a clean vote on chartering, whereas the 1991 vote on the omnibus education funding bill concerned multiple issues beyond chartering. More significantly, 1992 was an election year, and the teacher unions would be screening legislators for endorsement within a few months. In simple terms for quick comparison, however, I have generalized the votes as either "nay" or "yea" to chartering.

	DFL 1991	DFL 1992	Republican 1991	Republican 1992	Total 1991	Total 1992
"Nay" to chartering	42	52	18	8	60	60
"Yea" to chartering	33	24	31	45	64	69
Not voting	4	2	6	3	10	5
Total	**79**	**78****	**55**	**56****	**134**	**134**

** One seat shifted from DFL to Republican in a special election.

At first glance, chartering gained five more yeas from 1991 to 1992. But upon a closer look, there was a significant shift with DFLers. Of the fifteen members who went from "yea" in 1991 to "nay" in 1992, thirteen of them were DFLers. Conversely, of the seventeen members who changed their vote from "nay" in 1991 to "yea" in 1992, only six were DFLers. That is, fifty-two of the sixty total votes against chartering in 1992 were DFLers.

More than nine months had elapsed since chartering first passed the Minnesota legislature. Congress and several other states were now debating it. But on the home front, progress was painfully slow. Few local school boards were cooperating to make chartering a reality. While my Republican colleagues were coming on board, my DFL colleagues appeared to be moving away from chartering.

We needed to build the will of the public. If chartering were to survive, we needed to spread—and shape—the word about chartering.

The right words and the right tone could make all the difference in chartering's success in the policy world.

25

Shaping the Chartering Message: Setting the Tone for the Future

MAY 1992

The opportunity to introduce chartering to a supportive and influential audience came quickly. The Democratic Leadership Council (DLC) invited me to speak about chartering as part of a panel at the Democratic Leadership Conference in New Orleans on May 1, 1992. Here was the moment to shape the chartering message for opinion makers and lawmakers across the country. Attendees included members of Congress and state and local officials from around the nation, all sharing a commitment to problem solving and seeking a

"Third Way" to the most vexing issues of our day.

My speech would hopefully preempt the national conversation and frame the chartering message at the outset. If we supporters didn't frame the issue, others would no doubt frame it for us. But chartering is not the easiest concept to talk about. It's complicated. If not framed in terms of "values" or "benefits," eyes glaze over after the first minute or so.

The panel featured several policymakers who had been involved with "reinventing government" at the local and state levels. The moderator was David Osborne, author of 1988's *Laboratories of Democracy,* and most recently at the time, coauthor of 1992's *Reinventing Government: How the Entrepreneurial Spirit is Transforming the Public Sector.* A journalist, Osborne also served as advisor to two governors and to presidential candidate Bill Clinton. Frankly, I found his influence rather daunting. In *Reinventing Government,* Osborne and coauthor Ted Gaebler held up Minnesota's open enrollment and chartering initiatives as examples of the restructuring we needed within the public education system. Like me, they supported the creation of new public schools, including chartered schools, but rejected turning education over to the private marketplace in the form of vouchers.

As nervous as I was about this invitation, I felt deeply honored to join the panel. News about the upcoming speech was already making an impact. On April 29, 1992, Jon Schroeder wrote me, "Your trip to New Orleans couldn't be coming at a better time!" Representative Dave McCurdy was interested in offering a chartering amendment in the US House, but as Schroeder explained, McCurdy needed "encouragement from a fellow Democrat."

I had only ten minutes to introduce chartering to attendees, state and federal policymakers, the media, and the nation. How could I explain chartering and four years of history to this important audience in so short a speech? Every word counted. Language would be important. The wrong words or the wrong tone could hurt our chartering efforts for years to come. But the right words and the right tone could make all the difference in chartering's success in the policy world. For the first time in my adult career, I sought help from a messaging coach. I can't remember how many hours we spent preparing for this ten-minute speech, but it felt like days on end.

The most important—and most difficult—goal was finding that thirty-second "elevator speech" that described what a chartered school *is*:

> In short, a charter school is a new kind of public school that rewards innovation, empowers teachers and parents, and meets student needs without turning our existing school system upside down. It's simple: No results; no charter. Teachers trade away regulation for results, and bureaucracy for accountability.

Nearly as difficult was describing what a chartered school *is not*. I wanted to stress they were not vouchers, and they were not a diversion of public school dollars. But the most important point for this audience to hear was this:

> Charter schools *are not an indictment of our public school system*. They are a tool for innovative entrepreneurs to do the job better in times of scarce resources and demanding social agendas.

And finally, the call to action:

> Yes, being on the "bleeding edge of change" is painful. But it is critical for us as progressive Democrats to be there. Why? The public demands as much. A recent Harris Poll

found that education has moved to the top of the roster of political concerns in this year's election. . . . two-thirds of the American public support public school choice. As Democrats, what are we waiting for?

We must continue to [respond] to our changing times. . . . by reinventing public education. If we don't respond, this revolution may move beyond us—beyond our comfort level as Democrats.

The message got through. The response was excellent.

Most importantly, my appearance at the DLC conference was about much more than delivering that one speech. (See Appendix II for full transcript.) It was about creating the message and language of chartering that would serve me and hundreds of others for years to come. The US Department of Education, the DLC, and newspapers around Minnesota would use much of this language in their publications.

The impact of the speech was felt at the federal level as soon as May 15, 1992, when McCurdy's staff confirmed to Schroeder that he would be the lead Democratic cosponsor of a "yet-to-be-determined" chartering amendment in the House. But back home in Minnesota, the impact was not so much felt. Slowly, ever so slowly, supporters were just starting to make chartering a reality.

*City Academy became the first chartered school to open
in the United States on September 7, 1992. Yes!*

26

The First New Chartered Schools:
Outside the Mainstream

SUMMER 1992

Things were still moving slowly on the Minnesota front. By the end
of the 1992 legislative session in May, the Minnesota State Board
of Education had granted approval to only two of the eight allowed
chartered schools—Bluffview Montessori School in Winona and
Toivola-Meadowlands in northern Minnesota. That summer, the
State Board of Education would approve two more chartered schools.
They would be the final schools approved that year.

There was good news and less-than-good news about the third

and fourth approved charters. The less-than-good news was that both schools focused on special student populations, so they had little impact on the general school district populations. Clearly, local school boards were holding back any proposals that might serve the same students as they did. They were, ironically, helping to build our case for change in the 1993 legislature. The good news, though, was that both were *new* schools—consistent with the original intent of the chartering legislation. They were excellent proposals that met specific needs for the students and the community.

On June 9, 1992, the Minnesota State Board of Education granted approval to City Academy, which was previously approved by its sponsor, the St. Paul Board of Education. With an operations plan well in hand, City Academy was ready to open that fall. It became the first chartered school to open in the United States on September 7, 1992. Yes!

The school was created to attract hard-to-reach learners between the ages of sixteen and twenty-one who had dropped out or were at risk of dropping out. St. Paul mayor Jim Scheibel was instrumental in helping City Academy find a suitable, low-cost facility in a park-and-recreation building in a low-income neighborhood on the east side of St. Paul. St. Paul Superintendent Curman Gaines was also supportive. The school was the dream of two former Guadalupe Area Project teachers and Barron Chapman, a City of St. Paul recreation assistant. Teachers Milo Cutter and Terry Kraabel worked over a year on the proposal before they approached the St. Paul school board in March 1992. As reported in the March 11, 1992, *St. Paul Pioneer Press*:

> Teacher Terry Kraabel . . . said his school would not take away money from St. Paul schools because it would serve mostly dropouts.
>
> "We have seen a lot of kids fall through the cracks of the public school system," said Kraabel, who taught at the Red

School House, a private school for Indian children, for two years before teaching last year at Guadalupe. "We have finally figured out that we have to change the way we teach."

[In his school] he said. . . . [s]tudents would receive counseling, personalized instruction and hands-on learning.

As reported in the article, Gaines said he did not view the proposed charter as a competitor of the school district because the students it would serve were not in school anyway. That may have been a key factor in the St. Paul school board's decision to approve the charter. The local teacher union, however, was not supportive. As reported in the article, Gladys Westin, president of the St. Paul Federation of Teachers, said her group was opposed to any chartered schools. "We see it as the siphoning off of public dollars to private schools," she said.

In the fall, the school would open as a year-round program with thirty-five students. It had three full-time teachers and a first-year budget of $200,000. Cutter became its director. As the first and only chartered school to open in 1992, City Academy and Cutter pioneered a path for many others throughout the state and nation. The school was successful. At the end of its first year—spring 1993—fifteen of the seventeen graduates were registered to attend post-secondary institutions in the fall. And eight years later, in 2000, President Bill Clinton would travel to City Academy to recognize its long-term success as the first chartered school in the nation. It was a moving and well-deserved tribute to Cutter, the teachers, and alumni. City Academy was in a "class by itself."

On August 10, 1992, the Minnesota State Board of Education approved the fourth charter applicant, the Metro Deaf School, which was scheduled to open in the fall of 1993. Sponsored by the Forest Lake school district, the school would serve students in grades six through eight who were deaf and hard of hearing. It was the first chartered school specifically directed to students with disabilities.

Scott Haskins, co-chair of the parents' group that planned the school, had brought the proposal before the Forest Lake school board in April 1992. Haskins told the board that past sixth grade, the only program in the state for children who were deaf was the residential Minnesota State Academy for the Deaf in Faribault, about ninety minutes south of the Twin Cities. In the March 30, 1992, issue of the *St. Paul Pioneer Press,* reporter Linda Owen quoted Haskins as saying, "We're looking for an opportunity for our children to get on the bus, go to school and come home at night. It's not my liking to send my 13-year-old to live at school Monday through Friday and only come home on the weekend."

At Metro Deaf School, students as well as their families would be taught the language, culture, and history of the deaf community. Students would learn all content subjects in American Sign Language (ASL), with English as a second language. They would also participate in developing their own learning outcomes. Ideally, said Haskins, the majority of the school's teachers and administrators would be deaf or hard of hearing "so the children would have role models to follow." The school's steering committee was made up of four people who were deaf and three who were not. School officials hoped the school could expand to eventually serve students through the twelfth grade. That appeared feasible, with more than 1,500 students in Minnesota at the time who were deaf and hard of hearing.

After meeting with representatives of the deaf community, Governor Arne Carlson endorsed the deaf school. Forest Lake super-intendent Gerald Brynildsen, who had been cool to the chartering concept, was quoted in Owen's article as saying that this deaf school proposal would at least be a new idea "more in line with the intent" of the chartering law.

Ted Kolderie attended the hearing before the Minnesota State Board of Education and recalls it vividly:

It was summer. School was out. So a lot of students were there. Deaf students. And the student member of the state board. All the discussion was among the adults. When they were about to adjourn, at the "Any further questions?" point, this student member said: "Yes, I'd like to hear from the students." There was moderate consternation, and a half-dozen students filed over to the side of the room. Somebody was there to translate. "Why would you like to go to this school?" was the question. One kid just said, "I want to live at home where I can play with my dog and go to a school where I can talk to my friends." The application was approved without a dissenting vote.

True, this chartered school served a special population and was not a "mainstream" school—even in the chartering sense. Maybe this school wasn't exactly what we envisioned charters to be. But it was still a joy to watch the parents and their children realize their vision in creating this school uniquely suited to their needs.

With only four chartered schools approved in the first eighteen months following passage of the legislation, progress was indeed slow. The results had not exactly met our expectations. To Kolderie, more needed to be done. If chartering were to survive, a second state legislature—and not just *any* state legislature—needed to step up to the plate.

But when you get to say, "Now it's gone to California,
the biggest state in the country and a union stronghold,
and it was authored by a Democrat and signed into law
by a Republican" . . . it really gave it a lot more leg. . . .

ERIC PREMACK

27

Chartering Evolves in California: "A Policy Redwood"

FEBRUARY–SEPTEMBER 1992

By early 1992, a robust debate about school choice was underway in the California legislature and in the education and business communities. Voucher advocates were mobilizing—this time, with major funding from a top business leader. They hoped to go to the ballot in fall 1992 with a referendum initiative that would entitle parents to vouchers worth about $2,500 annually for every school-age child.

239

Parents could use these publicly funded vouchers to send their children to any school—public or private. As California state senator Gary Hart, a chartering proponent, later wrote in the September 1996 issue of *Kappan* magazine, "This was not a modest voucher pilot proposal, but a full-blown effort to reconstitute public education in California."

The voucher referendum threat in California had surfaced as early as the previous summer. It motivated state education leaders like Hart, Superintendent Bill Honig, and Assemblymember Delaine Eastin to search for education reform alternatives to propose for the 1992 legislative session. Not coincidentally, Ted Kolderie had connected in Washington, DC with a California business leader who invited him to talk to the California Business Roundtable education committee. Kolderie called Eric Premack, his longtime friend who had worked with the Citizens League and who was then a legislative analyst at the California legislature, to suggest that Premack set up meetings in Sacramento with legislators and others during his trip. The visits were successful. Said Kolderie, "They saw chartering as a way to generate innovative new schools and to catalyze the system, but *within* the general framework of public education." On the same day of the Kolderie visits, Premack received phone calls from staff members for both Democratic chairs of the education committees, saying, "We want to run a chartered school bill."

During this time, Kolderie also enlisted Jon Schroeder's help in circulating information about US Senator David Durenberger's chartering bill to a list of key Californians. One of them was Republican governor Pete Wilson. Durenberger and Wilson were close friends, having served together for twelve years in the US Senate. Durenberger wrote a personal letter to Wilson to encourage him to support state legislation in California on chartered schools.

Kolderie knew that passing chartering in a state like California would have great impact across the nation. As Premack explained in his May 2011 interview:

> Certain states [have] certain reputations. Minnesota's is sort of the "policy hothouse," where they get to grow interesting things that won't grow anywhere else or that are very difficult to transplant—sort of "policy orchids," if you will. But if you can do it in California, then it's a "policy redwood"—it's big and undeniable.
>
> When you say something happened in Minnesota, people say, "Isn't that cute?" and roll their eyes a little, with a degree of admiration, but [it's an] "It'll never fly here in Jersey" kind of [reaction]. But when you get to say, "Now it's gone to California, the biggest state in the country and a union stronghold and it was authored by a Democrat and signed into law by a Republican," . . . it really gave it a lot more leg, in my experience, in shopping the idea to other states.

Spurred by the growing threat of the voucher ballot initiative, the chairs of the education committees in both houses of the California legislature held a joint press conference on February 1, 1992, to publicly propose their respective chartered school bills. Hart proposed SB 1448; Eastin proposed AB 2585. Unlike in Minnesota, where Representative Becky Kelso and I worked from one bill, these were two very different and competing bills. The bills differed in their approaches to chartering, and chartering supporters felt Hart's was the stronger bill. Wilson favored Hart's bill as well.

Hart's proposed bill was similar to the Minnesota law, except that it allowed a local school board to approve a charter without needing second approval from the state board. Eastin's proposed bill was more prescriptive and union friendly, requiring sign-off by collective bargaining agents and a second approval by the state. Hart wanted to authorize one hundred chartered schools; Eastin's bill authorized twenty-five. Underlying these differences were the politics of ambition, as both legislators were unannounced candidates to run for state superintendent in 1994. Also, Eastin was up for reelection the coming fall; Hart was not.

Despite the differences in the bills, what was most important is that both came from Democratic education leaders who were committed to introducing a positive reform alternative to blunt the appeal of the voucher plan. In California, no legislator could afford to take the electorate for granted on ballot initiatives. As Premack so colorfully said, the voucher ballot initiative "gave some cover to Democrats, like Hart, to walk out on the charter plank. . . . It's what I call the 'crazy grandma' strategy: If you have a crazy grandma in the attic, then our idea looks that much more sane."

To keep chartering out of the political crossfire of the upcoming state superintendent election, Premack helped Hart and Eastin reach an unusual deal. They would allow one another's bills to go through the entire legislative process largely unscathed and then let a conference committee work out any differences. The "handshake deal" was that neither bill would emerge from the conference without the concurrence of both legislators.

First, of course, they had to get their bills to the conference committee. Hart and his staff assistant Sue Burr worked to keep their bill simple and with few restrictions, allowing as much flexibility as possible for chartered schools. As Hart and Burr described in their September 1996 article in *Kappan* magazine, the first hurdle was the senate education committee, where they needed six votes to pass the bill. As they met with committee members prior to the April 8 hearing, they were reminded of how confusing the chartering concept was and of the need for a sharp, clear message. So instead of focusing on how chartering worked, they focused on how the current educational system worked. They wrote,

To drive home the message that schools needed much greater flexibility, we hauled the 11-volume, 6,000 page education code to the committee hearing and stacked it on the table in a three-foot pile. This graphic display, with its implication of schools being crushed under prescriptive statutes, proved to be quite powerful, and, after an extremely lengthy and contentious hearing, the bill passed out of committee by a vote of 6 to 5.

Hart allowed very few amendments to his bill. As he and Burr wrote, "If we weren't careful, we would end up 'reinventing' that 11-volume education code we used so effectively as a prop."

Hart had long been interested in creating more flexibility for public schools. As noted in the *Kappan* article, he previously authored legislation for a program that granted approximately two hundred schools greater flexibility in exchange for greater accountability. He also sponsored a statewide pupil achievement test to ensure that schools given more freedom would still be held accountable through the use of a standard measurement tool.

To Hart, "a move toward charter schools seemed to be a natural evolution of the education reform process." As Premack told it in his interview, Hart had been growing weary of complaints from district staff and superintendents who said they couldn't do anything "outside the box instructionally," even with these new powers granted by Hart's sponsored programs. Premack explained, "To him . . . in part, [chartering] was sort of throwing down a challenge to school districts: 'Okay, if the restructuring bill that I ran a few years ago wasn't powerful enough to let you do what you need to do, we're going to give you the waiver to end all waivers, in the form of a chartered school bill.'"

Hart's focus on in-district innovation was a primary reason why California became the first state to consider "conversion" chartering,

a process whereby teachers of an existing district school could petition to convert into a chartered school. In Minnesota, we hadn't
really thought about this option. We were focused on creation of
"new" schools. According to Premack,

> I think [Hart] anticipated a certain number of "from-
> scratch" charters, but I don't think [he] anticipated the
> number and emphasis of "from-scratch" schools that we
> .actually did see. . . . I think his anticipation at the time was
> that a lot of this would be done by existing school staff, and
> perhaps, board members who wanted to push the envelope.

Already, the concept of chartering was evolving. I had long
thought chartered schools could be laboratories for innovation, but
the idea that the chartered school law itself might be the focus of
innovation hadn't really occurred to me. No doubt, though, it was
front and center to Kolderie, who had always focused on the innovation of "chartering" as a concept, rather than on the innovations
within the "chartered schools" themselves.

The two competing chartering bills were winding their way
through the legislative process to the conference committee, where
the goal was to work out the differences and produce a final bill.
Ironically, the voucher ballot initiative, which had stimulated the
chartering activity in the first place, failed to get enough signatures
by the April 27 deadline, so it would not appear on the November
1992 ballot. Would this remove the urgency for passage of chartering
legislation? Would the unions become more aggressive in their opposition to chartering and try to kill it?

The day of the conference committee arrived. As Premack
described it,

We all go into the conference committee, and they start going through [the bills] issue by issue. It is pretty clear they're not going to reconcile these big differences. I assumed at the time that it wasn't going to happen that year in California. The politics aren't happening, and the differences between these bills are so profound.

At that point, the education aide to Speaker of the Assembly Willie Brown walks into the room and whispers into Eastin's ear and the ears of all other assembly Democrats on the conference committee. They recess. Premack said,

We didn't know what was going on, but with Willie being really tight with the [California Teachers Association], we figured it was no good. They come back after the recess, and they essentially slam dunk and pass Eastin's bill out of committee and allow the bill later that day to pass the assembly.

Not only did we not get our bill, but we have the concept . . . caught in the superintendent [political] crossfire. We've got this bad bill hanging out there, which is worse than having no bill out there. So I thought it was just a lousy day.

This was all going on amidst the backdrop of a huge budget deficit in California. Most thought the chartering "war" between the two bills was now settled, and legislators were now working on the budget. But Senator Hart wasn't quite done. Premack continued the saga:

I remember a nighttime session on the budget. I'm standing outside the senate chamber watching a couple

TVs. . . . They were trying to slam dunk a budget that night. There was a lull on the floor. Gary Hart stood up and said, "Mr. President Pro Tem, I ask for unanimous consent to bring my bill SB 1448 back from conference committee."

Premack didn't think much of it. He thought Hart was bringing the bill back for the next year of the biennium, a routine procedure. "I wasn't paying close attention," said Premack. "Nobody was paying close attention." Then Hart continued: "I also ask for unanimous consent to adopt the assembly amendments to my bill." Again, Premack thought, "Not a biggie. The amendments were pretty innocuous because of the deal we had. I thought, he's just doing a little cleanup on the floor while he can, and I again thought nothing of it."

Finally, Senator Hart said, "I ask for unanimous approval of the measure and for immediate transmittal to the governor's desk." Now Premack was baffled. "I thought, what the . . . ? I had no idea! At that time, I could see some business cards floating down in front of the television camera. What I later learned is some of the education lobbyists up in the gallery were writing 'no' on the back of their business cards."

What Premack learned was that Burr and her boss, education committee chief of staff Bill Whiteneck, were "pissed off" that Eastin had reneged on her handshake deal at the behest of Brown's education aide. According to Premack, they were "grousing" about it when another senator, known as the "in-house guru" on parliamentary procedure, said, "Why don't you just call the bill back if you haven't really amended it much?" He explained how to do that. Shortly thereafter, Hart came out on the floor and, at a quiet time, slid it through. This parliamentary handspring was possible because of the unusual deal the two committee chairs had struck. Basically, both chartering bills had gone through both houses, largely untouched, and therefore were both primed to go to the governor. As Premack relayed the story,

> I'm standing outside, watching this on the television screen, and it's hard to hear, because everybody's talking about budget stuff. Glee Johnson, who was Governor Wilson's key staffer on education policy, walked out of the senate chamber door, and she's smiling ear to ear. . . .
>
> I still thought Hart was just bringing the bill back for reconsideration the following year of the biennium. I didn't quite get what this unanimous consent and immediate trans-mittal was about and why the governor would be involved at this point in the process.
>
> Glee came up to me and gave me a big hug, and I said, "What the hell's going on, Glee?"
>
> "It's out."
>
> "What do you mean, it's out."
>
> "I'm taking the bill to the governor's desk right now."
>
> "You have the actual bill?"
>
> "Yes. It's been signed as passed in both houses. I just got this from the chief clerk's desk."
>
> "But the Eastin bill is out too," I said, still thinking about this conference committee deal.
>
> Glee rolls her eyes and says, "What do you think the governor is going to do with *that* bill?"

Premack smiled as he remembered the story. He knew the governor disliked Eastin. They had great personal animosity. He concluded, "So Glee took the bill to the governor's office, he signed it, and vetoed the Eastin measure—and boom!"

Chartering was passed in California. Wilson signed the bill on September 20, 1992. The chartering bill would become effective on

January 1, 1993. Ten months after that, in November 1993, the voucher initiative would finally make its way to the California ballot, only to be rejected by the California electorate by a margin of almost two to one.

By the time of the chartered school bill signing, Premack had left his job as a legislative staff member and was working as a consultant. Inundated with requests for assistance, Premack turned his attention to chartering. As predicted, the California chartering legislation had national impact. Now there were three lead voices spreading the word on chartered schools across the nation . . . from Minnesota, Washington, DC, and California. The "chartering trifecta" of Kolderie, Schroeder, and Premack would eventually help write chartering laws in over half the states.

But first, things weren't going so well in Washington, DC.

In fact, this insistence on rewarding the status quo is a 180-degree turn from the direction that real education reform is now taking in virtually every state in this nation.

US SENATOR DAVID DURENBERGER

28

States Lead, Congress Lags

SEPTEMBER–OCTOBER 1992

On October 1, 1992, US Senator David Durenberger told his colleagues on the Senate floor that California governor Pete Wilson, their former colleague, had just signed a bill allowing the start-up of one hundred chartered schools in California. He told them, too, that Connecticut, Michigan, Massachusetts, and several other states had offered credible chartering proposals as part of broader education reform initiatives. Durenberger also reported on Minnesota's chartering progress, saying that "despite continued resistance on the part of some parts of the education establishment," four Minnesota chartered schools received approval. The first of these schools—City Academy—had just opened in September.

Durenberger played a role in each of these successes, either through his personal relationships or through his leadership in generating the chartering conversation throughout the nation. But he couldn't overcome the election-year politics in Washington, DC. The chartering provisions in S2—the bipartisan Senate education bill he, Senator Ted Kennedy, and Senator Joe Lieberman worked hard to pass—hit a brick wall in the House-Senate conference committee. The chartering provision would not be part of the final bill passed by the committee.

On October 1, Durenberger made a statement on the final passage of the conference committee report on S2. He used the opportunity to oppose the conference committee report as well as lay groundwork for action in the next Congress. Durenberger minced no words in his statement:

> The Senate's version of S2 included explicit authority for states to use federal funds to help start new schools, including new charter schools like those now emerging in Minnesota.
>
> And, when [the bill] last left this body, S2 explicitly recognized a role for states in expanding parent choices and in promoting real reform in how we teach and learn in our nation's public schools.
>
> Unfortunately, Mr. President, the Democratic majority in the House of Representatives did not share that vision for real reform in American education.
>
> The House majority refused to explicitly recognize a state role in starting new schools or encouraging new ways of

organizing and managing public schools outside the traditional local education agency monopoly.

The House Democratic leadership would not allow the word "choice" to be even included in the bill—not even the more limited extension of choice among public schools and between public school districts that the vast majority of Americans now either has or is eagerly demanding.

In fairness, Mr. President, I must acknowledge that this failure to acknowledge the importance of states in promoting school choice and new schools is not attributable only to the House Democratic leadership.

The Bush Administration has also contributed its share of rigid lines drawn in the sand. In particular, the Administration's insistence on centering its education reform initiative on a traditional and outdated definition of public and private education has also helped preclude passage of meaningful education reform legislation in this session of Congress. . . .

A quick reading of this bill easily pinpoints my single biggest concern with the conference committee's agreement on S2.

At least eight out of every ten dollars authorized by this legislation, must go to existing public schools through local public school boards and administrators. That was a condition insisted on by the House majority. But it is not a formula for promoting real education reform.

In fact, this insistence on rewarding the status quo is a 180-degree turn from the direction that real education reform is now taking in virtually every state in this nation.

Durenberger made it clear that he would be back the next year to try again. As he said on the Senate floor, "I honestly believe that, had we more closely followed the lead being taken by Minnesota and a number of states, we would have made much more progress this year in reaching consensus on this bill, and in reaching consensus on a new national government role in encouraging education reform." He outlined several key goals for the next year's reauthorization to help develop this new consensus on the national government's role in education reform. They included:

- Remove federal impediments to state and local reform initiatives. "That may be our most important goal—to get out of the way of states and local schools that are on the cutting edge of change," he said.

- Provide further federal support to states promoting school choice. He cited a new initiative in Minnesota called "School Choice Advisor" to provide essential information about schools to empower parents to make informed choices.

- Assist states encouraging emergence of more school choices. Start-up funding for new schools such as chartered schools was key.

Durenberger's leadership helped set the national stage for the next Congress. That was important. Both of the 1992 presidential candidates—Republican George H. W. Bush and Democrat Bill Clinton—would be friendly to public school choice in some form. It was the Democratic majority of the US House of Representatives that was the biggest resister on the federal level. It was the same dynamic that had occurred in the Minnesota House and the California State Assembly when chartering legislation passed in those states. The resistance to chartering and public school choice was always much stronger in state houses than in state senates. Perhaps it was due to the shorter terms and smaller districts, or the notion that the house is "closer to the people."

Even without successful passage of Durenberger's legislation, chartering in Minnesota was already becoming an opportunity and platform for new and creative partnerships on the state and federal levels. Joe Nathan organized a meeting for Durenberger on September 1, 1992, where chartering supporters could share their experiences on the ground level and counsel the senator on needed assistance. This particular meeting was also where Nathan shared news that a proposal by a Minnesota team—of which he was a part—had just been selected by the New American Schools Development Corporation, a private sector funder. It was one of just eleven proposals across the nation to receive a multimillion-dollar grant to "reinvent" public education. One theme of the proposal was to make schools community resources, especially in rural areas, and the proposal suggested using the Minnesota chartering law to start some of these new "break-the-mold" schools. This impressive national philanthropic grant was just one example of how chartering was benefitting from the growing interplay between the state-and federal-level focus on improving public education.

This interplay would be key to the rapidly accelerating expansion of chartering around the country—especially as the 1992 election neared.

Clinton responded, among other ideas, with a full endorsement of chartered schools. . . . I knew that the relationship between teacher unions and chartering would be changed forever.

29

1992 Election: Politics at Home and in Washington, DC

SUMMER–FALL 1992

Chartering wasn't much on my mind the summer and fall of 1992. It was election year—all legislators were up for election in newly redrawn districts after redistricting. It was my fourth election campaign to the Minnesota Senate. Running as an incumbent is always easier, and I had been serving my constituents for ten years.

My district wasn't changing much in redistricting, as only a few precincts were added. While my campaign team and I always worked hard during campaigns, the DFL considered my district a relatively safe seat. The presidential campaign was well underway, too, and to my great delight, it appeared that Governor Bill Clinton would be the Democratic nominee. I was heavy into politics at all levels.

As always, I sought endorsement from our labor allies early in the process, so we could display their endorsement in our campaign materials. In my past three elections, all the labor unions had endorsed me. I think it was June or July that I sought endorsement from the Robbinsdale Federation of Teachers (RFT), which screens for the Minnesota Federation of Teachers (MFT). I also sought endorsement from the Minnesota Education Association (MEA). While these organizations and I disagreed on chartering, I had a ten-year record on the Education Funding Division and the senate education committee as a strong advocate of education funding statewide and particularly for our suburban district. Beyond that record, I was majority whip of our DFL caucus and chair of a division on the tax committee—also important to education funding. So I honestly didn't expect a problem with endorsement.

I was wrong.

The generic screening questionnaire by the RFT asked for my position on chartering. The union's materials made clear that it supported repeal of chartering in the 1993 session. I talked with the union members at great length and indicated I not only would oppose repeal, but would try to strengthen the law in 1993 to add the Minnesota State Board of Education as a separate sponsor. On the remainder of their issues, our positions aligned.

To my surprise, I received a call several days later with the news that the RFT would not endorse in my race. That meant the MFT would also hold back. And soon, the MEA would do the same. Ironically, DFL Representative Becky Kelso, the house chartering bill author, received teacher union endorsement without any problem. I suspected it was because she ran in a tough Republican district and the unions knew she needed endorsement to win—regardless of her position on chartering. Not that the unions wanted my Republican opponent to win. He supported vouchers, so they certainly didn't want him elected.

MFT president Sandra Peterson confirmed in her 2011 interview that chartering caused the denial of my endorsement. She said, "They thought she was going too far and not listening. . . . For Ember, the unions were not always pleased with what she was doing. She kept pushing on the issue. She kept forging ahead."

The problem grew more complicated when the Minnesota AFL-CIO accepted the recommendation of its affiliate, the MFT. Now, that was something I never expected. Plenty of people in my labor-oriented district looked for the AFL-CIO logo on the literature. Twenty years later, the whole experience is hazy, and I don't remember details. I do remember that after I discussed the issue with DFL legislative leaders, the AFL-CIO finally granted its endorsement near the end of September—after most of my literature and mail pieces were printed. The teacher unions never endorsed me.

I knew the teacher unions were sending me a message. It was heard. But denying my endorsement wasn't a strategic move, especially on the part of the RFT. I was reelected—with a wide margin of 58.7 percent of the vote—without their support. I now had a certain freedom to pursue my intended course for chartering in the 1993 session.

Even as the union politics boiled up for my own reelection, I was also focused on representing Clinton's campaign throughout Minnesota. Back in October 1991, when Clinton announced his candidacy for president, I responded to calls from leaders of the Democratic Leadership Council (DLC) to sign onto his campaign. Along with Representative Becky Kelso and others, I became co-chair of the

Clinton presidential campaign in Minnesota. Few in Minnesota knew anything about Clinton, and from a political perspective, Minnesota was not a Clinton state. Most of my colleagues were supporting Senator Tom Harkin of neighboring Iowa, who served in the same liberal tradition as former vice president Walter Mondale.

I enjoyed being a surrogate speaker for Clinton during the primary and general election campaigns, because I liked his platform, including education reform. I talked often to DFL audiences and general voters about his support for Minnesota's open enrollment. As campaign co-chair, I also got several chances to meet with Clinton when he came to Minnesota for fundraisers and rallies during the spring and summer. I admired his leadership greatly. But it was his personal charisma and ability to communicate a message that impressed me most. In a one-on-one situation, like a conversation at a fundraiser, he made you feel like your issue was the most important issue in the world. We did talk about chartering. He was definitely committed to it. I knew if he were elected, he would support US Senator David Durenberger's initiative and include other chartering proposals in his own education policies. Still, I hadn't yet heard Clinton talk publicly about chartering at that point in the campaign. After what had just happened in my small political world, I totally understood why he was low key about it. I was just thrilled to know he was supportive.

A week or two after the Democratic National Convention, Clinton and vice presidential nominee Al Gore and his wife, Tipper, came through Minneapolis on their bus tour. A large stage was set up in a busy downtown Minneapolis intersection. Thousands of people attended the rally. Clinton energized the crowd in a way I had never seen before. It felt like the wind was at our back in this election. Maybe, after all these years, a Democrat could be elected to the White House. I was riding high that day, sharing the stage and visiting with Clinton and the Gores. It just didn't seem possible that my public school choice work would eventually lead to something like this. What an unlikely set of circumstances. What a joyful moment in my political career!

The rest of fall flew by. Between my campaign and Clinton's, my life was a blur. It was intense, crazy, and exhausting. But through all this, I still distinctly remember the one moment that would change the future of chartering forever: I was watching one of the televised debates between Clinton and George H. W. Bush. Someone asked a question about education reform. Clinton responded, among other ideas, with a full endorsement of chartered schools. On national television. Think of it! Here he was, endorsed by all the teacher unions, yet still giving full support to chartering. I couldn't believe it. My eyes welled with tears. I knew now, for sure, that chartering was here to stay. And I knew that the relationship between teacher unions and chartering would change forever.

In my heart, I also knew Clinton would be the next president. Together, we supporters could work to grow chartering from one school in Minnesota to hundreds or even thousands of schools around the country. The rocky road of change appeared to be paved with a fresh new layer of shiny sealcoat.

Promote charter schools and other state efforts to harness choice and competition to improve our public schools.

FROM *MANDATE FOR CHANGE*

30

Mandate for Change

WINTER 1992–1993

They were already mixing that new sealcoat in Washington, DC, at the Democratic Leadership Council (DLC) and Progressive Policy Institute (PPI). By September 1992, PPI asked Ted Kolderie to write a chartering portion for the education chapter of the book *Mandate for Change,* which would be the blueprint for the Clinton-Gore presidency. Kolderie now had the opportunity to help shape a presidential agenda.

The chapter was titled "Educating America: A New Compact for Opportunity and Citizenship." I never expected *this*. President-Elect

Bill Clinton was not only supporting chartering; he was making it one of three initiatives that would form "a new educational compact for work and citizenship." On pages 129–137, with help from Will Marshall, coeditor of *Mandate for Change*, Kolderie laid out the history leading to chartering, including Sy Fliegel's successes in New York's East Harlem; the urgent need to withdraw the districts' exclusive franchise; the public school choice experiments in Minnesota and around the nation; and the contrast between vouchers and public school choice.

What I found most interesting was how Marshall and Kolderie presented or "messaged" chartering as the answer to a problem with the *system,* not a problem with the people in it. Kolderie wrote, "What is needed is a *change of structure* and incentives that will push public schools to improve on the basis of their own initiative, in their own interest and from their own resources." This was significant. There was no finger pointing or blaming teachers, unions, or administrators. This was a systemic issue. The system was unfair to those who worked in it. Teachers were not identified as the barrier. Instead, they were encouraged to imagine possibilities that could open up with system change. Excerpts from the chapter describe this concept:

> Charter schools offer an alternative form of public education. They are not intended to replace the schools we have today. Their likely effect is to stimulate the existing system in ways that will cause districts to improve. They offer some reward for taking risks. The new schools will be small, so that mistakes, which will occur, will be small. They let parents and teachers volunteer for change. Most important: They let an innovation appear without having to secure the prior approval of those who will be threatened if it succeeds.
>
> The districts will not like this pressure. As when any business loses its exclusive they will not want others offering

public education within their borders. They will try to discourage this competition, saying "We can do this now."

But without some real stimulus they don't and won't. The central problem with public schools was put perfectly by Albert Shanker, the president of the American Federation of Teachers (AFT), at a meeting in Minnesota in 1988: "This is a system that can take its customers for granted." That's true. Children attend where they live. . . .

Pushing for change upsets people. It might cause a strike, cost an election, or end a career. Unfortunately, there is nothing that requires kids' interests to be put first. Principals who want to change their schools, but are blocked, have nowhere else to go; parents and students have nowhere else to go; nor do teachers. . . .

For a country that claims to be serious about improving its public schools this is an absurd arrangement. How can we expect teachers and administrators to make exceptional effort if we assure them their success whether they do or not?

This arrangement is unfair to those in education. It is wrong to give people incentives that are not aligned with the mission they have been given to perform. As Theodore Sizer says in Horace's Compromise, "The people are better than the system." The present system has the structure of reward backward.

After acknowledging that changing the structure of public education could be done only by changing state law, the author and editor declared a role for the president:

However, the new President has an opportunity to take the lead in activating the process of state lawmaking. . . . A progressive agenda for reinventing government may in fact depend on connecting the power of national leadership to the power of the state legislatures over the organization of major domestic and urban systems, including, but not limited to, public education.

In addition to the bully pulpit, the new President can use the leverage of federal education aid to promote public school choice. He should support a proposal by Senators Dave Durenberger (R-MN) and Joe Lieberman (D-CT), which would permit the states to use federal education grants to set up charter schools.

Finally, and most importantly, Kolderie and Marshall introduced new opportunities for teachers:

Teachers would also benefit greatly from chartered schools. They are hurt as much as the kids by the obstacles to change. They know there are other and better ways for students to learn. Some will be willing to take the risk involved.

Schools organized on the public charter model could change the reward system for teachers dramatically. Such schools could be provided a fixed sum of money, given the freedom to run their own instructional program, and allowed to keep whatever they do not need to spend. At the same time, they would be held accountable for results. This would provide a powerful incentive to adopt more economical and effective ways of learning. The teachers' success would be connected to the students' success.

The "Mandate for Action" section of the chapter provided specific action items for Clinton's administration. The first item immediately captured my attention:

MANDATE FOR ACTION

1. **Promote charter schools and other state efforts to harness choice and competition to improve our public schools.**

> President Clinton should put the resources of his Education Department behind state efforts to design and enact public school choice laws. He should further encourage the states by proposing that they be allowed to use a significant portion of federal education aid to set up innovative public schools. Presidential leadership also is essential for setting broad, national standards of performance for all public schools, including charter schools.

I read this chapter about one month after the November 3 election as I was readying for the 1993 legislative session. With a Democratic president supporting chartering on the national level—a powerful counter to the resistance from local school boards in Minnesota—I believed the time had come—at last—to improve Minnesota's law. I was preparing legislation to do two things: remove the cap limiting our charters to eight schools, and authorize the Minnesota State Board of Education to be an alternate sponsor to local school boards.

As I stepped back to reflect on the larger picture, a huge sense of relief washed over me. No longer was this just Minnesota's dream for only eight schools. Now we had California's law allowing one hundred schools. And now we had a Democratic president who wanted these dreams realized for students and teachers and families all over the country. I couldn't help but burst with pride that our work in the Minnesota legislature helped shape the president's education agenda for the nation.

On all counts, I couldn't have been happier.

Chartering, birthed near the source of the Mississippi River, was helping rebuild an entire education system at the river's mouth.

Epilogue

A Personal Journey through Chartering—Twenty Years of Highs and Lows

1992–2012

As 1992 came to a close, I told myself it was time to turn over the mantle of leadership on chartering. That's what I normally did whenever I authored bills into law during my eighteen years as a state senator. I should happily move on, I thought—chartering was safely established and championed by others in Minnesota and nationwide.

In the new 1993 legislative session, I would continue my service on the senate Education Funding Division and Education Committee, but I would also take on a new role as chair of the senate Judiciary Committee. As a lawyer, I loved the Judiciary Committee. I was passionate about preventing family violence and upholding human rights. It was time to delve into new issues.

Perhaps the most important reason for moving on from chartering was that at the age of thirty-nine, I was beginning a new chapter in my personal life. During the summer of 1992, I met Michael Junge. Mike, thirty-six, was the McLeod County attorney, having served in elected office for that rural county in central Minnesota since 1987. It didn't take long. On Christmas Eve, Mike and I got engaged, with our wedding date set for October 1993. Being with him, I realized just how intense my life had been for over a decade. So in January, Mike and I took time to celebrate our engagement, our 1992 election victories, and our new Democratic president by joining in the Clinton-Gore inaugural festivities in Washington, DC. What a joyful time!

Yes, it was time to put chartering to rest and move on to new life chapters. But that didn't happen. Something kept pulling me back.

1993–1999

First, I wanted to improve the Minnesota law. If the law were to have an impact, it had to allow *real* chartering to occur. In its original form, it didn't go far enough. So from 1993 to my retirement from the senate in 2000, I worked with my legislative colleagues to provide more independent authorizers (including postsecondary institutions), remove the cap on charters, provide start-up funding, and provide "lease aid" to help schools lease facilities. We faced the most resistance in our first attempt to improve the law in 1993, as only one chartered school had opened and many of our legislative champions had retired. But as more chartered schools opened, more states adopted chartering laws, and the federal government took a leading role, the improvements became easier to pass, resulting in a strong chartering law in Minnesota.

Second, I wanted to support the new champions of chartering, especially those in other states. Frankly, now it was harder for other states to pass chartering, because opponents were smarter about the issue. It was not uncommon, for example, for opponents to publicly proclaim their "support" for chartering, as long as the law contained conditions they wanted that were anything but chartering. I was especially committed to supporting other Democrats, who were always subject to pressure from unions—the allies-turned-foes. So, I traveled where I was asked to go. Ted Kolderie, Joe Nathan, and others started organizing national meetings on chartering. Policy organizations like the National Conference of State Legislatures planned speaking opportunities, and legislators from individual states requested counsel.

The state opportunities for chartering were opening up, in part, from work by Jon Schroeder and US Senator David Durenberger on the federal level. In 1994, the successor to the earlier Durenberger-Lieberman legislation appropriating start-up funding for chartered schools passed Congress. In a huge breakthrough, the funding was made available for chartered schools as defined by state law, not as defined—or restricted—by federal law, which had been championed by members of the House.

Some of my most enjoyable opportunities were working with the Clinton administration as they spread the word about chartering. Through the early years of chartering, I took part in satellite town hall meetings and conference telephone calls with US Education Secretary Richard Riley and Deputy Secretary Madeleine Kunin. In 1996, I served as a panel responder to President Bill Clinton's remarks about chartering at a National Conversation of the Democratic Leadership Council (DLC). In June 1997, I attended the Family Re-Union Conference at Vanderbilt University in Nashville, Tennessee, hosted by Vice President Al Gore. At one point, I spoke about chartering on the same stage with both Clinton and Gore. Now *that's* an experience! I was grateful that both of them took such a personal interest in creating new champions for chartering. I remember Clinton describing chartering this way: "It is a way to give people the power to change their own lives."

2000: Leaving Public Office

By the year 2000, chartering was well established and had passed into law in thirty-five states and the District of Columbia. That may have been why the Minnesota chartering law was declared a winner of the 2000 Innovations in American Government Award sponsored by the John F. Kennedy School of Government at Harvard University and the Ford Foundation. With much help from Ted Kolderie, I wrote the application on behalf of the Minnesota legislature, using language from my "Freedom to Be Better" speech from the 1992 DLC national conference. That award came with a $100,000 grant to further the innovation of chartering in Minnesota.

The 2000 legislative session was my last, as I had announced my intention to retire from the Minnesota Senate after eighteen years of service. It was time to move on. In media interviews and in an open letter to colleagues, I focused on lessons learned from the "gift of public service." Several of those lessons came from my chartering experience and its aftermath. Here are three of those lessons, with reflections from today:

- **There is more than one right answer.** Public service is about finding the next right answer—and allowing the public the freedom to do the same. If we look for more than one right answer, we look in comfort, not with fear or desperation. We free ourselves from the unreasonable fear of making a mistake or the fear of being "wrong." We unlock our creativity and allow ourselves to resolve seemingly irresolvable conflict. I wonder what might have happened if I had approached conversations with the teacher unions with a more open mind, looking for that next right answer. Could we have developed that final compromise together, allowing them to share in the ownership? Might that have smoothed the rocky road for charters ever since?

- **Celebrate the small victories.** Mountains are built one boulder at a time. Change in the public forum can be frustratingly slow. When the compromised chartering legislation passed, I did not think one chartered school could ever emerge from the "gutted" legislation. In retrospect, I could have celebrated that the most important part of the legislation stayed intact: the opportunity for someone other than a local school board to deliver public education services. Inherent in that concept was the separation from the district in all ways, including collective bargaining agreements. Perhaps I would have seen the pathway to improving the law over time—one change at a time.

- **Compromise is not defeat.** In writing this book, I've identified this third lesson that's particularly relevant in today's divisive political times. In my mind, the compromise of the 1991 conference committee meant total defeat of chartering. Today, I now know this: the compromise saved the legislation. Chartering might never have emerged without it. Others realized that; Representative Becky Kelso, the house author of the legislation, had thought the result was "spectacular." Twenty years later, I can finally agree.

The year 2000 was also the last year of Clinton's presidency. I was thrilled to learn he would highlight chartering in his final months. On May 4, 2000, during National Charter Schools Week, the president visited City Academy of St. Paul, Minnesota—the first chartered school in the country. Clinton and I hugged as we celebrated our long journey together to advance chartering. The timing was just two weeks before the end of my final legislative session. What a way to end my career in public service!

Clinton's speech at City Academy (see Appendix II) reaffirmed his goal of seeing three thousand chartered schools across the nation before the end of his term. As to Minnesota's chartering law, Clinton said, "Minnesota's law is right. You basically have struck the right balance. You have encouraged the growth of charter schools, but you do hold charter schools responsible for results. That's what every state in the country ought to do." The National Alliance for Public Charter Schools has since affirmed Clinton's view, ranking Minnesota's as the top chartering law in the country in 2010 and 2011 and as the second-best in 2012.

And so it was. In 2000, two champions of chartering retired from public office. What would that mean as the controversy raged on around the country?

The 2000s

I would find out soon enough. In 2001, Minnesota DFL legislators led a highly visible media and legislative effort to impose regulatory restrictions on chartering. Chartered schools were indeed vulnerable, as some had caused headlines for financial fraud. But the proposed response was overkill. Chartering supporters responded by proposing creation of an accountable system (within the state department of education or elsewhere) to better train and engage authorizers in their duties as sponsors of chartered schools. Some sponsors were derelict in their duties. In one case, the sponsor didn't even bother to read the minutes of the board meetings of the school. Inexcusable.

Once again, even though I had now retired from the legislature, I was called back to chartering. I worked primarily behind the scenes, supporting legislation that better defined the sponsor role in an attempt to counter the attacks. Still, proposed restrictions on charters kept coming in ensuing years—including the threat of a total moratorium on new charters. What a contrast: Throughout the 1990s, chartering proponents in Minnesota worked to pass legislation to provide more flexibility for chartering. How ironic that in the 2000s, they were constantly battling back legislation to restrict chartering. I needed to stay in this sometimes ugly debate.

The controversy around charters was continuing on the national scene as well. The chartering message wasn't breaking through. In response, several organizations were struggling to create a national voice and a national advocacy group for chartering. I agreed to help. I became a board member in the mid-2000s of what would evolve into the National Alliance for Public Charter Schools.

Somehow in all this highly visible turmoil around the country, chartering did in fact keep marching forward, state by state and school by school. By the year 2005, there were over one million students attending approximately 3,400 chartered schools around the country. It was the enormous power of "citizens taking the lead"—despite politicians and despite unions. Chartering was spreading around the country as a grassroots phenomenon. It was not coming from the "grass tops."

My favorite example of this grassroots effect came from ten-year-old Bubbles Auld, a Minnesota chartered school student, who in 2007 nominated chartered schools for eventual inclusion in the "MN150" permanent exhibit at the Minnesota Historical Society. The exhibit celebrated Minnesota's 150 years of statehood by featuring

150 people, places, things, and events that shaped Minnesota and the world beyond. Auld wrote in her nomination form: "Minnesota is the first state to have the charter school systems. Charter schools have made a big improvement in learning choices." Truly, chartering has survived because of the people whose lives it touches.

2006: My Congressional Campaign

In 2006, I found myself pulled back into the chartering controversy—though this time, not of my own accord. Recall that in 1992, the teacher unions chose not to endorse my reelection bid for the Minnesota Senate, due to my stance on chartering. But for elections thereafter, they did endorse me. I thought the chartering matter had been put to rest. Not so. Union leaders can have long memories. I learned that the hard way in 2006, when I ran in the DFL primary election for a seat in the US Congress. I ran in the urban, liberal district of Minneapolis and surrounding suburbs—where union influence was strong.

I was not surprised that the teacher unions chose to endorse one of my opponents in the race (now serving in Congress), because he had also been endorsed by the DFL party of that liberal district. What did surprise me was that the teacher unions mailed a negative attack piece against me—a DFLer—just a few days before the primary election. The piece claimed I was "anti–public education" and distorted the impact of chartering. This was no less than fifteen years after the chartering legislation first passed. As might be expected, my support numbers dropped immediately, with little time to recover.

While this was just one of many factors shaping the outcome of that election, it was one I could have mitigated. There's a lesson for other policymakers who take on tough issues: I should have been more prepared to respond to this last-minute political attack. I should have expected that the chartering conflict with the unions would resurface. I could have easily inoculated the issue with an earlier press conference, surrounded by hundreds of supporters from chartering families in the district. I just didn't do it.

In an ironic twist that will always mean a great deal to me, a union leader who opposed chartering in 1991 became one of my strongest supporters for Congress in 2006. Sandra Peterson, who served as president of the Minnesota Federation of Teachers in the 1990s, eventually ran as a DFLer for state representative in my legislative district and won. Peterson was one of several legislators who supported my campaign for Congress, even though the DFL party had endorsed my opponent. (She had no idea about the union attack piece until she was interviewed for this book.) So, despite all the tensions and disagreements that occurred between union leaders and me in the early 1990s, she and I could still remain friends over time. That doesn't happen often in today's political environment. I am very grateful to her for that.

2008: The National Charter Schools Hall of Fame

In 2008, I retired from the board of the National Alliance for Public Charter Schools. That same year, I was inducted into their National Charter Schools Hall of Fame. Kolderie had been inducted the year before, as part of the first group of inductees. I attended the induction ceremony in New Orleans, Louisiana, with my sister, Helene Johnson. My emotions that day are hard to describe. As I looked out over an audience of over 3,500 chartered school educators, students, and allies, I couldn't help but wonder if this conference could ever have happened if we hadn't passed the law in Minnesota. Maybe chartering would have passed somewhere else. Or maybe not.

For me, this recognition was especially meaningful. My husband

and I, now married over fifteen years, never had children. Yet I had a part in providing opportunity for the children of over a million families. And this white "limousine liberal from the suburbs" (as I was described by union leaders at the time) was at the root of a significant change in education for urban families, who experience challenges beyond anything I could imagine.

As I toured post–Hurricane Katrina New Orleans with my sister, I also realized there was a positive outcome to the hurricane recovery efforts: the city's failing education system could be reborn with chartered schools. Today, nearly three-quarters of the public schools in New Orleans are chartered schools, the highest percentage in the country. New Orleans is closer to being a "charter district"— a public school district consisting entirely of chartered schools—than anywhere in the country. Chartering, birthed near the source of the Mississippi River, was helping rebuild an entire education system at the river's mouth.

Later in 2008, seeking a new way to learn and grow in chartering, I accepted an invitation to join the board of directors of Charter Schools Development Corporation (CSDC), a national leader in helping charters find and develop facilities. In an unlikely alliance, or in yet another example of the bipartisan nature of chartering, I aligned with former California Republican congressman Frank Riggs, who successfully authored several chartered school facilities bills into law in Congress to create support for financing facilities. He is now CEO of CSDC. As noted in the Acknowledgments, I am grateful to him and the CSDC board of directors for their support with publication of this book. We are committed to spreading the story of chartered schools far and wide.

And to that, I am deeply grateful to you, the reader, who took time to learn the pioneering chartered school story. I hope you will pass it on to others.

Acknowledgments

This book would not have happened without the enormous help of two individuals: Ted Kolderie and Dana Schroeder. To them I am deeply grateful.

Ted's prolific writings before, during, and after the passage of chartering legislation captured the essence of the story and preserved it for over twenty years. His personal notes, memos, correspondence, news archives, and writings abound in both my files and his. He was always generous with his time and connections and continues to be so as cofounder and leader of Education|Evolving, an education policy think tank.

Ted's importance to this chartering story was affirmed in July 2011, when he traveled to Colorado to receive a prestigious award from the Education Commission of the States (ECS), a nonpartisan policy organization that provides education and policy information to lawmakers. ECS recognized chartering as a "significant contribution to American education" and also recognized Kolderie as key to the origins of chartering. As Beth Hawkins wrote in an August 19, 2011, article for MinnPost.com, "The James Bryant Conant Award recognizes individuals who have made an outstanding contribution to education. It places [Kolderie] in the company of Thurgood Marshall, Marian Wright Edelman, Fred Rogers, and a host of state governors." As the ECS press release noted, "A short paper Kolderie wrote in 1990, 'The States Will Have to Withdraw the Exclusive,' though not the first publication about chartering, is regarded by many as the founding document of the contemporary charter movement."

The second person who made this book possible is Dana Schroeder. As a longtime Citizens League member and editor for ten years of its monthly *Minnesota Journal,* Dana had written about chartering as early as 1992. She is married to Jon Schroeder, US Senator David Durenberger's policy aide who drafted the federal chartering legislation. Dana spent many hours researching legislative audiotapes and documents about chartering at the Minnesota Historical Society (not an easy task). She served as confidant and advisor. Most of all, she conducted all but one of the fifteen interviews with individuals involved in the story of chartering twenty years ago. Dana's transcripts of those interviews are interspersed everywhere within this book, bringing an objective, and, in many cases, surprising perspective to the history of chartering.

I am also deeply indebted to the individuals who, in addition to Ted, contributed their time and expertise by sitting for those interviews with Dana. On the state policy level, they include former Minnesota state representatives Becky Kelso, Ken Nelson, and Charlie Weaver; former speaker of the house Bob Vanasek; and former Minnesota state senator Ron Dicklich. Others interviewed who were deeply involved in these efforts included Dan Loritz, former advisor to Governor Rudy Perpich and assistant commissioner at the Minnesota Department of Education; Joe Nathan of the Center for School Change (now at Macalester College); Louise Sundin, then president of the Minneapolis Federation of Teachers; and Sandra Peterson, then president of the Minnesota Federation of Teachers and now a state representative.

Former US Senator David Durenberger and Jon Schroeder, then

his policy director, added in-depth perspective on the federal level. Al From, founder of the Democratic Leadership Council (DLC), and Will Marshall, president of the Progressive Policy Institute, then a project of the DLC, added enormous depth to the federal story. And Eric Premack, founder and executive director of the Charter Schools Development Center in Sacramento, California, related the incredulous story of the passage of chartering legislation in California, the first state to follow Minnesota's lead.

Publication of this book was made possible by the generous financial support of Charter Schools Development Corporation (CSDC), a nonprofit organization based in Hanover, Maryland. Now board vice chair, I first joined the CSDC board of directors in 2008 at the urging of former US Congressman Frank Riggs, its president and chief executive officer. Riggs and I both understood that financing chartered school facilities was and is a major challenge for the establishment and expansion of chartered schools. Over its fourteen-year history, CSDC has provided or procured roughly $590 million in capital financing and facilities for over 225 chartered schools in twenty-four states and the District of Columbia, improving educational opportunities for over three hundred thousand children.

I am grateful to Frank, board chair Tom Nida, executive vice president Michelle Liberati, and the CSDC board of directors for providing financial support for the publication costs of this book. We share a common commitment of growing a strong, high-quality chartered sector throughout the nation.

CSDC's support of this publication owes in part to a generous grant from the PNC Foundation to CSDC. The PNC Foundation is committed to assuring that millions of children "Grow Up Great" and are ready for school. The PNC Foundation is affiliated with the PNC Financial Services Group of Pittsburgh, Pennsylvania, and PNC Capital Markets, which support chartering through financing chartered school facilities around the country. I am especially grateful to Greg McKenna of PNC Capital Markets and Michael Labriola of the PNC Foundation for their support in facilitating the PNC Foundation's grant to CSDC.

There are others to be acknowledged. My staff assistants at the Minnesota Capitol—Marcia Seelhoff and Tom Krueger—helped organize chartering materials before I left the senate in 2000. Minnesota Senate photographer David J. Oakes and House of Representatives photographer Tom Olmscheid contributed black-and-white photos of lawmakers during the passage of the chartering legislation.

The monthly discussions of an informal Redesign Discussion Group, of which I am a member, helped me frame some of the redesign concepts and lessons that are part of this book. I am always heartened by these discussions of commonality among members from many different political perspectives. Discussion participants include Ted Kolderie, Curt Johnson, and Dan Loritz, among others.

I appreciate the support of Mark Peterson, former president and CEO of Lutheran Social Service of Minnesota (LSS). He recognized the power of chartering's redesign principles and tasked me and others on our executive team to apply them to delivery of human services in Minnesota, particularly in delivery of services for people with developmental disabilities. I also appreciate the support of my assistant at LSS, Jerica Price, who helped me with scheduling and other logistics throughout this process.

And finally, I am grateful for the support, love, and encouragement of my husband, Mike, and sister, Helene, who stood by me during this process and who know more than anyone else that completion of this book is a twenty-year dream come true.

Appendix I: Commentaries

A Serious Risk of Missing Its Potential

BY TED KOLDERIE
APRIL 2012

After California's legislation in 1992, the chartering idea spread rapidly. Six more states acted in 1993. By 1998, thirty-three states and the District of Columbia had some kind of chartering law.

Clearly, the idea had tapped into some powerful sentiments not visible before.

The media attention was remarkable, with no organized effort at all. And the legislative pickup was astonishing. In state after state, the bills defied all political reality—passing against the opposition of what state-capitol observers knew as the most powerful associations in state politics—again, with no organized national effort. Perhaps someday some political scientists will write a legislative case study weaving together the wonderful stories from the end of the sessions not only in Minnesota and California—as told here—but also in other critical states such as Michigan, Pennsylvania, and Colorado.

These were literally state capitol policy initiatives—led in some cases by governors, but mostly by individual legislators. There was a remarkable mix of Republicans and Democrats and of veterans like

Joe Doria and Jack Ewing in New Jersey and first-termers like Bob Perls in New Mexico and Joe Tedder in Florida.

Minnesota senate counsel Betsy Rice's draft went to legislative bill drafters elsewhere, and people from Minnesota visited other states. States began to link up—sharing drafts and the names of persons involved.

Quickly, it was clear what accounted for the interest.

Legislators were enormously frustrated by school districts' unresponsiveness to the pressure for improvement. They were aware of the voucher option. But if they did not want to do that—and most did not—they believed they had to take the system in its existing form. All it took was to say, "No, you don't. The legislature made this system; the legislature can change it. If the districts aren't giving you what you want, it is fully within your power to get somebody else who will."

In some ways, the most remarkable—and least-noted—response was the outpouring of people wanting to create new and different schools.

No law created any school. These were purely enabling laws. What produced the charter sector was the effort of thousands of educators and citizens to design, to get approved and to start schools. In the years before start-up grants appeared this was accomplished largely with sweat equity and often against significant bureaucratic and interest-group opposition.

In 1994, Congress and the Clinton administration began to provide start-up aid. Around the country, the state laws improved. The number of schools grew. In 2000, Harvard Kennedy School and the Ford Foundation cited Minnesota's chartering law as a "significant innovation in American government."

But powerful forces were working to change or to capture the chartering idea.

The Notion That a Chartered School Is a Kind of School

A proper history of the years that followed will no doubt be written someday. Here I can offer only a general interpretation of what happened—notes toward a history.

It does matter what things are called. When the effort began in Minnesota, *to charter* was a verb. The Citizens League titled its report "Chartered Schools." In the original 1991 law, the schools were "outcome-based schools."

Quickly, however, *charter* became an adjective. And the change distorted the original idea in a critically important way.

The laws were and are open as to the kind of school being created. A chartered school is not a kind of school. And no student learns anything from a charter. Students learn from what they read, see, hear, and do. So an effort to identify the learning effects of chartered schools must begin by asking: What do these schools have their students reading, seeing, hearing, and doing?

But as *charter* became an adjective, people everywhere began to believe *charter* was a kind of school. Ignoring the differences among schools, they began to ask, "What are students learning? Do students learn more in 'charters' than in district schools?" This made no more sense than asking whether eating out is better than eating at home or whether east-facing schools score higher than south-facing schools. But researchers and advocates—for chartering as well as for districts—plunged into the debate.

Since the schools being examined were different kinds of schools, the usual conclusion was, "The evidence is mixed." As of course it would be. Even so, those favoring chartering pointed to schools where scores were higher than in district schools, and those favoring district public education pointed to schools where scores were higher than in charter schools. This foolishness continues.

It is all about traditional school, "performing" or not performing. Lost was the sense of chartering as an opportunity for innovation and as a strategy for system change.

Standardization vs. Innovation

The idea at the start was to encourage teachers and others to find new, different, and better approaches to learning. That is why legislators tried to cut the chartered schools free from many, if not most, regulations. And why they left it open for the organizers to try new models. As a result, there has in fact been significant innovation in the chartered-schools sector. Not enough. But some significant new approaches.

Much of this focus on innovation was lost, however. Research never explored or inventoried the new models. And at least several developments began to inhibit innovation.

- **Bureaucratic resistance.** State departments, in charge of the new sector, have trouble with "different." Students not in their seats in the classroom? Can't have that. Teachers generalists, not subject-matter specialists? Horrors.

- **Narrow concepts of achievement.** Especially after 2002, with the accountability program in national law, schools were thought to be "quality charters" if they had high scores on English and math. Little credit was given for students learning or achieving anything else. Assessment is an assay, looking for the presence of some particular thing, when it should be an analysis that identifies all the elements present.

- **The pressure to standardize and "scale up."** Fairly early on, private companies appeared, seeking to manage the new (and nonprofit) schools. There was pressure to find "what works" and to create as many schools as possible on that model. Size is important to their profitability. So foundations and venture capitalists are now investing heavily in "charter management companies" that adopt "proven" models—as if all is known that can ever be known about teaching and learning. These have little interest in innovation or in school autonomy.

- **A failure to understand the process of change.** A stream of reports and proposals pours out, urging America to convert its K–12 system into the system used in Singapore, Shanghai, or Finland. This misunderstands the process of change. The K–12 system in this country—in a single state, even—cannot be "blown up and built over again," as some advocates sometimes say. Policy needs to be practical about the way systems change. Successful systems change through a process of innovation in a context of choice. Think about the systems you know. They are open to new models. People are free to try these. Those who prefer, say, to drive traditional cars may continue to do that, but they may not prohibit others from driving a Prius. For a time the different models run side by side. Over time, the mix changes; the system evolves. If public education does not open to innovation, the new models will appear outside it, will bypass it. Chartering is public education's principal platform for innovation. To try to suppress innovation with some effort to create a monoculture of "high-quality" traditional schools is madness.

- **Misdirected research.** Education researchers try to come to overall judgments: Does "X" work, or doesn't it? Is "X" better than "Y"? That can lead to bizarre conclusions. (When the Wright brothers reported they had flown for 120 yards, the conclusion from research would still have been that most heavier-than-air craft cannot fly. One case; who noticed? But what importance did that "most" have, once Wilbur and Orville had got it right?) Researchers should, but typically do not, look for individual cases of new-and-different schools, should identify and describe the learning programs in the schools that determine school and student performance.

Prospects

This needs to change. While clearly some known approaches to learning work better than other known approaches, it is absurd to believe that no more effective approaches can be found—at a time when the revolution in digital electronics is introducing a revolution in the handling of information, comparable to the introduction of printing. The way is now open to individualizing learning, changing pace, so that those who need more time can have more time, and so that those who can go faster do go faster, and to adapt to the aptitudes and learning styles that differ from student to student.

Certainly the turgid progress of conventional improvement argues the need to try new things. Student proficiency remains low. A quarter of the students still quit. The gaps in performance remain embarrassingly wide. Half the new teachers still leave within five years. These are not signs of a successful K–12 system.

People hope for better results with the next round of "improvement." And policy can still "do improvement," can replicate best practice from traditional school. But we cannot be certain that more of the same, done better, will get the country where it needs to go. So along with doing what works (today), we must also be looking for what might work better (tomorrow).

Chartering—properly understood and used—can do innovation better. They have some critical freedoms to be different. As autonomous organizations they can make more of their own decisions. They are small, so the impact of what doesn't work will be small. They can fix problems quickly, on site.

Chartering combines authority and accountability in the school. In the district system the two are separated, which results in management trying to hold teachers accountable for what they do not control. That produces the damaging conflict now so visible with the teacher unions.

In an important organizational innovation, the chartered sector is now demonstrating that a school can be run successfully when organized as a professional partnership of teachers. This was Albert Shanker's vision for teachers as professionals. I said to Eugenia Kemble of the Shanker Institute in 2008, "Chartering has finally produced what Al originally had in mind."

The teacher unions have wanted professional status for their members. Today it is clear that chartering provides a route to that goal, as Louise Sundin explains in her commentary, which follows. The leadership of the Minneapolis Federation of Teachers has created a "single-purpose authorizer," approved by the Minnesota Department of Education in November 2011. This authorizer will now be able to charter new schools in Minnesota that can be organized as teacher partnerships.

This year, too, the Education Commission of the States recognized chartering as an "outstanding contribution to American education."

Change does come. It is not a problem that it takes time. It is the effort now to divert it back into traditional channels that is a serious concern.

Coming Full Circle

BY LOUISE SUNDIN
APRIL 2012

Twenty years on, it is time for chartering to revisit its origins and to see where it is today and what the future can hold.

Our journey to education reform in the American Federation of Teachers (AFT) began in 1985 with AFT president Albert Shanker's National Press Club speech describing what would make teaching a true profession. As an AFT vice president, I joined in the vigorous discussion and debate, then rushed home to make it happen. During that period, we began labor-management committees to professionalize teaching: mentor programs, induction programs, professional standards, job-embedded professional development, and action research. We viewed ourselves as reformers, risk takers, and role models to lead the way to professionalism.

In 1988, the Minneapolis Foundation invited Shanker to its annual Itasca Seminar to talk about his new idea, charter schools. Shanker had a vision of these being communities of practice, where professionals rather than administrators ran the school. The professionals, as a community, would seek out, refine, and implement the newest innovations. They would keep up on emerging research, improving their practice and each other. He knew the constraints, but he envisioned charter schools as innovative, powerful schools that would improve student learning, reenergize dispirited urban teachers, and give the country's stagnating public education enterprise a boost—without costing more than taxpayers were willing to pay.

Minnesota was the first state to turn Shanker's dream into reality. But as legislators began to generate the bills to implement the concept, teachers and their union leadership became skeptical, if not outright hostile. They were concerned that:

- Schools started by "outsiders" would not be as good for children as schools started inside the district.

- A proliferation of chartered schools could take jobs away from district school teachers.

- The push for chartered schools was part of the campaign to privatize and profit from public education.

Shanker's original concept was for teacher-run schools that would be innovative, do things differently, and be a way for teachers and parents to start schools within the union. When he saw that Minnesota's bills were weak on union support, excluding teachers from leadership roles and normal legal protections, he was not supportive. There was also a battle to make sure teachers were licensed. It's hard to imagine a true profession without the professionals being licensed. Collective bargaining, professional licensure, and academic freedom were all strong positions for Shanker. Because the bills failed to meet these tests, Shanker did not support their passage.

Supporters of charter schools in Minnesota never understood why the unions wouldn't support them—how licensure and other legal processes protect the public as well as professionals. Teachers and other employees can be and have been fired at will for trying to unionize or challenging educational positions of a supervisor, among other things. The lack of protection is one of the causes of the teacher turnover, or "churning," at charters.

As Chartering Evolved ...

Despite educators' continuing worries, chartering has become a way of opening new schools and is popular, for several reasons:

- Charter schools have convinced parents that a small charter is like a big family and that belonging to that family is advantageous for their children.

- Families often look for other opportunities for their children if they are not succeeding in their current schools.

- Charters have start-up funds and financing that let them offer a stable, sustainable program.

- Teachers at charter schools are often young, enthusiastic, and committed to the program model offered (and without background knowledge of unions).

- Charters sometimes offer single-ethnic focus, attracting specific student populations.

- Families believe the negative publicity about their regular public schools, often advanced by trusted community-based organizations.

- People can start up a charter school when a district tries to close a school because of budget issues or consolidation.

The connectedness between school and family has been a success for charter schools. Even when students aren't doing well in charters, families feel they are a part of a whole where they are listened to and where they can change things. They often have the opposite experience with schools in a large system that feels immoveable and unresponsive. That is clearly one of the things that erodes the faith parents have in public schools. It was different when we had decision making at site-governed schools and schools of choice in the public system. It is a lesson from which district schools should learn. Ownership and partnership were lost in the century-old move from one-room schoolhouses to large school districts.

However, issues of concern remain, and many of teachers' original fears are being realized. Chartering has not lived up to the expectations even of its creators and strongest proponents. They saw getting away from unions and the bureaucracy as improvements in and of themselves. They have found that just getting away from something does not change student learning. Many who started charters thought it would be enough just to create a culture where the students felt comfortable, where they liked school and their teachers. But students who didn't learn in traditional schools generally did not overnight become happy and successful learners in charter schools selected by their concerned parents. Taxpayers who balked at fully funding neighborhood schools balked at funding charters too.

Some innovation is taking place in the charter sector, but not nearly enough. Most learning programs in charter schools are very traditional. Chartering ought to increase innovation, advance new approaches, and implement new research. Unfortunately, the majority of charter schools have just tinkered around the edges. Mainly this is because the folks who have the knowledge, research, experience, and passion are not the leaders of the schools. Innovations are usually successful where teachers are in charge and leading the learning.

Meanwhile, Back in the Districts ...

While reformers around the country were embracing the charter idea and opening charter schools, teachers and their unions were working collaboratively with their districts to create, expand, and implement the professional model: establishing peer review processes to replace top-down administrator check-list teacher evaluation, creating a teaching magnet, starting a professional-practice school, opening professional development centers, expanding teacher leadership, and introducing alternative systems for teacher compensation.

The era of choice in the 1970s had come closest to the idea of innovation. That began in Minneapolis with Southeast Alternatives and peaked with Minneapolis offering more than a dozen different educational choices to students and families. Minneapolis Public Schools

(MPS) offered one of everything and two of most; from fundamental to continuous progress, to Montessori, to math/science magnets, to environmental science, to fine-arts magnet. And the parents, teachers, and students loved it. They partnered to create unique and very different programs to serve the needs and different learning styles of the children. The result was trust and commitment.

In the '90s, "Schools of the Future" and "In-District Charters" were attempts at communities of practice in both Minneapolis and Saint Paul. The MFT collaborated in starting at least six innovative schools or "schools of the future," some of which were pushed by outside partners (demonstrating that innovation often comes from the outside): Chiron; School in the City; the Public School Academy; and the School of Extended Learning, a year-round school. In Saint Paul, the Saturn School was an example.

But the shelf life was short. Within about six years, all these wonderful schools had been sucked back into the district, their uniqueness eliminated, turned back into plain vanilla by a bureau-cracy that couldn't tolerate, or in some cases couldn't afford, differences in delivery or design. We learned that it is difficult, if not impossible, to run a school with full independence inside a centrally managed district. Despite our best efforts, the professionals were never fully in charge. Our fate was determined not by the merits of decisions at the schools, but by administrators in the central office. The decisions sometimes revolved around jealousy and politics, transportation schedules and costs, and perceived difficulty in communicating and keeping track of significantly different programs.

Also, some trends in K–12 education have changed teachers' work in the district schools and have slowly impacted the unions' view of chartering. It started with the standards movement. Decisions once made by teachers moved from the classrooms to the districts and to the state and federal level. It intensified with No Child Left Behind (NCLB). With the advent of School

Improvement Grants (SIGs), funds go from the US Department of Education to individual schools, essentially circumventing both states and districts. This significantly reduced teachers' discretion, judgment, and control. The job—and career—of teaching was now to carry out what their "superiors" wanted done. At the same time, the younger people coming into teaching were, and still are, wanting and expecting a more professional role.

So, you have these two trends clashing, pushing in opposite directions. Almost every experienced teacher is frustrated with decisions being made by persons who do not know teaching and who do not know the students.

Shanker's Dream of "Communities of Practice"

The professionals' school Shanker envisioned hasn't materialized. Twenty years after the first charter law, teachers are still longing for the opportunity to be true professionals. The charter-versus-district debate misunderstands the issue. *What really matters is the debate of professional ownership versus central management by administrators.*

Education has suffered from being patterned after the industrial model with line-supervisor, boss-worker assembly line analogies. Teaching has never gained the status of a true profession for several reasons:

- Teachers began with only a two-year degree from a "normal school" or teachers' college.

- Teachers were, and still are, overwhelmingly women.

- Administrators are trained in a separate curriculum with their own degree and title.

Few, if any, teachers-in-training ever thought they could be in charge of a school. Nobody offers to teachers the professional-partnership opportunity available to those training for other white-collar professions: law, medicine, engineering, architecture, accounting. If education is ever to be a true profession, teaching will be the only degree, training, or credential needed for the work. Leaders will be chosen by teachers, and advanced certification will be in teaching. That is the model of the true professions. And nothing so energizes professionals as being in charge of their work.

Where schools are organized as partnerships, teachers can select their colleagues, evaluate each other, help each other develop, work together on learning. This is impossible within the traditional organization. In the partnership schools, we see teachers willing to accept responsibility because they control what matters for school success. This contrasts with the difficulty in getting teachers to accept full responsibility and accountability for what matters, when they are not in control of the school and the learning.

An example was a group empowered as the first cohort of Minneapolis teachers to go together through the MFT/University of St. Thomas master's degree program in teacher leadership. All were teaching at Patrick Henry High School (PHHS). They became the nucleus and the leaders of the PHHS Professional Practice School; the PHHS Teacher Leadership Model, where teacher leaders ran the curricular programs as Patrick Henry Instructional Leaders (PHILS); and the PHHS Residency Program, where new teachers experienced a full-year residency under the tutelage of a skilled, on-site mentor/ colleague. But those successful programs, though showing significant improvement in student learning, are now innovations of the past. The initial administrators were followed by others who proclaimed support for teacher leadership, but proceeded to bring their own agendas and, eventually, emasculated the programs.

Chartering as a Route to Professional Status

Charter-like schools are beginning to appear around the country. The Boston Teachers Union (BTU) took the initiative to create Pilot

Schools right after Massachusetts set up a program that gave chartering authority only to the state. "Our in-district charter schools,"
Bob Pearlman of the BTU called them at the time. The Pilot Schools'
program allows significant authority to the school, gives significant
flexibility from the contract, and expands the teachers' role in decision making. Los Angeles Unified, with the leadership of United
Teachers of Los Angeles, has now imported the Boston model.

Union leaders are aware of the teacher-partnership model and see
the role it offers teachers. It has aroused their interest. Around 2000,
union teachers in Milwaukee brought the model to their city and
worked out ways for teacher-run schools to operate so the teachers
would remain district employees and under the master contract.
More recently, the BTU has helped create a teacher-run school. So
did the Denver Classroom Teachers Association three years ago.
Sometimes these schools are under the charter law; sometimes not.

When she headed the United Federation of Teachers (UFT) in
New York City, Randi Weingarten got two schools chartered. They
were not organized as partnerships. But the teacher interest was
remarkable. The first, an elementary school, had about seven hundred
applicants for its thirteen positions. The second, a secondary school
created later, had about 1,100 teachers apply. This says something
about the interest where teachers have a larger professional role. Last
fall, a Teachers in Professional Practice (TPP) school appeared in
Portland, Maine—the first conversion of an existing school. A TPP
school in Nashville is now being planned. In a TPP, teachers band
together in a professional partnership and sell their services to the
school district.

In 2005, the MFT worked with the Minnesota Business Partnership (against the opposition of the rest of the "education cartel") to
pass a law for site-governed schools. This law created the opportunity
for a charter-like program within the district, something like Boston's
Pilot Schools. When the opportunity was announced, groups of

teachers and parents submitted proposals for innovative schools for urban students. But four years went by with no real cooperation from the Minneapolis district to work out the delegation of authority needed for the schools to be "self-governed." In 2009, the MFT went back to the legislature to put the delegation of authority in law, so the question to the district would pretty much be a simple yes or no on a proposal. Teachers came up with five proposals with more in the wings. The district grudgingly approved one, and even that has yet to be started.

Why is it that Boston has a large number of Pilot Schools and Massachusetts has twenty-plus schools in planning under their new "Innovation Schools" law, but in Minnesota we have a stagnant effort? In Massachusetts, the Secretary of Education (who works for the governor, who is not the commissioner) barnstormed with consultants to identify teachers who might be interested in running schools. That office provided consultants in a limited capacity to show applicants how to develop a proposal, how to ask the right questions, and what to expect. This eases the process of starting a school. This advocacy appears essential and has been working for Massachusetts.

Without comparable executive leadership for innovation in K–12, Minnesota will have to find some third-party organization to help these schools form. This could be the teachers' organization, local or state. It has no formal power, but it has influence to help ensure the key autonomies for schools and to help teachers pick up sound practices. It could be a resource for the board and the teachers. That way every school starting wouldn't need to reinvent the wheel.

In 2011, under the leadership of president Lynn Nordgren, the MFT applied for a grant from the AFT Innovation Fund set up by Weingarten, now AFT president. In the competition, the MFT won a grant to design and create a nonprofit that would apply to be an authorizer of charter schools under Minnesota's new program for single-purpose charter school authorizers. The MFT believes teachers know good teaching and learning when they see it, so they will be good assessors of the achievement by the accountability program.

That application, creating the Minnesota Guild of Public Charter Schools, was approved by the Minnesota Department of Education on November 30, 2011. This is the first case in the nation of a union playing a key role in creating an authorizer of charter schools. Testifying to the Minnesota legislature in February 2011, I explained that the union was frustrated trying to create a professional role through the district. The union concluded they needed to move upstream to gain the ability to create schools themselves.

The Larger Task Remaining

Shanker's vision is still missing. It is time to bring that back; time to realize what he originally envisioned. School, as a *Community of Collective Practice,* has tremendous potential in some of the most important areas of education today:

- **Effective management of schools.** This means professional educators making management decisions and delegating tasks to administrators and professional managers. Research by Richard Ingersoll at the University of Pennsylvania has found that the more ownership teachers have in their work, the better the environment. There are as many top-down, nonownership schools in the chartered sector as in districts.

- **Innovation and improvement.** Those on the front lines are best positioned to know the differences among students and to know how those different needs can be met by different approaches to learning and different kinds of schools. The innovation we look for, support, and nurture is a Saturn-like innovation in which General Motors and the United Auto Workers jointly trusted and empowered employees to use their hands, their minds, and their hearts in improving their product.

- **Evolution of unions into professional partnerships.** The teacher union that is so vilified in today's political rhetoric is a just response to the central control of school districts that leaves teachers powerless. If teachers are empowered, there will be a need for a different kind of collective representation. The needs of professional partnerships will change the services, responses, and organization of the new union.

The "New Unionism" has been sought and described by both the American Federation of Teachers (AFT) and National Education Association (NEA) in recent decades. The AFT began with the Futures Report that articulated the responsibility of unions to provide and support the very best teaching professionals, to care equally about the results of student learning, and to care about the success of the institutions in which teachers and other education employees work. Then the NEA's Bob Chase identified "Third Stage Unionism."

As a founding member, I joined twenty-four other AFT and NEA locals fifteen years ago to create the Teacher Union Reform Network (TURN). Our locals, now greatly expanded, have led efforts to restructure the US teacher unions to promote reforms for better learning and higher achievement for America's children. TURN unions provide leadership for the collective voice of their members, but also assume responsibility to students, their families, and to society. Teacher unions are committed to public education as a vital element of our democracy. What unites these responsibilities is our commitment to help all children learn. We affirm the unions' responsibility to collaborate with other stakeholders in public education and to seek consistently higher levels of student achievement. TURN locals also challenge themselves to create a new union to complement the changes in reformed schools and districts. TURN has now expanded to meet regionally, where I co-chair Great Lakes TURN. We want to use this union as a force for change in schools, in public education, and in other unions. We advocate change that is bold, doable, and survivable.

In the discussions at TURN, the attitude toward charters is visibly changing. Members see opportunities in many of the models developing. They're frustrated with the "managed instruction" they see coming from the district, and with the inability of the district to generate good schools. They see reform going toward more centralization—the opposite direction from what teachers see as right for themselves and for students. Ingersoll has found an important truth: schools work better where teacher roles are larger. They are more orderly, have less student truancy, and have lower teacher turnover. The degree of power and control that practitioners hold over workplace decisions is one of the most important criteria distinguishing the degree of professionalization and the status of a particular occupation or line of work. The charter sector offers some hope as a place to get the professional status and the approach to learning that teachers believe is right.

Overcoming the final challenges regarding Shanker's vision of charters as teacher-led schools, as teacher/parent partnership schools, and as union-supported schools can illuminate what's possible for the future.

Key opportunities include:

- **A new era of management in school districts.** Help districts change from top-down, siloed, central administration to school-based decision making. Instead of "school boards" that run schools, create "education boards" that oversee schools that make decisions themselves. To empower teachers as professionals, the school has to be endowed with self-determination. It could be via charter or could be inside a district or a union school. The principle of "local control" is most effective at the level of the school and the professionals. Move away from a school board that runs schools through a central administration to one that oversees performance agreements with school sites that run themselves and are measured against the goals in the performance agreement with the district and the union.

- **A new era for boards.** District structure should evolve from central-control with uniform processes to a "modular" design whereby schools run themselves. This way, district school boards change their role from "management and superintending" of schools to overseeing and assessing schools responsible for their own management, subject to similar choice-based incentives as are schools in the chartered sector. In this model, board-level duties are clarified by the division of the oversight of schools and of their management, and schools are given self-determination through the combination of accountability for results with authority over their operation.

- **A new era for unions.** What does the future of unions look like as they respond to the reconfiguration of districts and to the opportunities for self-governed schools, union schools, in-district charters, performance agreements, and other communities of practice? Our thinking at this stage includes moving to a new model of professional unionism:

From blue-collar behaviors and beliefs	To white-collar behaviors and beliefs
From industrial, top-down organization	To professional, flattened organization
From employees tied to large employers	To single schools and individual professionals

Large groups of employees in one bargaining unit in one large district may still have a master agreement negotiated by the union. That contract will allow for many of the exemptions, guides, standards, and articulated collaborative processes, such as performance agreements, that may be used by school sites. Schools that choose to enter into a "reciprocal obligations" agreement and/or a teacher-led schools memorandum of agreement with the school board and the union may do so. (A reciprocal obligations compact is one in which the administration and the union acknowledge their shared responsibility to stop the reform churn and to establish an empowered school environment. This gives educators the resources, control, power, and autonomy to transform individual schools, so that students receive a genuine opportunity to obtain a quality education.) It has been tried by Steve Smith, president of the Providence, Rhode Island, Federation of Teachers.

Individual professionals who are at-large or associate members of the union may receive all the protections, standards of practice, current research, and professional development for individual professionals provided by the union (national, state, and/or local). These models are being tried out in some ways by the new regional TURN networks. Teacher advocates have begun to conceptualize that charter schools and teacher-run schools will potentially constitute the third way, a viable and effective alternative to both public and private education.

Final Thoughts

Some organizational reformers still believe that some other viable alternative can be found to spark substantial changes in the public system. Despite overwhelming evidence to the contrary—and despite two-and-a-half decades of reforming, then restructuring, then redesigning—the educational enterprise remains mired in its century-old industrial model. Whatever the role of charter schools, the true restructuring or redesign must be more than tinkering around the edges of the industrial institution of the "school district." It was an unrealistic expectation that this century-old system be changed overnight by watching smaller, nimbler, more innovative schools operate successfully. Innovation will result in models of education that embed technology and virtual tech; that assess students' aptitudes as well as intelligence; that organize students by interest and ability rather than by age; and that allow them to demonstrate their learning, not just their test-taking skills. Learning will be project based and holistic, not restricted to individual classes expecting students to make the appropriate connections. Shanker always touted the Boy Scout method of experiential learning by doing.

So, we have come full circle and are back to work to realize Shanker's dream of real charters where teachers and parents are partners and kids learn a lot. We're designing the fourth way, fourth-stage unionism, the true teaching profession. We realize that teachers must risk reaching well beyond their personal and professional comfort zones to have the true professional status that Shanker envisioned and that we have worked to create. Whether they organize themselves as teachers in private practice or in self-governed schools or charter schools or union-led schools or teacher-led schools, teaching professionals need to be innovators, leaders, and risk takers.

We began our journey of reform over twenty-five years ago with the goal we called the "New 3 Rs: Relationships, Responsibility, Respect." Teachers have since taken unprecedented responsibility for student results and for quality teaching by themselves and their colleagues, and they have gained new skills and knowledge to build close relationships with all students. The one "R" that has gotten worse, instead of better, is "Respect." Teachers feel attacked, blamed, and shamed as they struggle to meet every demand for layer upon layer of accountability. They are the "Rodney Dangerfields" of the professions.

The work of teachers, and their empowerment, needs to change drastically if teaching is to attract and keep the "best and the brightest." To that end, TURN locals nationwide are embracing changes, collaborating with parents, and creating their own schools that are models of communities of practice where teachers are in charge and *respected*. If these efforts are not successful in the future, who will teach the children?

It will take time. We won't truly discover a new world until we get far enough out to sea to lose sight of the old one.

Appendix II: Viewpoints

How Chartering Informs Redesign of Other Public Services

Throughout this book, I've shared observations about the journey of chartering over the last twenty years, as well as opportunities and challenges for its future. But I'm not drawn to chartering solely as a reform of the public education system. Over time, I've come to realize that its principles can serve as a government redesign model that can be applied to delivery of other government services. This creates exciting possibilities. What principles can be gleaned from the chartering experience as a successful redesign of public service? What cautions did chartering provide? And finally, how might the chartering experiment be applied to other government services?

Eight Principles to Chartering's Success

1. **Chartering was a bipartisan initiative.** Some would call it nonpartisan. Leaders who envisioned this restructure were committed to improved outcomes, not to a political agenda. The state legislative sponsors came from the Democratic (DFL) majority party, the party at most political risk if the initiative passed. Republican policymakers gave valuable support to the effort, but did

not trumpet it. Democratic president Bill Clinton's support was crucial "cover" to Democratic lawmakers around the country as they worked to replicate chartering in other states. Republican US senator David Durenberger's support enrolled conservatives who originally believed chartering did not go far enough in education reform.

2. **Moderates of both parties prevailed.** Twenty years ago, moderate politicians made up a significant portion of both the Republican and Democratic caucuses in the Minnesota legislature and in Congress. Moderates often worked across party lines to create new policy innovations. Chartering came from the center of the political spectrum. It was led and supported by moderate policymakers in both parties. Today, few moderates in either party are serving in public office at the state or federal level. In my view, a first-in-nation chartering law would not pass in today's political climate.

3. **System change coexisted with the existing system.** Imagine the launch of a small boat parallel to a large ocean liner. They both transport passengers to the same destination, but the skipper of the small boat can choose a different path or schedule, offer different services, and create a different experience, all without interfering with the ocean liner. In time, more passengers may choose to ride on the small boat. In time, the ocean liner may adopt new—and successful—services the small boat was offering. Now all passengers have more choices. So it was when the Minnesota legislature authorized an organization other than the public school district to deliver public education. And so it can be in other areas of government, such as delivery of human services. Significant change can

occur in delivery of government services without fear of "blowing up" the larger system.

4. **The innovation was the law itself, not an individual school.** The innovation wasn't the creation of any one individual school. The innovation was the restructuring of the system—the opportunity for someone other than a public school district to create and hold accountable a public school. Yes, some chartered schools will be very innovative. Others will not succeed at all. But here's the key: as long as the chartering law exists, new chartered schools will be created to try new ways of educating students. Will there be risk? Yes. And reward? Most definitely! The more the public understands and accepts this distinction, the more they will tolerate the occasional failed school. Controversy around chartering may diminish.

5. **The federal innovation was the law.** Minnesota's chartering legislation also changed the role of the federal government in education, usually the purview of the states. Durenberger and Clinton altered the federal-state relationship around public education by championing support and incentives to states that passed chartering laws. The feds did not mandate or pass a federal chartering law; the feds encouraged and defined "true" innovation through distribution of federal grants to states, which then passed them on to chartered schools. This was new. Not coincidentally, two moderate politicians of different parties led the way.

6. **Policymakers let citizens take the lead.** Sometimes the most important thing policymakers can do is remove barriers and let citizens take the lead. Policy entrepreneurs

and visionary educators brought chartering to the Minnesota legislature. It was supported by citizen organizations such as the Citizens League, the Urban Coalition, and the Minnesota Business Partnership. The chartering law itself removed barriers within the public education system. Educators and families were free to create new opportunities or eliminate existing gaps in the public education of their students. Policymakers allowed them "the freedom to be better."

7. **Performance outcomes defined success.** Recently, a policy colleague shared his view that the "single most important redesign of chartering was the notion of putting performance-based outcomes in a contract." This was rarely known at the time. A decade later, Governor Tom Vilsack of Iowa led his vision for "Transforming Iowa," which included the creation of "Charter Agencies," where state agency leaders could commit to contractual performance outcomes in return for greater flexibility. Currently in Minnesota, legislation is pending to create a performance-based organization—or charter agency—to provide more choices for people with disabilities. Developed by Lutheran Social Service of Minnesota and called "My Life, My Choices," the legislation would authorize the Department of Human Services, among other agencies, to enter into a performance-based contract with a nonprofit or local government to deliver agreed-upon outcomes for people with disabilities, without prescribing how to achieve them.

8. **Choices built constituency.** Who can argue with the power of choice? According to the September 2011 Phi Delta Kappa/Gallup Poll, 74 percent of Americans support

giving families access to public school choices. Minnesota governor Rudy Perpich instinctively knew this in 1985, when he directed his staff to ensure students would be able to enroll in the newly enacted postsecondary enrollment options program when the school year began. A constituency was built overnight, and it had impact. The next year, the legislature chose not to repeal the program, despite pressure for repeal from education groups.

Three Cautions for Sustaining Redesign

1. **Don't leave accountability to chance.** As an author of chartering legislation, I concede that we didn't think much about the role of "sponsors" during initial passage of the legislation. Now called authorizers, these are the public and nonprofit entities that oversee and hold the board of a chartered school accountable. I regret that the original legislation did not make clear the accountability responsibilities of the sponsor, including the training and execution of their duties. Today, organizations such as the National Association of Charter School Authorizers (NACSA) support authorizers around the country with training, financial tools, and best practices. Some states allow authorizers to collect fees for their administrative expenses or require approval of prospective authorizers by their state department of education.

2. **Don't leave description to chance.** A recent poll commissioned by the National Alliance for Public Charter Schools revealed that only 13 percent of respondents could accurately define a chartered school. Few Americans knew that chartered schools were public schools and that they do not charge tuition. I regret that the original legislation

identified these schools as "outcome-based schools" rather than "public chartered schools." (We thought the focus on outcomes and results would strengthen the legislation, connect it to the current focus on outcome-based education, and reduce overall opposition). Had we described them as public chartered schools in the first legislation, confusion might have been avoided.

3. **Resist temptation to legislate operations and governance.** The pressures to prescribe "protective" details are unending. Every interest group wants to prescribe in law their piece of the outcome. Because of that, unintended consequences result. Take Minnesota's law, where, due to union pressure, a majority of a chartered school's board must be teachers. The inherent conflict of interest still causes difficulties—teachers negotiate with themselves in setting salaries and benefits. But the greater, unforeseen problem is that the chartered school's board loses out on overall expertise. With teachers in majority, fewer board seats are available for outsiders with important skill sets in finance and governance. Especially in small chartered schools, the limited number of available teachers automatically limits board size and outside expertise. While charters in Minnesota can now "waive" this majority requirement, the point here is larger. Government's role is in setting broad policy and ensuring accountability. Legislating prescriptive measures can have unintended consequences and can suppress the creativity and innovation of the concept.

Six Recommendations for Redesigners of Today

1. **Ask different questions.** The most frequent question I heard during the chartering debates was, "Who wants this?

Who's asking for chartered schools?" Frankly, no one was asking for chartered schools—they didn't know what they were. The better question was, "What do parents want for their children from their public schools that they are not getting now?" Think Henry Ford: if his question was, "How can I get there more quickly?" his answer would have been "Faster horses." Policymakers of today will succeed with true redesign only if they ask the right questions. Stakeholders outside government—nonprofits, business, academics—can help frame those questions, just as Ted Kolderie and others did with chartering. Policymakers and state agency managers usually think within what they know. Many of them helped create the current system. So, they think in terms of "improving" the current system and call that redesign. Redesign is much more than "continuous improvement." It is about systemic change. The chartering legislation was not about, for example, prescribing new standards within the system. Chartering was about systemic change within public education because, for the first time, a new school could be created outside the existing system.

2. **Learn the rules.** Making legislation is like making sausage—learn how to cook! The best counsel I received as a new legislator was that "Rules are power." Learn the legislative rules and know the procedures. Passage of chartering legislation in Minnesota and California was not Civics 101. When we saw an opportunity to move the legislation in the process, we took it. Sometimes we made split-second decisions.

3. **Find common ground.** During this time of political gridlock and finger-pointing debates, redesign of

310

government services is one area where individuals of different points of view can find common ground. Policymakers and constituents often can agree on outcomes, and once people are committed to outcomes, it's easier to find common ground to accomplish them. But it is hard work. It takes a special kind of policymaker. Redesign work is not "sexy." It doesn't usually make headlines. It's not a talking point of the day. But when successful, it can create a major impact.

4. **Develop more policy entrepreneurs.** We need them in public office and in civic leadership—period. But policy entrepreneurs need the right development and training. We can teach them principles of redesign, including the right questions to ask. We can bring people of different points of view together to tackle a problem. Philanthropic funding can provide leadership training for policy entrepreneurs. The point is to train them before they run for office and are indoctrinated into the capitol cultural way of thinking. Candidates for office usually run because they are passionate about an issue. We need to encourage "passionate" candidates who are also skilled problem solvers. This policy orientation is not generally rewarded in elections. That must change.

5. **Term limits work against redesign.** In many states, lawmakers are limited to a certain number of terms they can serve in office, resulting in turnover of veteran lawmakers. When institutional memory in a legislature is lost, two things happen: New lawmakers continue with or recreate past failed solutions. And the views of state agency staff, many of whom have worked for years to create the

current systems, become even more powerful, wielding influence with uninformed legislators.

6.   **Don't make it personal.** Engage opponents and hear their point of view on the issue. Recognize that opposition isn't personal; it is a difference of opinion. Stay grounded. This isn't easy, and in 1991, I didn't succeed at it very well. If you find yourself taking matters too personally—with the good or the bad—it may help to step back and remember why you chose to follow your path in the first place. Reclaim the urgency of your mission. For me, Kolderie was the person who grounded me. For him, it wasn't about politics or personal gain; it was about providing a better education for kids. Sometimes I struggled to understand his points. But for me, he was a steady, calm, and passionate reminder of why we were there and where we were going. Every policymaker leading a difficult issue needs that personal compass.

Closing Advice to Redesigners of Today

- Ask different questions.

- Take a stand.

- Celebrate the small victories.

- Always look for the next right answer.

Public Viewpoint: Facts and Findings

Twenty years after the first chartering legislation was passed in Minnesota, what is the public's viewpoint on chartering? Here are findings and facts that shed some light on this question.

Chartered Schools, Vouchers, and Choice

The September 2011 *Kappan* magazine published the following conclusions from the Phi Delta Kappa/Gallup Poll, "What Americans said about the public schools."

> Americans continue to embrace the concept of charter schools. This year's poll shows an approval rating of 70%, the highest recorded since the question was first asked 10 years ago. Charter school support has increased steadily over that period. Support for public charter schools is strongest among Americans under age 40 (76%) and Republicans (77%).
>
> Americans increasingly support choice—allowing students and parents to choose which public schools to attend in their community regardless of where they live—and this support (74%) is consistent across age differences and political affiliation.
>
> But vouchers received the lowest approval rating in the past 10 years—only one of three Americans favor allowing students and parents to choose a private school to attend with public dollars.

Minnesota and School Choice

Table 1 shows the most recent data available from the Minnesota Department of Education. The figures are from the 2011–2012 school year, except where noted.

Type of School Program	Enrollment	Percent of Total
Total K–12 students	839,426	100%
Public chartered schools	39,143	4.7%
Nonpublic schools	72,458	8.6%
Open-enrolled in nonresident district (2010–2011)	58,408	7.1%
Students homeschooled (2010–2011)	17,247	2.1%

Table 1: Minnesota K-12 Students, 2011-2012 (except where noted). Source: Minnesota Department of Education

Table 2 below shows that chartered schools make up 7.5 percent of all public schools in Minnesota—a higher percentage than nationally (5.4 percent, as shown in Table 3).

Type of Schools	Number of Schools	Percent of Total
Public schools	1,968	100%
Nonchartered public schools	1,820	92.5%
Public chartered schools	148	7.5%

Table 2: Minnesota public schools, 2011-2012.
Source: Minnesota Department of Education

Chartered Public Schools in the United States

National data for 2010–2011, reported in Table 3, show that over 5 percent of the public schools in the country are chartered schools and that about 10 percent of those chartered schools were new in the fall of 2010. The data was provided by the National Alliance for Public Charter Schools, which at the time of this book's printing did not yet have comparable data for the 2011–2012 school year. The alliance did provide 2011–2012 estimates (as reported below) for the number of chartered schools and the number of new chartered schools in the fall of 2011.

Type of Schools	Number of Schools	Percent of Total
Total public schools	97,708	100%
Nonchartered public schools	92,431	94.6%
Chartered public schools	5,277	5.4%

Table 3: Chartered Schools in United States, 2010–2011
Source: National Alliance for Public Chartered Schools

According to the alliance, the average chartered school had been open for 7.1 years, as of 2010–2011. Many new chartered schools are starting up each year. In the fall of 2010, 518—9.8 percent—of the 5,277 chartered schools were new. The alliance estimates that 521 new chartered schools started up in the fall of 2011. The estimate of chartered schools in 2011–2012 is 5,637, serving over two million chartered school students. Data updates can be found at publiccharters.org.

The Freedom to Be Better: Speech to Democratic Leadership Conference

SEN. EMBER REICHGOTT
MAY 1, 1992

It's a pleasure to join the DLC today to talk about "reinventing public education." I want to update you on some things happening in Minnesota in the way of public school choice and charter schools.

If you're exploring these ideas in your state, you can thank the DLC for that. The DLC has been one of the strongest supporters of public school choice, and I want to extend my personal appreciation to Senators Joseph Lieberman and John Breaux for cosponsoring the charter schools initiative in the US Senate this past year. Together with Congressman Dave McCurdy, they helped lead the national debate on the issue, and they continue to be strongly committed to federal support for charter schools. We thank you for your leadership!

Mr. Osborne, you were kind enough to say nice things about Minnesota in your book. While I did not actually memorize the paragraph starting on the ninth line on page 101, I do remember your calling Minnesota's system a "revolution" in public education. Those are kind words. Today I want to briefly share how that revolution came about, where it is going, and why it is incumbent upon each of us as parents, public officials, and progressive Democrats to continue to battle. We call this battle "reinventing public education." What it means is, creating new opportunities for kids, teachers, and our communities.

As I was getting up this morning, I was reminded of a fellow named George back in Minnesota. He was having a devil of a time getting ready for school. His mother woke him; he went back to sleep. She woke him again, and he complained bitterly about having to go to school. She bothered him again, insisting that he get dressed and get off to school now. He screamed back, "I don't want to go to school. Why do I need to go?" His frustrated mother replied, "Because, George, you are forty-five years old and you are the principal!"

George exemplifies the crisis in our schools today. Teachers and principals are burned out. Learners are falling through the cracks. Test scores are decreasing, and American students are becoming less and less competitive.

We wonder why the public is crying out for change.

You were right, Mr. Osborne: crisis in education was fundamental to our revolution in Minnesota. The first volley was fired in 1985 when high school students were allowed to take college courses for credit. With the strong leadership of our Democratic governor Rudy Perpich, public school choice (otherwise known as open enrollment) became reality for all students by 1988. Together we were able to turn a firestorm of protest over public school choice to enthusiastic acceptance by nearly two-thirds of Minnesotans. Even 61 percent of the teachers of the Minnesota Education Association support choice.

Why is there such strong support? Because choice is working.

Today we have the data to prove it:

- In just two years, fifteen hundred dropouts came back to school.

- College-bound students in one program increased by 700 percent.

- Student satisfaction increased threefold in some programs.

With these results, the revolution was well underway. We were now ready for Phase II—the creation of charter schools. When I first introduced the legislation, it seemed a natural extension of all that was working under public school choice. It just wasn't enough to provide students more access to choices, if there weren't plenty of choices to access.

So, Minnesota authorized the formation of eight charter schools. (We hoped for an unlimited number, but politics are politics.) This isn't a new concept to states like California, New Jersey, Colorado, and Michigan, where various charter school alternatives are being explored. But for those not familiar with charter schools, let me tell you how they work.

A charter school is for those teachers who think they can do it better. With proposal in hand, these teachers and supportive parents apply to a local school board for a charter. If approved, these teachers will operate their school up to three years with total autonomy as to budget, staffing, curriculum, and teaching methods. The school is exempted from nearly all state and local regulation, with basic exceptions for special education and desegregation. In return, the teachers must meet outcome-based performance standards as agreed in the charter. It's simple. No results; no charter. Teachers trade away regulation for results, and bureaucracy for accountability. In short, a charter school is a new kind of public school that rewards innovation, empowers teachers and parents, and meets student needs without turning our existing school system upside down.

Now that you know what a charter school is, let me tell you what it is not. First, charter schools are not a voucher system for private schools. Charter schools are an expansion of public school choice. All charter schools are nonsectarian and nondiscriminatory in admission policies. Students are assured of equal access regardless of financial means, previous achievement, or behavior.

Second, charter schools are not a diversion of public school dollars, nor do they benefit the few at the expense of the many. While dollars may not directly feed the school system bureaucracy, they are "diverted" only to follow the very student they are intended to educate.

At the same time, the incentives created by choice and charter schools stimulate the entire system. Is it any coincidence that the number of Advanced Placement courses in Minnesota's high schools has doubled since high school students were given the chance to take college courses?

Third, charter schools are not an indictment of our public school system. They are a tool for innovative entrepreneurs to do the job better in times of scarce resources and demanding social agendas. Tom Peters, in his book *In Search of Excellence,* observed that large organizations are seldom if ever responsible for major advances in their industries. A National Science Foundation study found that small firms produced twenty-four times as many innovations per research dollar as large firms.

Now there are some innovative exceptions—like 3M, where initiative drives the company and small groups are encouraged "to create" on company time. About one-fourth of 3M's sales come from products that weren't invented five years earlier, and five years from now, another 25 percent will come from products that don't exist today. What if 50 percent of the methods by which kids can learn haven't been invented yet? How can we even know what those methods are without a system that gives innovation someplace to go?

I've told you what charter schools are and what they are not. The big question is, Do they work? In Minnesota, we are in the very early stages of finding out. The first charter—a plan to bring dropouts back to school—is expected to open in August of this year. Several other charter proposals are currently under negotiation with the school boards, including a tuition-free Montessori school, a rural "open" school with interactive television technology, and a school for deaf and hearing-impaired children who wish to learn American Sign Language. In all, more than twenty charter school proposals have been stimulated around this state in less than a year.

There have been successes, to be sure. But the road to change is always a rocky one. Some outstanding proposals haven't made it. They've been rejected by school boards afraid to take risks, to give up control, or to divert dollars from the bureaucracy to the children they are intended to educate. In rejecting one proposal, a superintendent commented, "It's hard for me to grasp that what is proposed could be better than the program offered in our elementary school." That reminds me of the much-quoted head of the US patent office who years ago said, "Everything that could ever be invented has already been invented."

Yes, it can be frustrating. One successful charter applicant put it best: "We are truly on the bleeding edge of change." Being on the "bleeding edge" is painful. But it is critical for us as progressive Democratic officials to be there. Why? The public demands as much. A recent Harris Poll found that education has moved to the top of the roster of political concerns in this year's election. We know, too, that two-thirds of the American public support public school choice.

As Democrats, what are we waiting for? We have always been the party considered most responsive to education needs. We must continue to earn that reputation by responding to our changing times. Yes, by reinventing public education.

If we don't respond, this revolution may move beyond us—beyond our comfort level. I suspect that many of you would agree with me that a private school voucher system is not the way to strengthen education in this country. Indeed, it could well be destructive to public education. We can't ignore the president's strong support of vouchers in education. We can't ignore the fact that a large citizens group has worked for months to obtain signatures to place the voucher proposal on the California ballot. California legislators are just one group considering charter schools as a progressive answer to the problems facing our schools—an answer more in keeping with the values we have always associated with our public education system.

We must act now. The public won't wait any longer. Our children deserve more from us. In the words of one member of the Minnesota State Board of Education: "We have talked the talk of educational innovation. Now it is time for us to walk the walk."

Thank you very much.

Speech at City Academy Chartered School
BY PRESIDENT BILL CLINTON
MAY 4, 2000

On May 4, 2000, during National Charter Schools Week, President Bill Clinton visited City Academy in St. Paul, which opened in 1992 as the nation's first chartered school. The following are his remarks.

REMARKS BY THE PRESIDENT TO THE ST. PAUL COMMUNITY

City Academy St. Paul, Minnesota

9:45 A.M. CDT

THE PRESIDENT: Thank you very much. Well, after Tom and Milo talked, I don't know that I need to say much of anything. I thank you for what you said and for the example you have set. And I want to say a little more about Milo and this school in a moment.

There are a number of other people I would like to acknowledge and doubtless I will miss some, but I'd like to thank Education Commissioner Jax for being here; and Superintendent Harvey; Majority Leader of the Senate Roger Moe; The Mayor of Minneapolis I think is here, Sharon Sayles Belton; former Attorney General Skip Humphrey. I'd like to thank State Senator Ember Reichgott Junge, a longtime friend of mine and former state representative Becky Kelso, who were the original co-sponsors of the charter school legislation. The Charter Friends National Network director Jon Schroeder, who drafted the original federal charter law, which we adopted. The Center for School Change director Joe Nathan, a longtime personal friend of mine with whom I worked for many years.

And I'd like to acknowledge some people who came on this tour with me, some of whom who have been very active in the charter school movement for a long time -the President of the Progressive Policy Institute in Washington, Will Marshall; the President of the New Schools Venture Fund, Kim Smith; the policy director of the National Urban League, Bill Spriggs, and a longtime friend and City Council member from New York City, Guillermo Linares. And they're over here to my right. They've come a long way to be with you to see this first charter school in the United States.

When I was listening to Milo Cutter and Tom Gonzalez talk first about this school, how it got started, what its mission is, and then hearing Tom talk about his life and how his then-girlfriend and present wife got him into this school, it reminded me of all the struggles that I have seen the charter school movement go through throughout the United States, and reaffirmed my conviction that every effort has been worth it.

It is true that when I ran for President in 1992, Minnesota had the only public charter school in the country -this one. And so when I went around the country talking about charter schools, most people thought I had landed from another planet, because most people hadn't been here. Most people still haven't been here, to this school. But I knew it was an idea that had enormous promise. And some of the people involved in this enterprise have been working with me for years on educational matters when I was the governor of Arkansas.

I also knew that if Minnesota was doing it, there was a pretty good chance it was a good idea, since the state already had some of the best-performing schools in the United States. And I think the state and this community deserve a lot of credit for the general direction of education reform and rising test scores. Minnesota really is about to become Lake Wobegon, where all the children are above average. And that's good for you. Good for you. (Laughter and applause.)

I'm here today because I want all of America to know about you -and through you, to understand what might be done in other communities with the charter school movement to give all of our children the education they need, and the education our country needs for them to have in a 21st century information economy.

This is a good time for us to be doing this. Our economy is in the best shape it's ever been. We have been working for 20 years on school reform; no one can claim anymore they don't know what works. We now have enough evidence that the charter school movement works if it's done right, as it has been done here. And we have the largest and most diverse student body in our history which means there are more different kinds of people that may learn in different ways and have different personal needs, but they all need -I will say again -a certain high level of educational attainment.

The strategy that clearly works is accountability for high standards, with a lot of personal attention and clear support for the education mission of every school. We've tried to support that now for seven years. The Vice President and I have supported everything from increasing Head Start to smaller classes in the early grades to funds to help all of our states and school districts set high standards and systems for implementing accountability for those standards; to opening up the doors of college to more Americans.

Here in St. Paul, our movement to put 100,000 teachers on the streets -in our schools, I mean -has led, I think to 23 more teachers being hired. And here in this city the average class size in the early grades is 18. If that were true in every place in America, the children would be learning and all of our 3rd graders would be able to read, more of them would stay in school, fewer of them would drop out, more of them would do well. So I want to congratulate you on making good use of that, as well. (Applause.)

We've also tried to make sure all of our schools were wired to the Internet. We're going to do a little work on the Internet later this morning. When the Vice President and I started and we got the so-called e-rate passed in Congress, which allows lower- income schools to get subsidies to be wired and to use the Internet, to access it, there were only 16 percent of the schools and 3 percent of the classrooms connected. Today, 95 percent of the schools and almost 75 percent of the classrooms are connected. And I think by the end of this year—certainly sometime next year—we will have every classroom in America, certainly every school connected, except those that are literally too old and decrepit to be wired—and unfortunately there are some and I've been out on another crusade to try to build new school facilities and have the federal government help in that regard, too.

But we've come a long way. And yet we know that there are still schools which aren't performing as they should, even though test scores are up, even though college-going is up, we know that there are schools which aren't performing. And I wanted to come here today because of what you've done, because you've proved that charter schools were a good idea. As I said, when I started running for president, there was a grand total of one charter school. You. You were it. Now there are over 1,700 in America. And we have invested almost half a billion dollars since 1994 to help communities start charter schools. That's why there are over 1,700 and I'm proud of that. (Applause).

And this is actually National Charter School Week, which is nice for me to be here by accident in this week. And I can say that -you know, my goal was to at least fund 3,000 or more by the time I left office. And I believe we are going to meet that goal, and one of the reasons is that you have set such a good example.

Now what I want to talk about today is how the charter schools work a little, I want to say a little about that. And then I want to answer -if you'll forgive me for doing it, since you don't have this problem -I want to answer some of the critics of the charter school movements who say that not all the schools have worked.

Schools like City Academy, as I said, have the flexibility to reach out to students who may have had trouble in ordinary school experiences. At the same time, very often we see charter schools provide an even greater atmosphere of competition that induces kids to work harder and harder to learn. Studies show that charter schools are at least as racially and economically diverse as the public schools, generally; and here in Minnesota, they're more diverse than average schools.

Surveys show the vast majority of parents with children in our 1,700 charter schools think their children are doing better academically in those schools than they were in their previous schools. There are long waiting lists to get in most charter schools all across the United States.

Now, does that mean every charter school is a stunning success? No. But I don't think that anyone can cite any endeavor of life where everybody is doing a great job. The idea behind the charter schools was never that they would all be perfect, but that because they were unlike traditional schools they had to be created with a charter and a mission that had to be fulfilled. If they were not successful in that mission, they could be shut down or changed or the children could go somewhere else.

And so that they would be under a lot more -pressure may be the wrong word - but the environment would be very different -that if they didn't work, that kids wouldn't be stuck there forever, that there would always be other options, and that they, themselves, could be dramatically transformed.

Now, the one problem we have had is that not every state has had the right kind of accountability for the charter schools. Some states have laws that are so loose that no matter whether the charter schools are doing their jobs or not they just get to stay open, and they become like another bureaucracy. Unfortunately, I think even worse, some states have laws that are so restrictive it's almost impossible to open a charter school in the first place.

So the second point I want to make to the people, especially to the press folks that are traveling with us who have to report this to the country, is that not only has this first charter school in America, City Academy, done great but Minnesota's law is right. You basically have struck the right balance. You have encouraged the growth of charter schools, but you do hold charter schools responsible for results. That's what every state in the country ought to do.

Let me finally say that there are some people who criticize charter schools by saying that even though they are Public schools they amount to draining money away from other public schools. That's just not true. You would be in school somewhere. And if you were, whether your school was doing an effective job or not, the tax money would be going there. The charter school movement, if it works, can help to save public education in this country, by proving that excellence can be provided to all children from all backgrounds no matter what experiences they bring to the school in the first place. That's what this whole thing is about. (Applause.)

My goal is to get more money and more people involved in the charter schools movement to break down the walls of resistance among all the educators to it, and to get community people all over the country more aware of it. Today, we are going to release about $137 million in grants to support new and existing charter schools in 31 states, the District of Columbia and Puerto Rico. I am going to ask the Secretary of Education today to develop guidelines for employers and faith-based groups so that they will know how they can be actively involved in supporting the charter school movement.

While charter schools have to be non-sectarian, there is a role, a positive role, that faith-based groups can play. And employers, we find around America, increasingly are willing to provide space and other resources to help charter schools get started. In nearby Rockford, Minnesota for instance, there is the Skills for Tomorrow School, sponsored jointly by the Teamsters Union and the Business Partnership. Union, corporate and small business leaders have helped to develop the school. They also provide students with internships and take part in judging whether they have met their academic requirements, to ensure that they have the skills they need to succeed. I think the guidelines I'm calling for today will get more businesses and more faith-based groups involved in the charter school movement.

We have learned now for seven years that charter schools will work if you have investment and accountability, and if you make them less bureaucratic and more mission oriented. I'm very proud of the fact that in our administration the Secretary of Education has reduced the regulatory burden on local schools and states in administering federal aid by about two-thirds, while we have doubled the investment in education for our schools.

And I'm very proud of the fact that long ago, even though I wasn't given the privilege of coming to this school, I heard about Milo, I heard about the City Academy, I heard about the charter schools movement; I talked to Joe Nathan, I talked to Ember about it and a number of other people. And I ran for President in 1992 pledging that if the people voted for me, we would have more of these schools. And over 1,700 schools later, thanks to your example, my commitment I think has been fulfilled and American education has been advanced. I only hope that my presence here today will help to get us to 3,000 and will help to get us to the point in America where every school operates like a charter school. Thank you very much. (Applause.) END 10:00 A.M. CDT

Why MEA Opposes Chartered Schools

BY MINNESOTA EDUCATION ASSOCIATION
May 1991

Why MEA Opposes Chartered Schools

Insulting

The concept of chartered schools implies that beneficial change cannot be brought about within the existing system of public education, and says that it is necessary to create an additional, untested, competing system. It is insulting because it ignores the success of Minnesota public schools.

The real issue is to provide quality education for all of Minnesota's public school students. The discussion of chartered schools diverts our attention. We need to provide the time, talent, and resources to support the efforts of communities and educators state-wide to restructure our schools to meet the needs of our students and the future of our state.

A costly hoax

The concept of charter schools is a hoax that could cost Minnesota taxpayers millions of dollars and place constitutional guarantees in jeopardy. Under proposals which have been presented in Minnesota, charter schools could be created which would then be supported by state funds. These schools could operate independently of existing school districts and free of most state regulations and safeguards of quality. Our state cannot afford to divert resources in this way.

The institution of a chartered school system could threaten accessibility to education—and even result jn abandonment of our state's constitutional duty to provide a "general and uniform" public school system. Chartered schools could be established by any group or organization that applied to the state and met minimal requirements. Once granted a charter, these "schools" would receive taxpayers' dollars to operate.

More bureaucracy

Under these proposals, a new level of bureaucracy would be created to facilitate the formation of chartered schools. In addition, these chartered schools would be able to spend public funds for travel and consulting services and would have access to funding and innovative programs that existing public schools are denied.

Nonlicensed teachers

Most disturbing to MEA, these schools would not be subject to the state safeguards that insure quality education for all children. In fact, they would be permitted to hire persons to teach who are not licensed and therefore not properly trained. MEA stands firmly behind licensure as a requirement to insure the qualifications of teachers. Teachers need not only be "smart" about a particular subject and have a proclivity toward nurturing; they need professional training . Other professions, from barbers to brain surgeons, are licensed by the state. Minnesota students deserve licensed teachers.

324

Six major flaws in the chartered schools concept

Multi-tiered system

First, the proposal risks creating elite academies for the few and second-rate schools for the many—a multi-tiered system of public education with no guarantee of equity in facilities or curriculum. We had such a multi-tiered system here in this country in the 19th century; we don't need to go backward to discover our future.

Democratic values

Second, we depend on public schools to teach society's democratic values. This important charge could be thwarted by chartered schools, which would set their own standards of curriculum planning and implementation. Would public policy interests be well served by using public funds to support schools which might use censorship—on either the left or the right—to keep from their students important ideas, issues or works of literature?

Lax standards

Third, among the many "freedoms" proposed for chartered schools is lax enforcement of standards. It is incredibly naive to expect the market to protect our children in a system with such a lack of accountability. Private trade schools have shown how easily the lack of accountability and regulations can lead to fraud, misrepresentation and corruption when money is up for grabs.

Nonlicensed teachers

Fourth, foremost among these lax standards would be the ability of chartered schools to hire nonlicensed teaching personnel. As previously stated, licensure is necessary to ensure that teachers are professionally trained and fully qualified.

Costly scheme

Fifth, the chartered school scheme would be costly. Additional layers of bureaucracy would be required to start up and oversee chartered schools. Local boards of education would have to approve charters, which will not reduce the number of administrative staff needed, and recordkeeping by officials could result in the need for even more bureaucratic staff positions at the state level. It could be chaotic. There is no evidence in the education community to suggest that competition would produce cost savings. In fact, although colleges compete, college costs continue to soar.

Open door to vouchers

Finally, chartered schools provide an open door to vouchers. The ability to procure funds could mean that leaders of private schools would seek charters to obtain public money for their particular institutions—under the guise of a chartered school.

Innovation is part of today's public schools

Proponents of chartered schools believe innovation in education cannot be achieved under the current system. But, in fact, individual teachers, schools, and even entire school districts all across Minnesota are already engaged in designing new programs for excellence which are recognized nation-wide.

Siphon off resources

Innovation and improvement are a real part of today's public schools in Minnesota. Chartered schools, however, are an idea which would obviously siphon valuable resources of time, talent, money and energy away from a creative, high quality system of education—and our children would be the guinea pigs.

Goes against the grain

The chartered school proposal goes against the grain of several positive trends in Minnesota public education: fewer school districts and bargaining units; less administrative bureaucracy rather than more; higher, rather than lower, standards for teaching and education; and more rather than less integration of students and curriculum.

Bad public policy

The hallmark of public education in our nation and state has been the goal—and largely demonstrated ability—to meet the needs of *all* students. Elitism is contrary to all fundamental American values. The stated goals of chartered schools—including improving education and implementing outcome-based eduction—are commendable, but they are achievable through the existing public school system. And all students should reap the benefits, not just a select few. Creating an additional side bureaucracy and system is unnecessary and unconscionable. It's just plain bad public policy.

MEA supports real restructuring

Benefits for all students

Minnesota has more than 400 independent school districts, and all are doing the best they can for their students. Some do more than others, but all are committed to their students. Minnesota owes *all* of these students something. MEA backs real restructuring efforts which would benefit all Minnesota students.

Proposals for chartered schools don't really do anything to restructure schools; they would just create a new, small subset of schools. If the differences inherent in chartered schools would really be so beneficial, then all of our students should share in them—we owe them that much.

MEA supports innovation and education reform for all students. Innovation and experimentation can be accomplished within the existing system. The goal of chartered school proponents may be to make an end-run around the existing bureaucracy, which some believe hampers public schools' ability to experiment and implement new policy. Ironically, as we've already shown, they would create even more bureaucracy in their attempt.

Unnecessary duplication

At a time when state and local funding sources are scarce, chartered school proposals would drain away state resources, as well as the time and energy of people. Chartered schools represent an unnecessary concept which merely duplicates that which is possible in the current school structure.

We cannot afford to waste precious resources. It is time to focus on fundamental initiatives which will bring the needed changes and strengthen our public schools. Such initiatives include:

Reorganize

• School district reorganization to aggregate and focus resources, cut down administrative inefficiencies and broaden current curriculum opportunities for all Minnesota students.

Empower

• Empower teachers through site-based decision-making. Teachers are best able to decide how to attain learner outcomes, and must be empowered to do so.

Support quality education

• Provide the time and resources necessary to support quality implementation of outcome-based education.

MINNESOTA
EDUCATION
ASSOCIATION

An affiliate of the National Education Association
41 Sherburne Avenue
St. Paul, Minnesota 55103
612-227-9541

Appendix III: Biographies and Chronologies

Biographies

Robert Astrup. President of Minnesota Education Association (MEA) in 1991. MEA actively opposed chartering legislation. Astrup worked with Sandra Peterson, president of Minnesota Federation of Teachers, to merge the two state associations which occurred in 1998.

Minnesota State Representative Jerry Bauerly (DFL-Sauk Rapids). Member of the 1991 conference committee on the omnibus education funding bill. One of two dissenting votes on conference committee against chartering. Bauerly represented a rural constituency in central Minnesota and served 1987–1994. He was an assistant majority leader in 1991.

Ray Budde. Assistant professor at School of Education at University of Massachusetts, Amherst. Proposed concept of chartering in 1974 paper, "Education by Charter." In 1988, elaborated on the concept in the book *Education by Charter: Restructuring School Districts.* Deceased.

Governor Arne Carlson. Republican governor of Minnesota 1991–1998. Carlson signed the 1991 omnibus education funding bill into law on June 4, 1991, which included the first chartering provisions. The governor did not actively support or oppose chartering in 1991. He became a supporter of chartering during later years in office.

President Bill Clinton. As Democratic Arkansas governor during the 1980s, was the first governor in the nation to propose and replicate Minnesota's open enrollment law. In 1990, Clinton became chair of the Democratic Leadership Council (DLC) and included public school choice and chartering in his DLC agenda as early as 1990. Clinton served as president of the United States 1993–2000. Clinton was an early and outspoken champion of chartering. He signed the federal chartering grant program into law as part of the 1994 reauthorization of the Elementary and Secondary Education Act (ESEA).

Minnesota State Senator Greg Dahl (DFL-Ham Lake). In 1991, chair of senate Education Committee, member of Education Funding Division, and member of conference committee on omnibus education funding bill. Supported chartering. Served in senate 1981–1992.

Minnesota State Senator Gary DeCramer (DFL-Ghent). In 1991, member of senate Education Funding Division and member of conference committee on omnibus education funding bill. Supported chartering. Served in senate 1982–1992. Deceased.

Minnesota State Senator Ron Dicklich (DFL-Hibbing). Chair of the senate Education Funding Division, lead senate sponsor of the omnibus education funding bill, and senate co-chair of the 1991 conference committee on omnibus education funding bill. Dicklich took a strong stand for chartering and was an advocate for chartering a school in his Iron Range district that would otherwise be closed. Dicklich served in the senate 1981–1992.

US Senator David Durenberger (R-Minnesota). Served in the US Senate 1979–1994. Within days of passage of Minnesota's chartering law in 1991, he acknowledged the bipartisan Minnesota legislative effort in a statement on the floor of the US Senate. Durenberger educated his colleagues and created national exposure for chartering. By Labor Day of 1991, he and US Senator Joe Lieberman (D-Conn.) introduced legislation creating what would later become the federal chartering grant program in the 1994 reauthorization of the federal Elementary and Secondary Education Act (ESEA).

Sy Fliegel. Deputy superintendent of District 4 (East Harlem) of New York City Schools. Spoke at 1988 Itasca Seminar regarding successful turnaround of East Harlem community schools.

Al From. Founder, in 1985, of the Washington, DC–based Democratic Leadership Council (DLC). He led the DLC 1985–2009. He played a prominent role in the 1992 election of President Bill Clinton and served as domestic policy advisor to the Clinton transition.

Cheryl Furrer. Lobbyist for Minnesota Education Association (MEA) during passage of chartered schools. MEA actively opposed the legislation.

Rose Hermodson. Lobbyist for the Minnesota Federation of Teachers (MFT) and its successor organization, Education Minnesota. MFT actively opposed the legislation. Hermodson was a constituent of Representative Ken Nelson. Today she serves as assistant commissioner at the Minnesota Department of Education, supervising the choice and charter area. Immediately prior to this position, Hermodson worked with the Minneapolis Federation of Teachers.

Curt Johnson. Succeeded Ted Kolderie as executive director of the Citizens League, serving in that role when the league's report on chartering was released in 1988. Johnson became policy advisor and later chief of staff to Governor Arne Carlson 1991–1994.

Minnesota State Representative Becky Kelso (DFL-Shakopee). Chief house author of the 1991 chartering law. In 1991, was a member of the house Education Finance Division, and the conference committee on omnibus education funding bill. A former school board member, Kelso served in the house 1987–1998.

Ted Kolderie. Executive director of the Citizens League 1967–1980. Kolderie worked with the committee that produced its chartering proposal in late 1988, and was involved with Senator Reichgott and others in design and passage of the 1991 Minnesota legislation. For six years following, he was active in explaining the idea in about twenty-five states. Kolderie coauthored with Will Marshall the chapter on education in *Mandate for Change*, the policy book the Progressive Policy Institute produced for President-Elect Clinton. Kolderie has remained active in Minnesota through Education|Evolving, working to get charter laws used for innovation. In 2007, the National Alliance for Public Charter Schools made him an inaugural member of the Charter Schools Hall of Fame, and in 2011, the Education Commission of the States gave him its James B. Conant award for an "outstanding contribution to American education."

Minnesota State Representative Connie Levi (R-Dellwood). House Majority Leader 1985–1986. House author of postsecondary enrollment options (PSEO) legislation during passage in 1985. Served in the house 1979–1986.

Dan Loritz. Director of governmental relations and assistant commissioner for instruction at the Minnesota Department of Education 1984–1986, when DFL Governor Rudy Perpich proposed two public school choice initiatives: postsecondary enrollment options and open enrollment. Loritz played a key role in passage of both. Loritz served as Perpich's director of government relations in 1987–1988 and deputy chief of staff in 1988–1990. Loritz currently serves as president and CEO of the Minnesota-based Center for Policy Studies.

Will Marshall. Founded in 1989 the Progressive Policy Institute (PPI), then a project of the Washington, DC–based Democratic Leadership Council (DLC). He continues to serve as president of PPI, the position he has held since its founding.

Minnesota State Representative Bob McEachern (DFL-Maple Lake). Chair of the house Education committee in 1991 and member of the conference committee on omnibus education funding bill. McEachern was an influential opponent of the chartering law. He served in the house 1973–1992. Deceased.

Joe Nathan. Nationally known advocate of chartering and other education reform. He was a key participant in the design and passage of Minnesota's 1991 chartering law. A former public school teacher and administrator, he authored in 1983 the first of three books, *Free to Teach,* which garnered national attention. For two years he worked for the National Governors Association on an education report produced in 1986 advocating that less regulation in public education would produce greater results. After passage of the chartering legislation, Nathan testified at more than twenty state legislatures and to several congressional committees. He founded the Center for School Change at the University of Minnesota's Humphrey Institute in 1988 and provided support to applicants for new chartered schools. He continues as director of the center, which is now located at Macalester College in St. Paul.

Minnesota State Representative Ken Nelson (DFL-Minneapolis). Chief house author of the 1989 and 1990 chartered school legislation, which did not pass the house. In 1991, Nelson was chair of the house Education Finance Division, lead house sponsor of the house omnibus education funding bill, and co-chair of the conference committee on the omnibus education funding bill. In the conference committee, Nelson offered a compromise chartering amendment, which the committee accepted and was voted into law. Nelson served from 1973 until his retirement from the house in 1992, when he became staff director for the National Goals Panel.

Commissioner of Education and Minnesota State Senator Tom Nelson (DFL-Austin). Chaired the senate Education Aids Subcommittee (later called Education Funding Division) 1983–1986, during passage of postsecondary enrollment options. Served in senate 1976–1986. In 1990, was appointed by Governor Rudy Perpich as commissioner of education. Nelson led a working group in 1990 to improve the chartering legislation for reintroduction in the 1991 session. From 1991 to date, Nelson served as superintendent or interim superintendent of several school districts in Wyoming and Minnesota.

Barry Noack. Executive secretary and lobbyist in 1991 for the Robbinsdale Federation of Teachers. Prior to that, he was a ninth-grade social studies teacher in the Robbinsdale school district.

Minnesota State Senator Gen Olson (R-Mound). Lead Republican senate coauthor of the chartering legislation. In 1991, served on the Education Funding Division and on the conference committee on omnibus education funding bill. Olson was elected to the senate in 1982 and still serves. She became chair of the senate Education Committee during the 2011–2012 legislative sessions.

Minnesota State Senator Sandra Pappas (DFL-St. Paul). In 1991, member of the senate Education Committee and conference committee on omnibus education funding bill. Supported chartering. Served in house 1985–1990, was elected to the senate in 1991, and still serves.

Governor Rudy Perpich. DFL governor of Minnesota 1976–1978 and 1983–1990. He was a strong advocate during the 1980s of two public school choice initiatives: postsecondary enrollment options (which became law in 1985) and open enrollment (which became law in 1988). Perpich did not publicly support or oppose chartering. Perpich was defeated by Arne Carlson in the 1990 election. Deceased.

Minnesota State Senator Randy Peterson (DFL-Wyoming). Chair of senate Education Funding Division 1987–1990, during passage of open enrollment in 1988. Served in senate 1981–1990. Appointed to judgeship on the Intermediate Court of Appeals in December 1990.

Sandra Peterson. President of the Minnesota Federation of Teachers (MFT) and vice president of the American Federation of Teachers (AFT) during passage of chartering legislation. Previously was president of the Robbinsdale Federation of Teachers 1976–1987 and was a constituent of Senator Reichgott. Peterson led efforts to merge the MFT with the Minnesota Education Association (MEA), and was copresident of the merged entity, Education Minnesota, 1998–2001. Since 2005, Peterson has served as a Minnesota state representative (DFL-New Hope).

Eric Premack. Native of Minnesota, former staff member of Citizens League, and active proponent of chartering since its inception in the 1980s. In 1992 he closely followed passage of California's chartering law on staff of the California Legislative Analyst's Office and later as a consultant. Premack has since helped draft and implement chartering legislation in numerous states and at the federal level. Currently he is founder and executive director of the Charter Schools Development Center in Sacramento, Calif.

Minnesota State Senator Ember Reichgott (DFL-New Hope). Chief senate author of chartering legislation in 1989, 1990, and 1991 legislative sessions. Authored open enrollment legislation into law in 1988. At the time was a member of the senate Education Funding Division, chair of the Property Tax Division of the senate Tax Committee, and a majority whip. Served in senate 1983–2000. (Last name became Reichgott Junge in 1993.)

Betsy Rice. Senate counsel to senate Education Committee and chief drafter of the chartering legislation in 1989, 1990, and 1991. Rice's work has been replicated in states across the country. Deceased.

Minnesota State Representative Gary Schafer (R-Gibbon). In 1991, was a member of the house Education Finance Division and a member of the conference committee on omnibus education funding bill. Supported chartering. Served in house 1981–1992.

Jon Schroeder. Former staff member of the Citizens League and senior staff member to US Senator David Durenberger (R-Minn.) 1984–1994. In 1991, as Durenberger's director of policy development, he drafted the legislation creating what became the federal chartering grant program. He worked closely with a growing chartering community in Minnesota and other states to help secure inclusion of the federal grant program in the 1994 reauthorization of the federal Elementary and Secondary Education Act (ESEA). He directed the Charter Friends National Network 1997–2004.

Albert Shanker. President of American Federation of Teachers (AFT) from 1974 until his death in 1997. Floated the charter idea first before the National Press Club in Washington, DC on March 31, 1988. He spoke about the chartering concept at the Itasca Seminar near Brainerd, Minn., in October 1988. Shanker was interested in education reform to allow teachers more autonomy and greater professional status in exchange for greater accountability.

Louise Sundin. President of the Minneapolis Federation of Teachers, vice president of the Minnesota Federation of Teachers (MFT), and vice president of the American Federation of Teachers (AFT) during passage of chartering legislation. Retired from union leadership in 2006. Currently serves as chair of the Minnesota Guild of Public Charter Schools, an organization growing out of the Minneapolis Federation, which won state approval in November 2011 as a single-purpose, chartered school authorizer.

Minnesota State Representative Robert Vanasek (DFL-New Prague). Speaker of the House of Representatives in 1991, during passage of chartering legislation. Served in the house 1973–1992. Vanasek currently lobbies at the state legislature with his own governmental affairs firm.

Minnesota State Representative Charlie Weaver (R-Champlin). House coauthor of the 1991 chartering legislation and member of the house Education Finance Division. Served in house 1983–1998. Currently executive director of the Minnesota Business Partnership, a proponent of the original chartering legislation.

Chronology

1974: Ray Budde presents "Education by Charter: Restructuring School Districts" paper to Society for General Systems Research.

1983: President Ronald Reagan's National Commission on Excellence in Education publishes *A Nation at Risk*.

January 1983: Minnesota governor Rudy Perpich is inaugurated for second, nonconsecutive term.

Fall 1984: Minnesota Business Partnership includes "choice" in its proposal for K–12 education reform.

January 1985: Perpich proposes "Access to Excellence" education reform agenda, including postsecondary enrollment options (PSEO) and open enrollment.

January 29, 1985: AFT president Albert Shanker delivers National Press Club Speech proposing a national certification system to move teaching toward a profession.

June 27, 1985: Perpich signs PSEO into law.

1986: Attempt to repeal PSEO fails in Minnesota legislature.

1987: Minnesota legislature passes voluntary open enrollment into law.

February 1988: The Citizens League creates policy committee to develop education reform proposals.

March 31, 1988: Shanker introduces the charter school idea to National Press Club.

May 1988: Minnesota legislature passes statewide mandatory open enrollment into law.

July 10, 1988: Shanker writes "A Charter for Change," a *New York Times* column about charter schools.

October 2–5, 1988: Itasca Seminar, hosted by Minneapolis Foundation, focuses on public education; Shanker is a featured speaker.

December 15, 1988: Citizens League releases report urging creation of chartered schools.

January 1989: Senator Ember Reichgott introduces first chartering bill into Minnesota legislature.

March 6 and April 4, 1989: First public hearings on chartering in Minnesota Senate.

September 27–28, 1989: President George H. W. Bush invites nation's governors to Education Summit to establish national education goals.

February 25, 1990: National Governors Association issues recommendations to address "major crisis in education."

Spring 1990: Wisconsin Democratic representative Polly Williams obtains legislative approval of a private school voucher program for low-income Milwaukee families.

July 1990: Ted Kolderie sets out fundamentals of chartering in paper entitled, *The States Will Have to Withdraw the Exclusive.*

November 1990: Will Marshall of Progressive Policy Institute (PPI) teams with Kolderie to publish PPI Policy Report *Beyond Choice to New Public Schools: Withdrawing the Exclusive Franchise in Public Education.*

November 6, 1990: Minnesota Republican governor Arne Carlson is elected, defeating DFL incumbent Perpich.

December 1990: New draft of chartered school legislation emerges from working group, headed by Commissioner of Education Tom Nelson.

March 7, 1991: Senator Ember Reichgott introduces revised chartering bill into Minnesota Senate.

March 11, 1991: Representative Becky Kelso introduces revised chartering bill into Minnesota House.

March 20, 1991: Hearing in subcommittee of senate Education Committee; chartering provisions later incorporated into senate omnibus education funding bill.

April 10, 1991: Hearing in house Education Committee; no vote taken.

May 6, 1991: Governor Bill Clinton presents "New Democrat Agenda" in keynote address at the Democratic Leadership Council (DLC) national convention, promoting more public school choice options.

May 7, 1991: DLC convention delegates pass resolution entitled "Making Public Education Work," which includes language describing a chartered school.

May 10–17, 1991: Conference committee meets on omnibus education funding bill.

May 17, 1991: Conference committee adopts compromised chartering provisions as part of final omnibus education funding bill.

May 18, 1991: Final house vote on omnibus education funding bill.

May 20, 1991: Final senate vote on omnibus education funding bill.

May 22, 1991: US Senator David Durenberger enters statement in record of US Senate lauding Minnesota legislature for passing chartering legislation.

June 4, 1991: Carlson signs omnibus education funding bill into law, including the chartering provisions.

June 5, 1991: Clinton, DLC chair, issues press release announcing passage of chartering legislation in Minnesota.

July 31, 1991: Durenberger introduces "Public School Redefinition Act of 1991" into US Senate, the precursor to the federal chartering grant program which would be passed in 1994.

November 18, 1991: Winona School Board approves Bluffview Montessori Charter School proposal, the first charter request to be presented and approved.

December 10, 1991: Minnesota State Board of Education approves Bluffview Montessori Charter School proposal; the school would open fall 1993.

December 1991–January 1992: Local and state boards approve Toivola-Meadowlands Charter School proposal; the school would open September 7, 1993.

January 24, 1992: US Senator Ted Kennedy accepts the chartering concept as proposed by Durenberger and Senator Joe Lieberman into S2, the Senate's education act.

February 1, 1992: California assembly and senate Education Committee chairs propose two chartering bills at a press conference.

April 2, 1992: Amendment to repeal Minnesota chartering legislation fails by nine votes in the Minnesota House of Representatives.

May 1, 1992: DLC invites Senator Ember Reichgott to introduce chartering to national audience at 1992 Democratic Leadership Council Conference.

June 9, 1992: Minnesota State Board of Education approves City Academy charter school proposal following approval by St. Paul School Board.

August 10, 1992: Minnesota State Board of Education approves Metro Deaf chartered school proposal following approval by Forest Lake School Board.

September 7, 1992: City Academy opens as the first chartered school in the nation.

September 20, 1992: Governor Pete Wilson signs legislation into law authorizing 100 chartered schools in California.

October 1992: Democratic presidential nominee Clinton endorses chartering in national televised debate.

November 3, 1992: Clinton is elected president of the United States.

December 7, 1992: PPI releases *Mandate for Change* as blueprint for Clinton-Gore presidency, with chartering as one of three recommendations for "Educating America."

States with Chartering Laws by Years Passed

1991	Minnesota
1992	California
1993	Colorado, Massachusetts, Michigan, New Mexico, Wisconsin
1994	Arizona, Hawaii, Kansas
1995	Alaska, Arkansas, Delaware, Louisiana, New Hampshire, Rhode Island, Texas, Wyoming
1996	Connecticut, District of Columbia, Florida, Illinois, New Jersey, North Carolina, South Carolina
1997	Nevada, Ohio, Pennsylvania
1998	Georgia, Idaho, Missouri, New York, Utah, Virginia
1999	Oklahoma, Oregon
2001	Indiana
2002	Iowa, Tennessee
2003	Maryland
2010	Mississippi
2011	Maine

Appendix IV: Legislation

1991 Minnesota Law Creating Chartered (Outcome-Based) Schools

✱ 9   Sec. 3. [120.064] [OUTCOME-BASED SCHOOLS.]

10   Subdivision 1. [PURPOSES.] The purpose of this section is

11 to:

12   (1) improve pupil learning;

13   (2) increase learning opportunities for pupils;

14   (3) encourage the use of different and innovative teaching

15 methods;

16   (4) require the measurement of learning outcomes and create

17 different and innovative forms of measuring outcomes;

18   (5) establish new forms of accountability for schools; or

19   (6) create new professional opportunities for teachers,

20 including the opportunity to be responsible for the learning

21 program at the school site.

22   Subd. 2. [APPLICABILITY.] This section applies only to

23 outcome-based schools formed and operated under this section.

24   Subd. 3. [SPONSOR.] (a) A school board may sponsor an

25 outcome-based school.

26   (b) A school board may authorize a maximum of two

27 outcome-based schools. No more than a total of eight

28 outcome-based schools may be authorized. The state board of

29 education shall advise potential sponsors when the maximum

30 number of outcome-based schools has been authorized.

31   Subd. 4. [FORMATION OF SCHOOL.] (a) A sponsor may

32 authorize one or more licensed teachers under section 215.182,

33 subdivision 2, to form and operate an outcome-based school

34 subject to approval by the state board of education. The

35 teachers shall organize and operate a school as a cooperative

36 under chapter 308A or nonprofit corporation under chapter 317A.

1   (b) Before a teacher may begin to form and operate a

2 school, the sponsor must file an affidavit with the state board

3 of education stating its intent to authorize an outcome-based

4 school. The affidavit must state the terms and conditions under

5 which the sponsor would authorize an outcome-based school. The

6 state board must approve or disapprove the sponsor's proposed

7 authorization within 30 days of receipt of the affidavit.

8 Failure to obtain state board approval precludes a sponsor from

9 authorizing the outcome-based school that was the subject of the

10 affidavit.

11   (c) The teachers authorized to organize and operate a

12 school shall hold an election for members of the school's board

13 of directors. All staff members employed at the school and all

14 parents of children enrolled in the school may participate in

15 the election. Licensed teachers employed at the school must be

16 a majority of the members of the board of directors.

17   (d) The sponsor's authorization for an outcome-based school

18 shall be in the form of a written contract signed by the sponsor

19 and the board of directors of the outcome-based school.

20   Subd. 5. [CONTRACT.] The contract for an outcome-based

21 school shall be in writing and contain at least the following:

22   (1) a description of a program that carries out one or more

23 of the purposes in subdivision 1;

24   (2) specific outcomes pupils are to achieve under

25 subdivision 10;

26   (3) admission policies and procedures;

27   (4) management and administration of the school;

28   (5) requirements and procedures for program and financial

29 audits;

30   (6) how the school will comply with subdivisions 8, 13, 15,

31 and 21;

32   (7) assumption of liability by the outcome-based school;

33   (8) types and amounts of insurance coverage to be obtained

34 by the outcome-based school; and

35   (9) the term of the contract which may be up to three years.

36   Subd. 6. [ADVISORY COMMITTEE.] (a) The state board of

05/18/91   [REVISOR] RJS/AT CCRHF0700

1 education shall appoint an advisory committee comprised of ten

2 members. At least two members shall be African American, two

3 members shall be American Indian, two members shall be Asian

4 Pacific American, and two members shall be Hispanic. One of

5 each of the two members shall reside within the seven-county

6 metropolitan area and one shall reside within Minnesota but

7 outside of the seven-county metropolitan area. In addition, at

8 least one of each of the two members shall be a parent of a

9 child in any of the grades kindergarten through 12. As least

10 five of the ten members shall have family incomes that would

11 make them eligible for free or reduced school lunches.

12   (b) Each sponsor listed in subdivision 3 shall request the

13 advisory committee to review and make recommendations about a

14 proposal it receives from an individual or organization that is

15 predominately Caucasian to establish an outcome-based school in

16 which one-half or more of the pupils are expected to be

17 non-Caucasian.

18   (c) Each sponsor listed in subdivision 3 may request the

19 advisory committee to review and make recommendations about a

20 proposal it receives from an individual or organization that is

21 predominately non-Caucasian if requested to do so by the

22 individual or organization.

23   Subd. 7. [EXEMPTION FROM STATUTES AND RULES.] Except as

24 provided in this section, an outcome-based school is exempt from

25 all statutes and rules applicable to a school board or school

26 district, although it may elect to comply with one or more

27 provisions of statutes or rules.

28   Subd. 8. [REQUIREMENTS.] (a) An outcome-based school shall

29 meet the same health and safety requirements required of a

30 school district.

31   (b) The school must be located in Minnesota. Its specific

32 location may not be prescribed or limited by a sponsor or other

33 authority except a zoning authority.

34   (c) The school must be nonsectarian in its programs,

35 admission policies, employment practices, and all other

36 operations. A sponsor may not authorize an outcome-based school

05/18/91   [REVISOR]   RJS/AT   CCRHF0700

1 or program that is affiliated with a nonpublic sectarian school

2 or a religious institution.

3   (d) The primary focus of the school must be to provide a

4 comprehensive program of instruction for at least one grade or

5 age group from five through 18 years of age.   Instruction may be

6 provided to people younger than five years and older than 18

7 years of age.

8   (e) The school may not charge tuition.

9   (f) The school is subject to and shall comply with chapter

10 363 and section 126.21.

11   (g) The school is subject to and shall comply with the

12 pupil fair dismissal act, sections 127.26 to 127.39, and the

13 Minnesota public school fee law, sections 120.71 to 120.76.

14   (h) The school is subject to the same financial audits,

15 audit procedures, and audit requirements as a school district.

16 The audit must be consistent with the requirements of sections

17 121.901 to 121.917, except to the extent deviations are

18 necessary because of the program at the school. The department

19 of education, state auditor, or legislative auditor may conduct

20 financial, program, or compliance audits.

21   (i) The school is a school district for the purposes of

22 tort liability under chapter 466.

23   Subd. 9.   [ADMISSION REQUIREMENTS.] The school may limit

24 admission to:

25   (1) pupils within an age group or grade level;

26   (2) people who are eligible to participate in the high

27 school graduation incentives program under section 126.22;

28   (3) pupils who have a specific affinity for the school's

29 teaching methods, the school's learning philosophy, or a subject

30 such as mathematics, science, fine arts, performing arts, or a

31 foreign language; or

32   (4) residents of a specific geographic area if the

33 percentage of the population of non-Caucasian people in the

34 geographic area is greater than the percentage of the

35 non-Caucasian population in the congressional district in which

36 the geographic area is located, as long as the school reflects

1   the racial and ethnic diversity of that area.

2   The school shall enroll an eligible pupil who submits a

3   timely application, unless the number of applications exceeds

4   the capacity of a program, class, grade level, or building. In

5   this case, pupils shall be accepted by lot.

6   The school may not limit admission to pupils on the basis

7   of intellectual ability, measures of achievement or aptitude, or

8   athletic ability.

9   Subd. 10. [PUPIL PERFORMANCE.] An outcome-based school

10 must design its programs to at least meet the outcomes adopted

11 by the state board of education. In the absence of state board

12 requirements, the school must meet the outcomes contained in the

13 contract with the sponsor. The achievement levels of the

14 outcomes contained in the contract may exceed the achievement

15 levels of any outcomes adopted by the state board.

16   Subd. 11. [EMPLOYMENT AND OTHER OPERATING MATTERS.] The

17 school's board of directors shall employ and contract with

18 necessary teachers, as defined by section 125.03, subdivision 1,

19 who hold valid licenses to perform the particular service for

20 which they are employed in the school. The board may employ

21 necessary employees who are not required to hold teaching

22 licenses to perform duties other than teaching and may contract

23 for other services. The board may discharge teachers and

24 nonlicensed employees.

25   The board of directors also shall decide matters related to

26 the operation of the school, including budgeting, curriculum and

27 operating procedures.

28   Subd. 12. [HANDICAPPED PUPILS.] The school must comply

29 with sections 120.03 and 120.17 and rules relating to the

30 education of handicapped pupils as though it were a school

31 district.

32   Subd. 13. [LENGTH OF SCHOOL YEAR.] An outcome-based school

33 shall provide instruction each year for at least the number of

34 days required by section 120.101, subdivision 5. It may provide

35 instruction throughout the year according to sections 120.59 to

36 120.67 or 121.585.

1   Subd. 14. [REPORTS.] An outcome-based school must report

2   at least annually to its sponsor and the state board of

3   education the information required by the sponsor or the state

4   board. The reports are public data under chapter 13.

5   Subd. 15. [TRANSPORTATION.] Transportation for pupils

6   enrolled at a school shall be provided by the district in which

7   the school is located, according to sections 120.062,

8   subdivision 9, and 123.39, subdivision 6, for a pupil residing

9   in the same district in which the outcome-based school is

10   located. Transportation may be provided by the district in

11   which the school is located, according to sections 120.062,

12   subdivision 9, and 123.39, subdivision 6, for a pupil residing

13   in a different district.

14   Subd. 16. [LEASED SPACE.] The school may lease space from

15   a board eligible to be a sponsor or other public or private

16   nonprofit nonsectarian organization.

17   Subd. 17. [INITIAL COSTS.] A sponsor may authorize a

18   school before the applicant has secured its space, equipment,

19   facilities, and personnel if the applicant indicates the

20   authority is necessary for it to raise working capital. A

21   sponsor may not authorize a school before the state board of

22   education has approved the authorization.

23   Subd. 18. [DISSEMINATE INFORMATION.] The department of

24   education must disseminate information to the public, directly

25   and through sponsors, on how to form and operate an

26   outcome-based school and how to utilize the offerings of an

27   outcome-based school.

28   Subd. 19. [LEAVE TO TEACH IN A SCHOOL.] If a teacher

29   employed by a school district makes a written request for an

30   extended leave of absence to teach at an outcome-based school,

31   the school district must grant the leave. The school district

32   must grant a leave for any number of years requested by the

33   teacher, and must extend the leave at the teacher's request.

34   The school district may require that the request for a leave or

35   extension of leave be made up to 90 days before the teacher

36   would otherwise have to report for duty. Except as otherwise

05/18/91   [REVISOR] RJS/AT CCRHF0700

1 provided in this subdivision and except for section 125.60,

2 subdivision 6a, the leave is governed by section 125.60,

3 including, but not limited to, reinstatement, notice of

4 intention to return, seniority, salary, and insurance.

5   During a leave, the teacher may continue to aggregate

6 benefits and credits in the teachers' retirement association

7 account by paying both the employer and employee contributions

8 based upon the annual salary of the teacher for the last full

9 pay period before the leave began. The retirement association

10 may impose reasonable requirements to efficiently administer

11 this subdivision.

12   Subd. 20. [COLLECTIVE BARGAINING.] Employees of the board

13 of directors of the school may, if otherwise eligible, organize

14 under chapter 179A and comply with its provisions. The board of

15 directors of the school is a public employer, for the purposes

16 of chapter 179A, upon formation of one or more bargaining units

17 at the school. Bargaining units at the school are separate from

18 any other units.

19   Subd. 21. [CAUSES FOR NONRENEWAL OR TERMINATION.] (a) The

20 duration of the contract with a sponsor shall be for the term

21 contained in the contract according to subdivision 5. The

22 sponsor, subject to state board of education approval, may or

23 may not renew a contract at the end of the term for any ground

24 listed in paragraph (b). A sponsor or the state board may

25 unilaterally terminate a contract during the term of the

26 contract for any ground listed in paragraph (b). At least 60

27 days before not renewing or terminating a contract, the sponsor,

28 or the state board if the state board is acting to terminate a

29 contract, shall notify the board of directors of the school of

30 the proposed action in writing. The notice shall state the

31 grounds for the proposed action in reasonable detail and that

32 the school's board of directors may request in writing an

33 informal hearing before the sponsor or the state board within 14

34 days of receiving notice of nonrenewal or termination of the

35 contract. Failure by the board of directors to make a written

36 request for a hearing within the 14 day period shall be treated

1   as acquiescence to the proposed action. Upon receiving a timely

2   written request for a hearing, the sponsor or the state board

3   shall give reasonable notice to the school's board of directors

4   of the hearing date. The sponsor or the state board shall

5   conduct an informal hearing before taking final action. The

6   sponsor shall take final action to renew or not renew a contract

7   by the last day of classes in the school year.

8   (b) A contract may be terminated or not renewed upon any of

9   the following grounds:

10   (1) failure to meet the requirements for pupil performance

11 contained in the contract;

12   (2) failure to meet generally accepted standards of fiscal

13 management;

14   (3) for violations of law; or

15   (4) other good cause shown.

16   If a contract is terminated or not renewed, the school

17 shall be dissolved according to the applicable provisions of

18 chapter 308A or 317A.

19   Subd. 22. [PUPIL ENROLLMENT.] If a contract is not renewed

20 or is terminated according to subdivision 21, a pupil who

21 attended the school, siblings of the pupil, or another pupil who

22 resides in the same place as the pupil may enroll in the

23 resident district or may submit an application to a nonresident

24 district according to section 120.062 at any time. Applications

25 and notices required by section 120.062 shall be processed and

26 provided in a prompt manner. The application and notice

27 deadlines in section 120.062 do not apply under these

28 circumstances.

29   Subd. 23. [GENERAL AUTHORITY.] The board of directors of

30 an outcome-based school may sue and be sued. The board may not

31 levy taxes or issue bonds.

32   Subd. 24. [IMMUNITY.] The state board of education,

33 members of the state board, a sponsor, members of the board of a

34 sponsor in their official capacity, and employees of a sponsor

35 are immune from civil or criminal liability with respect to all

36 activities related to an outcome-based school they approve or

To Ember
With thanks
Bill Clinton

Democratic presidential candidate Bill Clinton visits in Minnesota with Clinton campaign co-chair Sen. Ember Reichgott during summer 1992.

US Secretary of Education Lamar Alexander; Jon Schroeder, policy director for Sen. Durenberger; US Senator David Durenberger, R-Minnesota (L to R).

Minnesota elected officials and DFL party leaders rally for the Clinton presidential campaign in 1992.

Reichgott and her fiancé, Michael Junge, join festivities for the 1993 inauguration of President Bill Clinton in Washington, DC.

Minnesota US Senator Paul Wellstone greets a student at A Chance to Grow Charter School in 1995, during a visit by US Education Secretary Richard Riley (center). In photo below, Reichgott Junge visits with students.

Students from City Academy and director Milo Cutter tour the senate chambers at the Minnesota capitol.

City Academy student Treandos Moore, Reichgott Junge, and City Academy director Milo Cutter join a 1995 conference call with US Education Secretary Richard Riley.

US Secretary of Education Richard Riley, Reichgott Junge, and Deputy Secretary of Education Madeleine Kunin participate in a March 19, 1996, satellite town hall meeting about chartered schools.

Reichgott Junge joins US Secretary of Education Richard Riley (second from left) and Vice President Al Gore (third from left) in a panel discussion at Gore's 1997 Family Re-Union Conference in Nashville.

Reichgott Junge greets Minnesota Federation of Teachers president Sandra Peterson (left) and Minnesota Education Association president Judy Schaubach during the 1997 MEA/MFT Fall Professional Conference.

President Bill Clinton visits St. Paul's City Academy, the
first chartered school in the nation, on May 4, 2000.
Jeremy Hall is shown meeting with the president.

Chartered school students join (L to R) Sen. Gen Olson, Reichgott Junge, chartered school association leader Steve Dess, and Rep. Alice Seagren for a press conference in support of improvements to the chartering law.

Nelson Smith, president of the National Alliance for Public Charter Schools, presents to national conference attendees in New Orleans the 2008 inductees of the National Charter Schools Hall of Fame: (L to R) Yvonne Chan, Linda Brown, and Reichgott Junge.

David R. Gergen (Center), National Selection Committee chair, presents Citizens League executive director Lyle Wray and Reichgott Junge a 2000 Innovations in American Government Award from the John F. Kennedy School of Government at Harvard University for Minnesota's chartered school law.

Milo Cutter (center), founder and director of City Academy High School, celebrates the first chartered school in the nation with students (L to R) Xai Her, Benito Lopez-Sanchez, Janette Castro, Jeyn Cid, and Deatrice Banks.

Students Chloe Chang, Arfii Theophilos, Weedduu Theophilos, Rejat Krishnan, and Azariah Wohler join second-grade teacher Rebecca Lund from Nova Classical Academy, St. Paul.